CASSIAN THE MONK
Columba Stewart

IMAGES AND RELICS
*Theological Perceptions and Visual Images
in Sixteenth-Century Europe*
John Dillenberger

THE BODY BROKEN
*The Calvinist Doctrine of the Eucharist
and the Symbolization of Power
in Sixteenth-Century France*
Christopher Elwood

WHAT PURE EYES COULD SEE
*Calvin's Doctrine of Faith in Its
Exegetical Context*
Barbara Pitkin

THE UNACCOMMODATED
CALVIN
*Studies in the Foundation of a Theological
Tradition*
Richard A. Muller

THE CONFESSIONALIZATION
OF HUMANISM IN REFORMATION
GERMANY
Erika Rummel

THE PLEASURE OF DISCERNMENT
Marguerite de Navarre as Theologian
Carol Thysell

REFORMATION READINGS
OF THE APOCALYPSE
Geneva, Zurich, and Wittenberg
Irena Backus

WRITING THE WRONGS
*Women of the Old Testament among
Biblical Commentators from Philo
through the Reformation*
John L. Thompson

THE HUNGRY ARE DYING
Beggars and Bishops in Roman Cappadocia
Susan R. Holman

RESCUE FOR THE DEAD
*The Posthumous Salvation
of Non-Christians in Early Christianity*
Jeffrey A. Trumbower

AFTER CALVIN
*Studies in the Development
of a Theological Tradition*
Richard A. Muller

THE POVERTY OF RICHES
St. Francis of Assisi Reconsidered
Kenneth Baxter Wolf

REFORMING MARY
*Changing Images of the Virgin Mary in
Lutheran Sermons of the Sixteenth Century*
Beth Kreitzer

TEACHING THE REFORMATION
*Ministers and Their Message
in Basel, 1529–1629*
Amy Nelson Burnett

GREGORY OF NAZIANZUS
ON THE TRINITY AND THE
KNOWLEDGE OF GOD
In Your Light We Shall See Light
Christopher A. Beeley

Reforming Saints

Saints' Lives and Their Authors in Germany, 1470–1530

DAVID J. COLLINS

OXFORD
UNIVERSITY PRESS

2008

OXFORD

UNIVERSITY PRESS

Oxford University Press, Inc., publishes works that further
Oxford University's objective of excellence
in research, scholarship, and education.

Oxford   New York
Auckland   Cape Town   Dar es Salaam   Hong Kong   Karachi
Kuala Lumpur   Madrid   Melbourne   Mexico City   Nairobi
New Delhi   Shanghai   Taipei   Toronto

With offices in
Argentina   Austria   Brazil   Chile   Czech Republic   France   Greece
Guatemala   Hungary   Italy   Japan   Poland   Portugal   Singapore
South Korea   Switzerland   Thailand   Turkey   Ukraine   Vietnam

Copyright © 2008 by Oxford University Press, Inc.

Published by Oxford University Press, Inc.
198 Madison Avenue, New York, New York 10016

www.oup.com

Library of Congress Cataloging-in-Publication Data
Collins, David J.
Reforming saints : saint's lives and their authors in Germany, 1470–1530 / David J. Collins.
    p. cm.—(Oxford studies in historical theology)
Includes bibliographical references and index.
ISBN 978-0-19-532953-7
1. Christian saints—Germany.   2. Authors.   3. Authorship.   4. Humanism—Germany.
5. Renaissance—Germany.   I. Title.
BX4659.G3C65   2007
235'.2094309024—dc22   2007014781

9 8 7 6 5 4 3 2 1

Printed in the United States of America
on acid-free paper

To my mother and father

Acknowledgments

Receiving the generous help of so many colleagues, friends, teachers, and scholarly institutions has been a source of great pleasure in writing this book. I hope that my expressions of gratitude here will be accepted in return for a debt that otherwise I cannot hope to repay. My first thanks go to the three scholar-teachers who bear the greatest responsibility for inspiring me to the advanced study of history. Thomas F. X. Noble introduced me to the Middle Ages and taught me as an undergraduate the hard but rewarding lesson that foreign countries have to be studied with foreign languages; John O'Malley imparted to me his love of the Renaissance humanists; and Bob Scribner drew my attention to Germany, the Reformations, and popular religion in the last two seminars he offered before his untimely death in 1998. I undertook the initial research for this monograph as a doctoral student under the supervision of Richard Kieckhefer, with the additional counsel of Robert Lerner, William Monter, and Edward Muir. They could not have guided this project in its earliest phase with more care or enthusiasm. I greatly value their mentoring and friendship.

In the course of my research I was also aided at several important junctures by colleagues in North America and Europe. They helped me better understand the larger issues on which my research touched and gave me invaluable assistance in the more recondite requirements of medieval and early modern scholarship. In this regard I am especially grateful to Eckhard Bernstein, Randolph Head, Erika

Rummel, and James Weiss. While abroad, I incurred similar debts to Robert Godding and Bernard Joussard, *bollandistes*; Guy Philippart and his former assistant Michel Trigalet of the Université Notre-Dame de la Paix in Namur; Monika Rener of the Philipps-Universität in Marburg; Gabrieli Signori of the Universität Konstanz; Markus Müller of the Albert-Ludwigs-Universität in Freiburg; Stephanie Haarländer of the Johannes-Gutenberg-Universität in Mainz; and Klaus Herbers and Dieter Bauer in association with the Arbeitskreis für Hagiographische Fragen. The editors and readers at Oxford University Press also greatly improved this book. I am especially grateful to Alison K. Frazier for her painstaking reading of and thoughtful commentary on the book in draft. I credit these colleagues' and friends' *sodalitas* for making the book better, and I take full responsibility for any remaining errors, oversights, and misapprehensions.

A number of institutions supported my research in essential ways. Fellowships and grants from the Deutscher Akademischer Austauschdienst, the Charlotte Newcombe Foundation, and Georgetown and Northwestern universities made two years and several summers of research abroad possible. The Monumenta Germaniae Historica, under the presidency of Rudolf Schieffer, generously extended its hospitality to me during a two-year residence in Munich. The staff members of the Herzog-August-Bibliothek in Wolfenbüttel, the Institut für Europäische Geschichte in Mainz, and the Staatsbibliothek in Berlin (in particular the Incunabula Division *unter den Linden*), where I worked for fruitful, if briefer, periods of time, extended me a similar hospitality. I am obliged as well to a host of librarians and archivists, many of whom I know only "virtually" on the internet. Their institutions include the Manuscripts and Old Books Division of the Bayerische Staatsbibliothek, the Stadtarchiv in Nuremberg, the Landesarchiv in Münster, the Historisches Archiv der Stadt in Cologne, the Stadtbibliothek in Trier, and the Universitäts- und Landesbibliothek Sachsen Anhalt in Halle a. Saale, as well as the interlibrary loan staffs at Northwestern and Georgetown universities. My colleagues in the History Department and Medieval Studies Program at Georgetown continue to help me—on and off duty, *verbo et exemplo*—negotiate a balance between researching and teaching. No chapter in this book has been previously published, but some preliminary research and analysis have appeared in print elsewhere: on Saint Benno, in *La Revue Bénédictine* in 2000; on Saint Ida of Herzfeld, in Gabrieli Signori's *Heiliges Westfalen* in 2003 and in the *Analecta Bollandiana* in 2006; and on late medieval German hagiography in general, in Guy Philippart's *Hagiographies* in 2006. Editors and readers caught mistakes, alerted me to oversights, and sharpened hypotheses, thereby improving the overall project and indebting me to them in the process.

On a personal note, I wish to express my gratitude to the several communities of the Jesuit order, especially in Brussels, Chicago, Munich, and Washington, D.C., where I did most of my research and writing. They supported me in more ways than I could ever enumerate. My *Kommilitonen* in the MGH-*Lesesaal*—Annette Wiesheu, Jochen Johrendt, and Christian Jostmann— as well as MGH-*Mitarbeiterin* Veronika Lukas, helped make Munich a home-away-from-home for the two years I was there. Seeming at every turn to enjoy my stories of late medieval saints and Renaissance humanists, the Clifton-Soderstrom and Langford-Collier families did the same for me in Chicago. Their friendship continues to be a source of great happiness. Lastly, I thank my family—parents, siblings, in-laws, abundant nieces, and two nephews—who learned more about what they least expected and who supported me with love in this as in all of my endeavors.

Contents

Abbreviations

AASS   *Acta sanctorum quotquot tot orbe coluntur*, ed. Société des
Bollandistes. Antwerp and Brussels, 1643–.

BHL   *Bibliotheca hagiographica latina*, 2 vols. and supplement.
Brussels: Société des Bollandistes, 1899–1901, 1998.

BHRR   *Die Bischöfe des Heiligen Römischen Reiches*, ed. Erwin
Gatz. Vol. 1 (1198–1448) and vol. 2 (1448–1648). Berlin:
Duncker und Humblot, 1996, 2001.

BK   *Bruder Klaus: Die ältesten Quellen über den seligen Nikolaus
von Flüe, sein Leben und seinen Einfluss*, ed. Robert
Durrer. Vols. 1 and 2. Sarnen, Switzerland: Louis Ehrli,
1917–1921 (repr., 1981), and *Bruder Klaus: Ergänzungsband
zum Quellenwerk von Robert Durrer*, ed. Rupert Amschwand. Vol. 3. Sarnen, Switzerland: Regierungsrat des
Kantons Obwalden, 1987.

BSB-Ink   *Bayerische Staatsbibliothek Inkunabelkatalog*, 5 vols.
Wiesbaden: Ludwig Reichert, 1988–2000.

BSS   *Bibliotheca sanctorum*, 13 vols. Rome: Istituto Giovanni
XXIII nella Pontificia Università lateranense,
1961–1969.

CB   "Katalog der Cincinnius-Bibliothek." In Johannes
Freitäger, *Johannes Cincinnius von Lippstadt*, 347–79.
Münster, Germany: Aschendorff, 2000.

DHGE   *Dictionnaire d'histoire et de géographie ecclésiastique.* Paris:
Letouzey et Ané, 1912–.

DSAM   *Dictionnaire de spiritualité ascétique et mystique: Doctrine et histoire.* Paris: Beauchesne, 1937–.

GW   *Gesamtkatalog der Wiegendrucke.* Stuttgart: Anton Hiersemann, 1968–.

Hagiogr.   *Hagiographies: Histoire internationale de la littérature hagiographique latine et vernaculaire en Occident des origines à 1550,* ed. Guy Philippart., Turnhout, Belgium: Brepols, 1994–.

Kurth   *The Complete Woodcuts of Albrecht Dürer,* ed. Willi Kurth. New York: Dover, 1963.

MGH   *Monumenta Germaniae Historica*
SRG: *Scriptores rerum Germanicarum in usum scholarum separatim editi*
SS: *Scriptores*
SSf: *Scriptores* (in folio)

RFHMA   *Repertorium fontium historiae medii aevi.* Rome: Istituto storico italiano per il medio evo, 1962–.

Schoch   *Albrecht Dürer: Das druckgraphische Werk,* ed. Rainer Schoch, Matthias Mende, and Anna Scherbaum. Vol. 2. Munich: Prestel, 2002.

Strauss   *Albrecht Dürer, Woodcuts and Wood Blocks,* ed. Walter L. Strauss. New York: Abaris Books, 1980.

UHM   *Das Urkundenbuch des Hochstifts Meißen,* ed. Ernst Gotthelf Gersdorf, 3 vols. *Codex Diplomaticus Saxoniae Regiae,* Section II. Leipzig: Giesecke and Devrient, 1864–1867.

VD16   *Verzeichnis der im deutschen Sprachbereich erschienenen Drucke des XVI. Jahrhunderts.* Stuttgart: Heisemann, 1983–1995.

VL   *Die deutsche Literatur des Mittelalters: Verfasserlexikon,* ed. Wolfgang Stammler and Karl Langosch, 2d rev. ed., 10 vols. plus supplements. Berlin: Walter de Gruyter, 1978–.

WA   Luther, Martin. *Werke.* Weimar, Germany: Böhlau, 1883–.

Figures

Reforming Saints

Introduction

The Case of Holy Benno, Bishop of Meissen

The Last Medieval Canonization

No one in the later Middle Ages could have foretold the prominence that the holy eleventh-century bishop of Meissen, Benno, would assume in the religious polemics of the sixteenth century.[1] The veneration that he had received in Saxony was unexceptional: Local bishops granted indulgences to pilgrims at his tomb, the cathedral clergy recorded reports of healings through his intercession, Meissen celebrated an annual feast day in his honor, an endowed lamp flickered at his grave, and the local Wettin nobility buried their deceased near his sepulcher.[2] By the standards of the later Middle Ages Benno was an unremarkable local saint.

The turning point came with Pope Hadrian VI's canonization of Benno in 1523. The rarity of canonization—no pope before the mid-nineteenth century proclaimed more than ten—added to the prestige of the honor.[3] In Benno's case, the dignity was all the more uncommon: he was only the third person from German lands canonized in a century.[4] In consequence, the local lord, George, the duke of Albertine Saxony, spared no expense in preparing the celebrations in Meissen for the feast day following the papal decree. At the same time, the canonization was attracting another kind of attention, and not what its proponents in Rome or Saxony were

anticipating. In his first extended critique of the cult of the saints, Martin
Luther, who had all but ignored the activities leading up to the canonization,
denounced the impending celebrations with the tract "Against the New Idol
and Old Devil to Be Elevated in Meissen."[5] Luther took especially sharp aim at
the account of Benno's life then circulating throughout Saxony, authored by
an official in Duke George's court, Jerome Emser.[6]

The subsequent sixteenth-century reaction to Benno's canonization
within Evangelical and Catholic circles is among the most colorful episodes of
its kind.[7] It illustrates the opposing ways that the newly forming confessions
used traditional devotions as propaganda. Luther's denunciations instigated
an exchange not only of polemical tracts but also of musical compositions.[8]
Then in 1539, following Duke George's succession by his Evangelical brother
Henry the Pious, armed men broke into the Meissen cathedral under orders
from the new duke and John Frederick, Elector of Saxony, to raze Benno's
sepulcher (see figure I.1), which stood in the nave of the gothic edifice. Un-
beknownst to the vandals, the story goes, the Catholic bishop of Meissen, John
von Maltitz, had already secreted the episcopal remains outside the city in
anticipation of just such a spoliation. The relics stayed hidden for more than
three decades until the duke of Bavaria, Albert V (1550–1579), having committed himself to the Catholic side of Germany's religious conflicts, negotiated their acquisition. The relics arrived in Munich with great ceremony in
1576. They reposed in the court chapel for four years until Duke William V
(1579–1597), Albert's successor and another ardent Catholic, used a dynastic
anniversary as the occasion to solemnly deposit them in Munich's Church of
Our Lady and to have Saint Benno declared the patron of Munich and Old
Bavaria. Decrees from the Wittelsbach court, new grave-site rituals for the
faithful, hagiographical treatises by Jesuits, and dramas performed by Munich's elite collegians invigorated Benno's cult anew and transformed it as his
devotees a half century earlier could never have imagined.[9]

Approaches to Benno of Meissen: The Historiography

When nineteenth-century historians began searching for the documentary
remains of Benno's eleventh-century life, they found little more than the
sixteenth-century texts and judged them seriously wanting. The reviews of
Emser's *Life of Holy Benno* were especially harsh: After several unsparing
articles in the 1880s and a dismissive Munich dissertation in 1911, the
question was no longer how accurate the work was but how culpable Emser
was for the deception.[10] This modern criticism—aimed in the first instance at

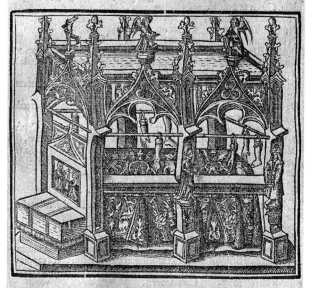
FIGURE I.I. Title page. Hieronymus Emser, *Divi Bennonis Misnensis quondam episcopi vita miracula et alia quedam non tam Misnensibus quam Germanis omnibus decora* (Leipzig: Melchior Lotter the Elder, 1512). Call number: Res/2 J. can. p. 201 g/1. Reproduced by permission of the Bayerische Staatsbibliothek, Munich.

The title page of Emser's *Life of Holy Benno* (1512) brings together traditional and innovative elements. The woodcut shows Benno's sepulcher, which stood in the nave of the Meissen cathedral from its installation in 1270 until its desecration in 1539. Hanging from the tomb are pilgrims' *ex votos* (votive offerings) representing the body parts that were healed through the saint's intercession. Emser's three couplets, a classicizing touch, read as follows: *Blessed Father Benno, take this life in return for a life. Nothing has meant more to me than this restitution. You prolonged my mortal life with your prayers when I was beyond all medical help. I give life back to you. Your name shall be immortal, for you will live more famously through my writings.*

Benno's sixteenth-century devotees rather than the eleventh-century bishop—echoed a distinction made by the canonization's first staunch critic. At the opening of his tract "Against the New Idol" Luther wrote that he had no desire to judge Benno himself: The eleventh-century bishop of Meissen "like all the dead has his judge already." Luther's expressed target was rather "Satan, arrayed in silver and gold, raised up and worshiped under the name of Benno," an abominable figure that popes and legend writers had created and that distracted the faithful from the worship singularly owed to God.[11]

A sixteenth-century distinction between the cultic figure and the historical one was not Luther's alone. Catholic proponents of the cult—the monastic author of a fifteenth-century life in Hildesheim, Emser, the dukes of Bavaria, and the Munich Jesuits—acted on a similar presupposition. In literature such as the vitae and in rituals such as the civil processions and Jesuit dramas in Munich, Benno's leading supporters fashioned the object of their religious devotion several times over, each time adjusting the portrayal to suit a different set of circumstances and group of actual or potential fans. Unlike Luther, of course, Benno's enthusiasts were committed to the direct and morally efficacious relationship between the historical Benno and the cultic one. They also rejected Luther's refusal to augur favorable divine judgment from biographical artifact. Still, their works and revisions give evidence of a distinction analogous to Luther's between, on the one hand, the Benno who existed and his biographical artifacts and, on the other, the Benno of literary and artistic portrayal.

The very distinction between artifacts drawn from the past and their fashioning into literary and artistic portrayals has attracted attention in our own day from scholars across the disciplines. The new interest invites a return to Emser's text and favors a new set of questions focused on the author and the vita rather than, as a century ago, on the bishop and his eleventh-century world. The practice of examining how and why writers fashioned their saintly subjects as they did—their use and invention of historical data; their reliance on antecedent narratives; their adoption of a specific literary form and its crafting in a particular rhetorical style; the participation of other interested parties, especially the patrons, in constructing the new narratives; and the instrumentalization of the saintly portrayals—has in the last half century turned writings about the saints into a highly fruitful source for the social and cultural history of the Middle Ages and the early modern period.[12] From this vantage Emser's *Life of Holy Benno* holds out scholarly promise for reasons that were beside the point to the sixteenth-century critics of Benno's canonization and of little interest to the medievalists more recently in search of the historical Benno.

Traces of Renaissance Humanism

Beginning with Emser's text, we find that characteristics of its language point in a promising direction for further investigation. Emser frequently favored an antiquated, classical diction and grammar over the conventions of late medieval scholarly Latin; the text is decorated with references to ancient literature and citations to Quattrocento historians; the vita's protagonists deliver moving, otherwise undocumented orations at crucial moments in the story; an ingratiating dedication and prologue introduce the vita; and elegiac distichs and epigrams precede and follow the text of the printed vita. In these respects *The Life of Holy Benno* is clearly shaped by the Renaissance humanist culture that flourished in German lands as Emser wrote the saint's life. Renaissance humanism was a literary and educational movement that gained strength in fourteenth-century Italy and began to have notable influence on German learning in the last quarter of the fifteenth century.[13] Humanists preferred the study of grammar, rhetoric, poetry, history, and moral philosophy—the *studia humanitatis*—over the study of theology, law, medicine, and natural philosophy.[14] They also favored the forms of expression taught by the ancient masters of rhetoric, such as Cicero and Quintilian, over the Aristotelian logic of the medieval schoolmen. Above all else, humanists loved the ancient languages, a love that was part of a more general enchantment with all things Greek and Roman.

A glance at Emser's own life confirms what the text suggests, namely, that he was a humanist. Humanism's cultural resources and preferences had inspired his training at schools in Tübingen and Basel, and his early career further reveals strong ties to humanist culture. Before his arrival at the ducal court he had tutored the sons of the famed humanist printer John Amerbach,[15] collaborated with Jacob Wimpfeling on editing Giovanni Pico della Mirandola's works, served as secretary to the papal nuncius Raimund Cardinal Peraudi, and lectured in Erfurt on John Reuchlin's classicizing comedy *Sergius*.[16] His publishing efforts included a Latin edition of Xenophon, the first German edition of Erasmus's *Handbook of a Christian Soldier,* and a vernacular edition of the New Testament. These occupations and accomplishments suggest that this Schwabian cleric was not only a humanist but also one of no mean achievement.

That an early sixteenth-century Saxon prince should employ a humanist as his secretary is not surprising. That a humanist would author a saint's life is. Indeed, when we consider the kind of literature *The Life of Holy Benno* was, the humanist style in which Emser wrote it turns the work into a puzzle. This vita was not simply a biography, a sort of literature that humanists commonly wrote for the sake of providing readers moral examples from the past to praise and imitate (if good) and to condemn and avoid (if bad). Rather, *The Life of Holy Benno* was hagiographical: biographical and moral to be sure, but also connected to the cult of the saints and penned as part of a canonization campaign.[17] Renaissance humanists, far from being associated with devotional literature like hagiography, have been associated with its rejection. In this regard, Erasmus of Rotterdam's *Life of Saint Jerome* (1516) is often taken as a model of a new Renaissance sacred biography. Erasmus included in it a manifesto against the elements of traditional saints' lives that he considered objectionable. With his signature wit, Erasmus condemned the "decorated tales" of saints' legends as historically slipshod and spiritually useless. He pointedly excluded several standard components of Jerome's medieval legends that were unlikely or impossible, such as his taming of a lion, his creation as cardinal, and accounts of miracles. Dubbing the vita the West's first modern biography, later scholars lauded it for breaking the medieval mold of fantastic and superstitious writing about saints and holiness.[18]

If we accept, for the moment, Erasmus's disapproval in *The Life of Saint Jerome* as normative for and typical of humanists, then the blame for Emser's literary participation in the cult of Saint Benno might be placed on the shoulders of Emser's employer. The influence of the Maecenas on the artist in this era cannot be overestimated. To blame Duke George, however, begs one question and overlooks another. It begs the question of why he assigned this task to his secretary in the first place. Composing a canonization vita was a delicate matter, and centuries of precedent would have pointed the duke toward more conventional composers of *vitae sanctorum,* to be found in this instance among the monks and clergy of the Saxon ecclesiastical institutions that had long made direct biographical, historical, and devotional claims on the holy bishop. That George instead chose a humanist newly at his court requires closer investigation.

The question that risks being omitted is more basic yet all the more crucial: How common was it for humanists to be composing hagiography? In fact, Emser and his *Life of Holy Benno* were not at all anomalous. Dozens of early German humanists composed and revised hundreds of works in Latin and the vernacular about scores of saints in all of the usual forms—narrative, poetic, dramatic, and liturgical. The authors included humanists as prominent as Jacob Wimpfeling, Conrad Celtis, Joannes Trithemius, and even (if he may be numbered among the Germans) Erasmus himself. Their saintly subjects included men and women venerated broadly across late medieval Germany, such as Saint Boniface and Saint Ann—the mother of the Virgin Mary—and locally in single cities or regions, such as Saint Basin of Trier and Saint Simpert of Augsburg.

The patrons who turned to these humanists ranged from the generous benefactor of the arts and infamous sponsor of indulgence sales, Archbishop Albert of Brandenburg, to an abbot humbly situated at Fischingen in Swiss Thurgau. The humanists dedicated their works to a similarly broad range of persons, from the Holy Roman emperor to the pastor of a pilgrimage church in Westphalia. Many of the works were sent to press; others found their way into canonization acts; still others remain to this day in manuscript form, having left their site of origin, if at all, only in the process of nineteenth-century archival centralization. In short, early German humanists, in league with diverse elements of their contemporaneous society, were among the most prolific composers and editors of hagiographical texts in the decades leading up to the Reformations in Germany.

Humanists and Saints

The purpose of the present volume is to investigate how and why the early German humanists composed so much about the saints. *Reforming Saints* examines the intersection of a kind of writer (the humanist) and a kind of literature (hagiography) at a defining moment for both. By exploring salient themes in the humanists' hagiographical writings and relating them to the general religious culture of the era, *Reforming Saints* discovers the unexpected yet coherent extent of humanist engagement in the cult of the saints and exposes the strategic ways that these authors made writings about the saints into a literature for religious and cultural reforms that German humanists promoted through much else of their activity. Despite the abundance of this material and its promise to shed light on humanist culture in pre-Reformation German society, it has not attracted much scholarly attention or positive evaluation. The historiographical preterition and misapprehension have three principal causes. Examining them here briefly will bring into focus the presuppositions and alternative approach of *Reforming Saints*.

Humanists Crafting Vitae Sanctorum

The derogation of Emser that we saw in the nineteenth-century scholarship has already pointed us toward one cause of the neglect of the literature: It tends not to be a reliable source for historical and biographical information about its medieval subjects. Despite the authors' frequently expressed concern for biographical accuracy, little evidence in support of the claim accumulates in the lives themselves. *Reforming Saints*, however, interrogates the vitae for something else, namely, what they reveal about the cultures where they were written and read.[19] On these grounds, I do not mine Emser's *Life of Holy Benno,* as well as mutatis mutandis the other writings, for information about the eleventh-century bishop and his diocese but rather for evidence of the sixteenth-century mentalities and cultural aspirations of those who commissioned, wrote, and read it.

But even if understanding eleventh-century Meissen is not a goal, determining how Emser crafted the vita out of sources at his disposal is central. That nearly all of the saints the early German humanists wrote about had well-established hagiographical dossiers that were accessible to the authors then and extant today makes this task possible. Indeed, most authors did not compose the lives de novo from snippets of information collected from medieval chronicles and catalogues, but rather revised intact older vitae. Many of the resulting works retained strong resemblances to their antecedents, regardless of whether the authors admitted their reliance. The similarities led subsequent researchers to treat the later works as insignificant Renaissance editions of more noteworthy medieval lives. Direct comparison of the authors' final products to the older vitae, however, usually renders confusing the earlier and the later works impossible. The differences accumulate and expose patterns of alteration to the biography and sanctity of the particular holy man or woman, to the saintly markers of a type of holy man or woman, and to the way of writing about the saints.

Even when the variations seem minor, they can still reveal much about why the humanists were writing the material.[20] Literature about the saints was by nature conservative. Older legends benefited from their antiquity, real or imagined, among devotees. Authors who altered, abandoned, or added to the established stories risked alienating their readers. Analyzing how humanists took that risk—in their writings about saints no less than in other historical texts—promises to yield information about two important relationships:[21] first, between humanists and the medieval past and, second, between humanists and their readerships. Analysis of the variations works against the conventional understanding of a characteristic hostility of humanists to the medieval past because it ultimately reveals the positive and creative ways in which humanists drew their saintly subjects out of that past. The variations also give us evidence of how authors and readers shared a respect for contemporary religious custom and popular piety. Repeatedly we see that humanists did not follow the older materials they found. In consequence, authors, patrons, and other readers sometimes disagreed over the narrative results. Further corrections and revisions could be required, as could the undoing of revisions once made. Especially when we have multiple drafts of an author's work on a single saint, we can discern the negotiations and compromises that could be made by diverse segments of a society that had a common devotion to its holy men and women. Variants, corrections, and recorrections are thus important data for this study.

A Problem of Periodization: Between Medieval and Early Modern

A second cause of the neglect of the literature has to do with its fit into the history of a kind of writing. A half century of research across the disciplines has made it axiomatic that the sources for the medieval cult of the saints— literary, artistic, and archeological—offer precious access to Europe's social and cultural past. The question then arises whether the humanist literature about the saints offers fresh insight into the society of its day. Hesitancy in an affirmative response stems in no small part from a certain betwixt-and-between quality of these writings: The humanist works have fallen victim to the problem of periodization, specifically to the ambiguous line separating medieval and early modern. For all the energetic attention that sources on the saints receive today, most studies of them are still conceived as either medieval or early modern. In practice, this means that the former reach only as far as the early fifteenth century and the latter begin only after the mid-sixteenth-century Council of Trent.[22] Up to now the most stimulating scholarship on devotion to holy men and women during the so-called long sixteenth century has focused on its transformed manifestation in Protestant Europe in sermons on feast days, funeral orations, and martyrologies.[23] In contrast, Catholic writing about the saints in this period has been left largely unexplored, leaving the strange impression that Catholic authors fell asleep one evening appending newly concocted, miracle-laden vitae to *The Golden Legend* and woke up the next morning to begin critically editing the January lives of the *Acta sanctorum*.[24]

Although the lines connecting the thirteenth-century *Golden Legend* and the seventeenth-century *Acta sanctorum* were neither straight nor unambiguous, they did traverse the humanists. *Reforming Saints* explains the transitions made along that tortuous development to the extent that humanists were their agents. This study's starting point corresponds to a resurgence of saintly life writing that began in the 1470s after a half century of its scarcity. This interruption was peculiar to Germany.[25] In part the interruption is related to the turmoil in German lands caused by the Councils of Constance and Basel coupled with the burgeoning of several new religious movements such as the Modern Devotion, monastic reform, and the Observant branches of mendicant orders. In the mid-fifteenth century these movements were busy establishing themselves across the Holy Roman Empire, articulating new religious visions, and developing new devotional customs. Their efforts at setting roots in German society may have drawn their writers away from devotional writing about saints, ambiguously regarded as it was at the time in many ecclesiastical circles. Whereas in earlier centuries monks and mendicants were the principal authors of texts about saints, in the period under consideration here secular priests were the most common authors. Moreover, themes associated with the Modern Devotion—emphasis on the inner life of the individual and meditation on the life and passion of Christ—rarely surface in the vitae sanctorum.[26]

The study ends in the 1520s. Luther's break with Rome and the consequent religious turmoil may make this caesura obvious. It is, however, easy to overestimate and misunderstand. On the one hand, although Luther opposed events such as Benno's canonization with vigorous rhetoric and subtle theology, opposition to the veneration of the saints—at the level of doctrine and practice—was neither newly his nor at the center of his reforming program. One finds in the Middle Ages a recurrent skepticism toward saintly veneration's theological justification and harsh criticism of abuses in its common practice. Calvin and Zwingli eradicated the cult of the saints with far greater determination than Luther. And although the Council of Trent affirmed the veneration of the saints in theory and condemned certain abuses, it did so quietly and not until its twenty-fifth and last session in 1563.[27] The first canonization thereafter was promulgated in 1588, sixty-five years after Benno's. Throughout *Reforming Saints* and in particular in the Conclusion, an eye is kept on the ways later polemicists, devotional writers, and scholars produced new writings about the saints through the tumultuous sixteenth century, relied on the earlier humanists as they did this, and acknowledged that debt.

What Ought Humanists to Have Written?

HUMANISM ACROSS THE ALPS. A third problem in studying humanist writings about the saints is much related to the second and has to do with more recent ideas of what the humanists ought to have been writing. The usual approach to Renaissance humanists begins with an examination of what they were writing in Latin on pagan or secular themes in Italy. From this vantage, writings by early German humanists about saints could not reasonably hope for much notice. Indeed, the conventional interpretation holds that the best humanists were not writing it; when they did, it was not their best material, and what was written is not worth closer historical analysis.[28] Only the most recent research into Italian humanism has begun to suggest something different. As a result, we now have a better grasp of not only the sheer quantity of such materials but also the forces that brought Italian humanists to write about the saints and the strategies that these authors employed in composing their legends.[29] The newly analyzed Italian phenomenon provides *Reforming Saints* with a model against which to compare the German texts. The similarities and differences are complex: Northerners and southerners preferred different saintly types, experimented with and structured narratives differently, and put their compositions to different uses. Moreover, the Italians mastered a level of classicizing that the Germans did not achieve in these decades. Still, a comparison of their engagement with literature about the saints sheds significant new light on the vexed relationship between Italian and German humanists and shows it, at least here, to be harmonious. Writing about saints made the early German humanists more, not less, like their Italian counterparts.

HUMANISTS IN GERMAN SOCIETY. An analogous problem arises when attention turns to the relationship of German humanists to broader German society. For humanists north of the Alps (and nowhere more than in the Holy Roman Empire) the plans to reanimate Western society began with reforming Christianity.[30] Conventional understandings of how the humanists contributed to sixteenth-century religious reform have taught us to look in two directions for those contributions. First, the humanist interest in religious reform has long inspired investigation into the ways that early humanists anticipated and inspired Luther and his reforming program. That there was something substantive and not merely accidental or coincidental to the relationship between humanists and Evangelicals finds confirmation in the sixteenth-century quip (likely of Catholic origin) that Erasmus "laid the egg that Luther hatched."[31] This saying takes its modern, scholarly form in the dictum "no Reformation without humanism."[32] From this the uberous hypothesis has been devised that humanism in Germany existed in a privileged, causal relationship to the Reformation and was fundamentally more at home with Protestantism, even before the fact in the fifteenth century, than with Catholicism.[33] Recent attempts to show how the humanist movement in Germany, in fact, went through a profound process of confessionalization that divided it and sapped it of considerable creative energy have helped attenuate the conventional interpretation of German humanists as proto-Reformers (whether intended as compliment or disparagement).[34] Still, when it comes to appreciating humanism's first appropriations into a German context and its participants' attitudes to late medieval religion, old prejudices still hold. By these lights no early humanist qua humanist would have had anything to do with the veneration of saints.[35]

An alternative insistence that the early German humanists be understood not as precursors to Luther but as anticipators of Erasmus does not shed any more flattering light on their hagiographical compositions. Although he maintained his religious allegiance to Rome despite strained relationships with many of Catholicism's most fervid adherents, Erasmus leveled much criticism against the cult of the saints in general and hagiography in particular, as in his life of Saint Jerome. In this regard he was like many late medieval learned elites. But to take Erasmus's pronouncements in *The Life of Saint Jerome* as normative simply excludes too much of what the earlier humanists wrote, to say nothing of Erasmus's other, sometimes even exuberant, writings about saints.[36] Furthermore, since so much hagiography appeared before Erasmus took center stage in the world of German humanism, applying an Erasmian standard to the earlier writings is as anachronistic as applying the Lutheran one.

Humanism in the empire was a far more complex phenomenon than the example of Erasmus could give us to understand. Non-Erasmian elements in the hagiography such as patriotism and sympathy for common devotions did not make these texts any less humanist than similar manifestations in humanists' other works. Such penchants were not antithetic to or digressions from humanism as it took root in Germany but intrinsic to it.[37] A central principle of *Reforming Saints* follows from this observation, namely, that these writings about the saints must, in the first instance, be analyzed on their own terms in the context of their composition and reception rather than in anticipation of Luther or Erasmus. When we allow the humanist authors to speak in their own voice, what we find is that they were exuberant writers about the saints. That such literary activity on their part may startle us surely has more to do with the limitations of our training than theirs: For such consummate rhetoricians as the humanists, who would by nature have an eye for the most genial ways to move their audience's heart, and in a society where people named their children, coped with illness, mourned their dead, kept time, honored their cities, and evaluated their rulers, all with the help of the saints, what could be more suitable than to turn to the cult of the saints and the abundant ways of writing about them? Like learned Christians for centuries before, the Renaissance humanists did just that and used writing about the saints to raise issues of both great moment and common human experience.

German Humanists and German Vitae Sanctorum

Reforming Saints proceeds by strategically focusing on forty freestanding Latin lives, composed new or revised between 1470 and 1530, of holy men and women who had been active in the German lands of the Holy Roman Empire.[38] These writings have been singled out for several reasons. The free-standing, prose, Latin life has a privileged place in the history of writings about the saints. Extensive study of similar vitae from previous centuries allows for more reliable comparison over time than, say, poetic and liturgical writings. Whereas contemporaneous vernacular lives in Germany have received much scholarly attention in recent years, the Latin lives, for reasons outlined earlier, have been neglected.[39] Their analysis promises nonetheless to shed light on and beyond the learned milieus in which they were composed.

The focus on German saints heightens the challenge by inquiring into the nature of humanists' engagement with local religious culture. On the one hand, historians have long looked to humanists for the ways that they were most strikingly detached from late medieval culture, its popular, religious dimensions more than any other. On the other hand, it was at the local level that the cult of the saints was at its most serviceable in shaping medieval and early modern European society. Indeed, as Peter Brown highlights with the notion of *praesentia*, a cult without a strong and specific locality would be anomalous, even absurd.[40] Indeed, *Reforming Saints* shows how Brown's observations on late Antiquity apply to early modern Christianity as well.

I have attempted to ensure that all such lives would be accounted for in this study. The five centuries in which vitae have had time to be lost, destroyed, dispersed, and even reedited beyond recognition caution against making a claim of exhaustiveness. The chapters concentrate on specific cases, but I have taken care to emphasize aspects of the highlighted cases that find resonance elsewhere within the literature. Furthermore, I have endeavored to trace connections between the narrative writings and those in other genres, precisely because these different forms were never composed in isolation. In point of fact, the single largest number of humanist works on the saints was poetic.[41] Frequently decorating the printed vitae, the poetry can tip off the modern-day researcher to the humanist origins of a text.

Judging a vita to be humanist is not an easy task. It generally begins with the determination of its classicizing language, marks of which include a restrictive classical diction and grammar, some hellenization of vocabulary, and the use of classical imagery. Aspects of style are dealt with throughout the study. Discussion of the use of neo-Latin, the relation of Latin to the vernaculars, and panegyrical strategies occurs throughout the following chapters. If the text can be characterized as "classicizing," then further confirmation of its humanist fit is sought in the training, employment, and literary oeuvre of the author. Additionally, attending to the patrons and dedicatees can give further indication of the cultural contexts in and for which the authors worked.

Compared with each other and the canon of humanist literature, these vitae can be judged along a scale of more and less "humanist," as can the authors themselves: Emser's *Life of Holy Benno* is a more elaborate, confident humanist text than John Scheckmann's *Life of Saint Basin, Bishop of Trier*. And whereas Abbot Joannes Trithemius, who wrote four vitae sanctorum, clearly numbered among the early German humanists, Abbot Andrew Lang, who twice revised *The Life of Saint Otto of Bamberg* and obviously had some exposure to the new learning, did not. In order to highlight the variety of ways that authors show their humanist colors in connection with the works they produced and the readerships they aspired to, as well as to avoid the implicit construction of an ideal humanist, I leave the introduction of the authors to the chapters themselves. Furthermore, including the range of more and less humanist texts in this study respects the varied ways in which the humanist program was appropriated in Germany both by a segment of the learned population and by a larger population not beholden to the entirety of the program even if enamored of large parts of it. By the same token, *Reforming Saints* remains attentive to the ways that in these writings the humanist authors, for all the diversity in their approaches, tools, and texts, were at their most accessible and intimately linked to broader (and at times less learned) culture and belief. Produced in socially mixed situations, classicizing saints' lives were not an elite aberration.

Exploring the complicated relationships, social and intellectual, that resulted in the composition of the texts is the task of the following chapters. The first two chapters draw attention to the types of saints that appeared most frequently in the new texts: bishops and recluses. The holy bishops in these vitae consistently modeled a way of achieving church reform, predicated on a common sense of Christianity's lamentable state and the bishops' proper role as the catalyst of reform. The lives of the holy bishops articulated the perceived problem and proposed the solution: The German peoples needed a reevangelization in the fifteenth century analogous to the evangelization of pagan tribes by missionary bishops centuries before. Not limited to humanists in its attractiveness, this reforming conviction drew the authors into alliances with patrons and devotees beyond narrow humanist circles.

A second large group of vitae had as subjects monks and nuns whose cults were geographically limited to single churches and small regions. Even at this local level, however, new ambitions to have official legends written in the latest style were emerging. Leaders of these local cults sought out humanist authors. Local attraction to the humanist style, however, did not obviate the need to respect local traditions about the saints. An examination of two pairs of lives, each including an original life by a humanist and his own later revision, exposes a fundamental tension between the appeal of a new style and a respect for traditional narratives that was intrinsic to the cult of the saints. The results of revisions in different, nearly opposite directions—Albert von Bonstetten's second vita of Saint Ida and Sigmund Meisterlin's second vita of Saint Sebald—show how complicated the interactions between humanist authors and their patrons could be.

A common kind of amendment humanists made to the narratives, regardless of the type of saint being addressed, was to the historical, social, and geographical setting. The third chapter demonstrates how humanist authors amended the civic and cultural affiliations of the saints in novel and ahistorical ways. I demonstrate that these changes associated their hagiography with the *Germania illustrata* project, a wider movement among German humanists to investigate, construct, and glorify an ancient and a medieval past that was "German."

While the humanists never managed to create a patron saint for *Germania,* chapter four examines how the Swiss did—or at least began to. The very ambiguities that make it difficult to define "Switzerland" in this period appear in the abundant hagiography written about the peasant-turned-hermit Nicholas of Flue. Nicholas became an exemplar of Swiss character that retained its appeal even as confessional divisions between Catholics and the Reformed hardened through the sixteenth century. Chapter four reads the humanist compositions about Nicholas of Flue as an indicator of how the cities and regions making up the Swiss Confederation increasingly conceived of themselves as a unit in this transitional period and of how Nicholas could posthumously attenuate the religious, political, and social stresses across the confederation that threatened its unity. In short, the case of Nicholas shows how authors could turn saints into civic patrons in a new humanist mode.

In the final analysis *Reforming Saints* shows that there is no single answer to the question of why the early humanists in Germany wrote hagiography in the first place. Humanists, even early ones in Germany, do not let themselves be categorized so simply, and their writing about saints served a variety of uses. In dimensions outlined earlier, humanist attention to saints continued medieval practice. At the same time, we can discern new patterns in the vitae: The humanists who were writing hagiography took this most popular of medieval religious genres and transposed it in a humanist mode, changing aspects of it to better suit their standards of good literature, to explain why the past was worth studying and how good examples might be drawn from this past and presented for emulation and even more so for praise, and to illustrate how religious and secular society should be transformed by reflection on the lives of the saints. Furthermore, *Reforming Saints* shows that, despite their elitist reputation, the humanists were not composing in ivory towers detached from broader society. Rather, many different cultural forces were engaging them with their patrons and readers, real and anticipated, as well as the devotees who heard the new stories read from pulpits. The humanists were attentive to many of these forces and shaped their compositions accordingly in the hope of enhancing their persuasive power. In this light, these authors, who as humanists have so often been simplistically cast as the great harbingers of the modern and scorners of things medieval, were doing what learned Christian authors had done throughout the medieval era. Thus the real question is not, Did the early German humanists write hagiography?—and certainly not, as those who want the humanists to be something other than they were ask with disappointment, How could they write hagiography?—because they so obviously did. Rather, given that they did write hagiography, how and to what ends did they convert it into a humanist genre? These are the questions I seek to answer in the following pages.

I

Reforming the Church

Humanist Authors and Bishop Saints

Bishops make war and cause unrest in the world; they behave like secular lords, which are, of course, what they are. . . . A bishop ought to take up permanent residence in the principal church of his diocese and lead a spiritual life there.

—"Reformatio Sigismundi" (1439)

The author of "Emperor Sigismund's Reformation" did not likely have the Introduction's eleventh-century protagonist Bishop Benno of Meissen in mind when he sketched his aspirations for the late medieval Imperial church in 1439. Nonetheless, similar concerns inspired Duke George of Saxony to begin petitioning Benno's canonization sixty years later and Emser to author the vita. The single most striking dimension of Benno's saintly persona in the new portrayals of him was his efforts at reforming Christian society by spreading and implementing authentic Christian religion. This aspect of Emser's composition points chapter one toward its first goal, namely, to investigate how Emser crafted Benno's portrayal to serve reforming ideals advocated by both his noble employer and his humanist colleagues. At the same time, the chapter is more than simply a case study: The most common subject of the forty vitae of German saints composed new or revised between 1470 and 1530 was the holy bishop, and the most common kind of author was a humanist. This observation immediately suggests the two broader goals that are at the heart of this chapter: first, explaining the popularity of the bishop as a particular saintly type and the humanist as a particular type of author; and second, identifying the concerns about Christian society that guided the writing of this largest single group of vitae and made holy bishops a key part of the solution within and beyond humanist circles.

There is also a practical reason for taking the vitae of episcopal saints as our starting point. There is abundant material about holy bishops composed in other regions and time periods that lends itself to comparative analysis with what our later German authors composed. Comparative analysis brings into focus the historically and culturally specific ways in which the authors were appropriating and transforming traditions about bishop saints as a group and traditions about individual holy bishops.[1] The accumulated results of such comparisons suggest the development of a new way of thinking about reform that exposes a new kind of historical consciousness and in turn suited humanists particularly well, namely, that fifteenth and early-sixteenth-century society required a reform akin to the earliest missionary efforts to the pagan Germanic tribes that the German humanists understood to be the antecedents of their own society. Consideration in this chapter of the authors' intellectual and social backgrounds and their relationships to patrons and readerships also establishes a groundwork that serves as a touchstone for analysis of other saintly types and contextual issues in the later chapters.

Medieval Bishops and Renaissance Lives

Bishops had been central in the propagation of Christianity and the administration of the church from its earliest centuries. This was especially true in the Holy Roman Empire, where the prince-bishop exercised temporal and spiritual authority as nowhere else in Christendom. Medieval bishops' rights and obligations were frequently articulated not only in laws and legal treatises, as might be expected, but also in narrative works such as diocesan chronicles, catalogues of bishops, gesta episcoporum, and vitae.[2] Biographical assertions about bishops, in addition to encouraging popular devotion and contributing to a canonization petition, could be used to establish legal claims in conflicts within and between dioceses, between dioceses and other ecclesiastical entities, and between spiritual and temporal authorities. Moreover, the power of bishops made writing about them suitable for addressing issues of local and regional importance in a variety of spheres—the religious, cultural, and political among them. In short, episcopal vitae were important because they were about important people whose influence affected so many dimensions of medieval society. In consequence, some of the most widely distributed vitae sanctorum in the Middle Ages were about holy bishops.[3]

The wide-ranging implications of episcopal vitae made their composition tricky affairs. Claims about a bishop needed to be justified. The strongest justification for the authors of episcopal lives was often found in the precedent of earlier vitae and other sources, both written documents and contemporaneous, popular convictions. Written precedent provides the first important points of comparison – and hence the continuities and the alterations between older and newer vitae – with which to judge what the later authors were trying to accomplish with their new compositions. The vitae we are considering can be divided into three groups along lines of their dependence on preceding writings. The first group consists of original and largely original vitae. Emser's life of Benno belongs to this group. Other original vitae are the first two freestanding vitae of the scholastic philosopher and bishop of Regensburg, Albertus Magnus, in the 1480s;[4] an anonymously composed life of Boniface, the well-known eighth-century missionary to Germany and founding bishop of Mainz;[5] the vitae of the early bishops of Trier Basin (seventh century) and Poppo (eleventh century) by John Scheckmann, a monk of the Saint Maximinus monastery in Trier;[6] and the lives of the bishops of Mainz, Maximus and Rhabanus Maurus, by the reforming Benedictine abbot and humanist Joannes Trithemius.[7] The amount of documentary evidence that the authors possessed in each of these instances varied: There were few older references to Basin or Benno, but Albertus Magnus was remembered in brief biographical passages in several late medieval Dominican chronicles, as well as in his own abundant philosophical corpus. Only the vitae of Albert and Benno were printed in their own day. The others were written as manuscripts and remained so through the sixteenth century. Moreover, only a few new vitae have as their subject a recently deceased holy bishop, as for example the vita of John Schallermann, bishop of Gurk, who died in 1465.[8]

A second category of vitae consists of works that count as minimally altered editions of older lives. Veit "Acropolitanus" Bild (1481–1529), a monk in Augsburg, edited a collection of the lives of Augsburg's three patron-saints— the bishops Ulrich and Simpert and the virgin-martyr Afra—in *Stories of the Patrons of the See of Augsburg: Christ's Glorious Confessors Ulrich and Simpert as well as the Blessed Martyr Afra,* which was printed in Augsburg in 1516 and then again in German translation later the same year. Bild did not treat his holy subjects all in the same way. The chapters on Saint Ulrich and Saint Afra barely diverge from these saints' principal medieval vitae.[9] Another minimally altered life would appear to be Jacob Wimpfeling's edition of an anonymous

Life of Saint Adelph that was printed in Strassburg in 1506. The preface, a dedicatory letter to a local noble, was Wimpfeling's principal addition. Heraldic devices representing the lord to whom Wimpfeling dedicated the vita adorn the title page (see figure 1.1).[10] The 1508 printed edition of *The Life of Saint Swithbert, Apostle to the Frisians and Bishop of Verden* represents a variation within this category. It is based on a late fourteenth- or early fifteenth-century counterfeit ascribed to an early medieval priest Marcellinus, discovered in the monastery at Kaiserwerth (on the Rhine, downstream from Düsseldorf), and prepared for publication in the early sixteenth century by two professors from Cologne.[11]

The third and largest group comprises the range of vitae that were the result of significant reworkings of older lives. In these cases, the author's reliance on an older life is consistent and obvious; but when they are compared there is no mistaking newer life for the older. Bild's vita of Saint Simpert, a ninth-century bishop of Augsburg, included in his *Stories of the Patrons*, is, for example, a marked revision Adilbert's tenth-century vita.[12] The Carthusian Werner Rolevinck's abbreviation and revision of an older life of the fourth-century bishop of Tongeren Saint Servatius, which was printed in Cologne in 1471, likewise falls into this category.[13] Andrew Lang, an abbot of the Michaelsberg monastery in Bamberg, twice redacted earlier lives of Otto, a twelfth-century bishop of Bamberg: the first time in 1474, the second in 1498 and 1499.[14] Joannes Cincinnius's *Life of Saint Ludger of Münster* (1515) was the author's own translation and revision of his German life of Saint Ludger (1512), which was itself a revision of Altfrid's ninth-century vita and its two principal medieval revisions.[15]

Shortly before his death in 1520, John Freiburger, a canon in Freising, reworked an older life of Saint Corbinian, an eighth-century missionary to Bavaria and Tyrol.[16] Saint Wolfgang, a tenth-century bishop of Regensburg, was the subject of two printed lives, both derived from Othlo's eleventh-century vita. The first was published in Burgdorf, Switzerland, in 1475. The other appeared in Landshut in 1516, followed by its German translation the same year. The Landshut abbot Wolfgang Haberl commissioned the work, and a local poet with a humanist education, Wolfgang Seidel, contributed to the vita by appending a couplet to the title page and a short panegyrical poem after the miracle accounts.[17]

Poetry's special appeal to humanists accounts for its appearance as the most common form of writing in honor of the saints in this period. Poems and epigrams decorated all of the printed vitae. Jacob of Gouda composed a *vita metrica* of Albertus Magnus in elegiac distichs that appeared as an appendix to Rudolf of Nijmegen's vita of 1490.[18] Sometimes a poetic work was the prin-

Vita sancti Adelphi patroni Colle
gij Nouillaren. In dominio Liechtenbergen: Dyo
cesis Argentinensis. Obi et corpus eius requiescit.

VIRTVTI AVITAE

FIGURE I.I. Title page. Jacob Wimpfeling, *Vita sancti Adelphi patroni Collegii No-villarensis* (Strassburg, 1506). Call number: an Ink A 22 (7). Reproduced by permission of the Universitäts- und Landesbibliothek Sachsen Anhalt, Halle a. Saale, Germany.

The title page of Wimpfeling's *Life of Saint Adelph* bears the arms not of the bishop-saint's family or see but rather of the local Alsatian count Philip III of Hanau-Lichtenberg, for whom the Strassburg humanist had prepared the vita. The count's recent installation occasioned the dedication. The connection between the count and bishop was the saint's tomb, which was in the count's territory.

cipal component of a printed book, such as Philip "Engentinus" Engelbrecht's *Life of Saint Lambert*. One of the longest poems about a saint from the period, it consisted of more than 750 lines of dactylic hexameter, the meter of classical epic poetry such as *The Illiad* and *The Aeneid*. Engentinus preceded the poem with a dedicatory epistle to the "consuls and senate" of Freiburg in Breisgau, where he lectured in poetry. He followed the dedication with a letter in elegiac couplets addressed to a humanist colleague in praise of the city and a poem to Mnemosyne, the mother of the muses and the ancient Greek goddess of memory.[19] Sebastian Brant, a leading early humanist in Basel, composed much hagiographical poetry and often published these poems either singly on broadsheets or in collections, yet other forms that writing about the saints could take in the hands of a humanist author.[20]

The majority of the episcopal vitae—as opposed to the vitae of recluses in chapter two—were printed. Few of the vitae had as their subject a recently deceased holy bishop, and none of these was printed. The less original the vita, the more likely that the bishop-saint lived in the early Middle Ages. All of the bishops enjoyed established saintly veneration before the new vitae were written. A certain number of vernacular lives appeared alongside the Latin lives, but there was no general rule of linguistic priority: For example, Cincinnius's German life of Ludger preceded the Latin version, but in the case of Bild's *Stories of the Patrons*, the German followed the Latin.

These observations begin to suggest intended readerships, or at least exclude some. In view of the fact that the saintly subjects already enjoyed veneration and few vitae were associated with canonization petitions, for example, one can infer that the vitae were not written for an otherwise decisive readership of saints' vitae, the Roman curia.[21] Neither Benno's veneration nor the petition for his canonization was an unusual event at this time in the empire. His actual canonization was, however. The most recent canonization of a German saint had been that of Leopold the Pious, margrave of Austria, in 1485. Leopold's canonization, like Benno's, had required the intensive efforts of a coalition of leading political and ecclesiastical figures—Emperor Frederick III and the canons regular at Klosterneuburg (north of Vienna). The petitioners called into service prominent Roman churchmen to craft the vita that would effectively persuade the papal curia of Leopold's suitability for canonization. Frederick had turned to Leopold in his search for an Austrian patron saint only after the pope had rejected the petition for the eleventh-century noble widow and monastery foundress Hemma of Gurk.[22]

The Cologne Dominicans wrote their two lives of Albertus Magnus (printed in Cologne, 1486–1487 and 1490) for a canonization that did not occur for another four and a half centuries. A similar Carthusian attempt in the

1510s to arrange the canonization of their founder, Bruno of Cologne, resulted only in the pope's verbal approval of his veneration within houses of the order. These rejected petitions need to be understood, however, in the context of a period in which canonizations were rare.[23]

The Authors and Their Patrons

Associating an author with Renaissance humanism is a delicate task because there is so little consensus about how to identify a humanist or define humanism. The principal definitions in use today differ in how they give relative weight to philosophical, rhetorical, and sociological dimensions of humanism.[24] Without giving outright precedence to any of these dimensions, I favor admitting both *degrees* and *kinds* of humanism in evaluating the hagiographical authors and their writings. Appreciating degrees and kinds of humanism allows for an analysis of the historical phenomenon that both accounts for most of the writing and accommodates variations within it. Likewise, it steers us clear of stylizing "the humanist" in a way that fundamentally distorts evaluation of these authors' writings.

Varieties of Humanist Association

Emser, shown in the Introduction to have been an accomplished and a recognized humanist, shared this clear association with many other authors of saints' lives. Some of them, referred to already, were yet more prominent: Wimpfeling and Trithemius played key roles in fostering the *studia humanitatis* in the empire, Wimpfeling within the context of the Sodalitas Rhenana, Trithemius within the context of Benedictine monasticism. Wimpfeling dedicated *The Life of Saint Adelph* to the Alsatian noble in whose territory the bishop's relics were preserved. Trithemius received his commission to write the lives of Saints Maximus and Rhabanus Maurus from Albert, archbishop-elector of Mainz (r. 1514–1545), on the occasion of these saints' translation to Mainz in 1516.[25] Veit Bild, another devotee of the studia humanitatis, had been a prized student of Jacob "Philomusus" Locher and poet laureate Joannes Stabius at the University of Ingolstadt. He was employed as a parish scribe at Saint Ulrich's in Augsburg and was ordained a deacon in 1503. Shortly thereafter he entered the monastery of Saint Ulrich in Augsburg. He studied the sacred languages of Hebrew, Greek, and Latin, authored works on music, historiography, philosophy, mathematics, and astronomy, and became a bulwark of Augsburg's humanist circle. He calculated astrological calendars and became an accomplished maker of sundials. Like most humanists, he was an avid writer of letters, and his correspondents included Conrad Peutinger, George Spalatin, Willibald Pirckheimer, Joannes Oecolampadius and Martin Luther. The correspondence with the two last figures reveals a sympathy for the reformers that waned after the Peasants' War in 1525. Bild's hagiographical compositions included, in addition to *Stories of the Patrons,* a liturgical life of Saint Jerome.[26]

It is difficult to identify other authors as humanist; indeed, some were not. One learned author without clear humanist training or sensibilities was the Trier monk John Scheckmann (d. 1531), who wrote lives of Trier bishops Basin and Poppo. Scheckmann wrote prolifically on devotional and historical topics: When it was wondrously discovered in 1512, he composed a work on the Holy Tunic, a garment that Christ himself reputedly wore. The same year he completed a history of the archdiocese of Trier, *The Tract in Praise of the Holy Church of Trier.* Around 1515 Scheckmann compiled descriptive catalogues of the relics kept at his own monastery and at the neighboring monastery of Saint Paulinus. He revised Bishop Johannes Enen's *A Short History of Trier,* translating it from its original vernacular into Latin and adding numerous references and allusions from classical literature; the resulting *A Brief History of Events in Trier* was printed in 1517. The epistolary preface of Scheckmann's *Life of Saint Basin* was addressed to the abbot of the monastery of Saint Maximinus, Vincent Cochineus. In it he explained that the composition was meant for use in the monastery where Basin lay buried and so for the encouragement of devotion to the seventh-century bishop as a matter of prestige for the monastery. The recent translations of several additional saints in other monasteries in Trier gave a competitive dimension to such encouragement. All of his writings betray classicizing tendencies and an interest in regional history akin to many of the authors who were humanists. Furthermore, he was a monk active in a monastery with a school with a humanist curriculum in place in the early sixteenth century. At the same time there is no indication he was formally educated in the studia humanitatis, traveled or corresponded with self-identifying humanists, or supported other programs associated with them.[27]

Like Scheckmann, Andrew Lang (1440/1450–1502) authored a bishop's vita, wrote in somewhat classicizing Latin, and had some contact with humanist scholars but lacked any strong association with humanism as a program of learning or scholarly milieu. One is on surer ground identifying evidence of humanist influence on him and in his writing than in identifying him tout court as a humanist. The abbot of the Michaelsberg monastery in Bamberg from 1483 until his death, Lang composed a catalogue of his abbatial predecessors in 1494, a chronicle of Bamberg's bishops between 1487 and

1494, a catalogue of Benedictine saints, and catalogues of Bamberg's bishops. With the encouragement of Trithemius he wrote a defense of the Immaculate Conception in 1497, a disputed Christian doctrine at the time, but much esteemed by humanists. His *Life of Saint Otto, Bishop of Bamberg* synthesized two older lives of the saint, who had led a reform of the Michaelsberg abbey in the twelfth century and was later buried there. In 1487 Lang sent the first vita to the duke of Pomerania, a region that Otto had extensively evangelized. The second, in 1499, went to the superior of the Bamberg Dominicans. A concern to reconcile the two medieval lives (the earliest, the commonly named Prüfeninger vita, made yet a third[28]) could have been a motivation in its own right.[29] Moreover, the town council of Nuremberg, in lengthy rivalry with nearby Bamberg, had been hard at work fostering its own local cults in an attempt to extract the city, at least symbolically, from Bamberg's oppressive shadow. In such a context, the need to promote afresh Bamberg's foremost saint was clearly also a motivation for so prominent a churchman to revise the saint's vitae.[30]

Scholastic Humanists and Saint Swithbert

The Life of Saint Swithbert (Cologne, 1508) finds itself in an entirely different milieu, yet with intriguing humanist connections. The author of the prologue reported that Gerhard Harderwijk—a member of the Laurentian Burse in Cologne, a dean of the faculty of the arts, and a rector of the university—had discovered a manuscript of the vita during a brief stay in the monastery at Kaiserswerth, where he and his students had taken refuge during a regional outbreak of the plague. Swithbert had been an Anglo-Saxon missionary bishop to Friesland and Westphalia in the late seventh and early eighth centuries and had founded the Kaiserswerth monastery. Harderwijk determined that a broader public deserved access to the manuscript and prepared the text for publication. According to the result's preface, "He took those books by holy authors, for so many centuries neglected and sought after, now discovered and diligently studied. He spent a month of correcting, tearing out the mistakes, with which the books were teeming; and he resolved that they advance into the light of day by being published."[31] Harderwijk died in 1503 before completing his work, so the task was adopted by the author of the preface.

The author of this letter was no less than Ortwinus Gratius (ca. 1480–1542), the archetype of the so-called scholastic humanist.[32] He encapsulated the seeming contradictions of that label in his own intellectual biography: On the one hand, he was a loyal student of Alexander Hegius (1433–1498), the humanist schoolmaster of Saint Lebuinus in Deventer.[33] In Cologne

Gratius taught poetry and rhetoric, and was a skilled editor of Latin texts for the Quentel printing house. On the other hand, when his colleagues—usually humanists and including Hermann Busch—diverged from the established medieval rules of grammar and dialectic, his criticism could be withering. Moreover, Gratius aligned himself firmly on the side of John Pfefferkorn during the Reuchlin controversy (i.e., the scholastic, antihumanist side), and translated many of Pfefferkorn's vernacular tracts into Latin. For this he was vilified in the *Letters of Obscure Men* (1515–1517), the definitive humanist denunciation of the scholastically inclined. In the final analysis, Gratius is more fairly characterized as a synthesizer who was confident in the ultimate reconciliation of scholastic and humanist pedagogies. He advocated amending the university curricula in Cologne accordingly. These revised programs provide the standard by which "scholastic humanism" is defined and judged in the modern scholarly literature.[34]

In 1881 this supposedly eighth-century vita of Saint Swithbert was revealed to be a late fourteenth- or early fifteenth-century counterfeit.[35] That does not appear to have been Gerhard's or Gratius's understanding; and we should not suspect Swithbert's promoters of duplicity, even if knowledge of its spurious origins would not have made it unacceptable to the monks at Kaiserswerth. By the moral reckoning of the time, even a counterfeit vita could point the readers to a holy person who had lived in this world no less than they themselves. This pious conviction raises the question, however, of how much latitude an author might allow himself in interpreting the sources that were available and accounting for aspects of the story when sources were not available.

Fashioning the Bishops

Appropriating the Past

In her study of Quattrocento vitae sanctorum, Alison K. Frazier has called what the Italian authors were doing a return "to the old for new reasons," rather than an invention of the past.[36] In general this holds true of the vitae sanctorum by the early German humanists, but the case of Emser's life of Benno is illustrative of the tension in which many authors worked. At the very period when Emser turned to Benno, the advocates of Benno's canonization found themselves in need of a vita—a necessary element in a canonization petition—but with few textual artifacts on which to draw. Until 1510 those involved in the canonization campaign knew of only a few scattered pieces of medieval evidence about Benno, mostly gleaned from chronicles such as that by Lampert of Hersfeld.[37]

As Duke George assigned Emser to the task of composing a life, the interested parties realized that the hagiographer needed to determine on what documentary basis he could write it. And so, commissioned in August 1510 by the cathedral chapter in Meissen, Emser traveled with the chapter dean, John Hennig, through Saxony researching Benno's life. Several documents surfaced at the monastery of Saint Michael in Hildesheim: a catalogue of abbots in Hildesheim that listed Benno among them, the certificate of his monastic vows, his coat of arms, a sketched likeness, and a booklet with a legend.[38] Emser rejected many of these new discoveries as spurious, which they likely were. However, he later cited a "very ancient little book" in his own vita.[39] A Hildesheim monk had composed this short vita of Benno in the mid-fifteenth century. The monastic author had taken the information about Benno that was known (for example, chronicles such as Lampert's and pieces of local chronography such as catalogues of abbots and bishops) and drawn on the medieval lives of two local eleventh-century bishops. The monastic legend emphasized Benno's life as a devoted monk in Hildesheim even though no verifiable evidence exists today that Benno was ever a monk there or anywhere else. More to the point, it contained almost nothing about his four-decade tenure as bishop of Meissen, which was then, as it is now, the best-documented period of Benno's life. Instead, the Benno of the Hildesheim legend led the idealized life of a reformed monk not unlike what the papal legate and cardinal Nicholas of Cusa had initiated in the Hildesheim monastery in the early 1450s. This vita, of which only one copy is known to exist, was probably not read outside the monastery in which it was composed until it was brought to Emser's attention around 1510.[40]

Having greatly expanded on the Hildesheim vita, Emser published his new vita in 1512 and five years later saw through press a German translation and revision. As one might expect of a vernacular saint's life, the biographical content was abbreviated, and the miracles were extended by fifty-four entries.[41] The process by which Emser prepared his work exposes an ambivalence characteristic of hagiography in general. On the one hand, great efforts were expended trying to find reliable documentation of Benno's life and personality. Correspondence between canonization advocates, as well as Emser's own writings and other documents, indicates that Emser, the canons, and the duke all shared this drive to research Benno's life. These letters also show that Emser and his assistants tested what they found for authenticity and rejected several claims deemed unreliable. On the other hand, they greatly exerted themselves in creating a record that is, at best, unsubstantiated: speaking where the sources were silent, altering them, and even omitting elements of what was, to begin with, a small body of information. Despite the efforts of Benno's advocates to find authoritative documentation, they manipulated their sources with a heavy hand, filling in troublesome lacunae and working around embarrassing facts.

Sources and Inventions

A similar ambivalence affected the other episcopal vitae, too. Indeed, like Emser, all of the authors, editors, and compilers stressed the lengths to which they had gone to gather the pertinent documents; yet few were hesitant to supplement and change what they found. For example, even as Scheckmann included chronicle and catalogue information of Basin's episcopal tenure in his *Life of Saint Basin,* he frequently reproduced claims and passages from a late eleventh-century vita about Basin's nephew, Saint Lutwin.[42] Not a falsification per se, this heavy borrowing was a common way documents were used and for which explicit citation was not necessary; other, older hagiographical writings were of enormous authority in the composition of later ones.[43] In the most flagrant case, a hagiographer not only forged a source but also invented an entire authority: In writing his life of Saint Maximus, Trithemius enthusiastically cited the Benedictine chronicler Meginfrid of Fulda. Meginfrid (as well as his confrère Hunibald, who appeared in other historical writings by Trithemius), however, was a chronicler entirely of the author's imagination.[44]

Some authors evade the charge of falsification on account of a lack of evidence. No manuscripts, for example, remain against which to judge Wimpfeling's *Life of Saint Adelph.* The life depends in large part on a medieval *Life of Saint Arnulf of Metz,* one of Adelph's predecessors in Metz. Wimpfeling's reputation as a scholar might lead one to assume that he had honestly and accurately copied an older *Life of Saint Adelph,* yet it seems unlikely that he knew about this other vita.[45] Sometimes, however, the few changes that were made were the most flagrant inventions, as for example in Cincinnius's *Vita s. Ludgeri,* when he asserted, for the first time, that another regionally venerated saint, Ida of Herzfeld, had served as Saint Ludger's godmother.[46]

Most authors treated in this study used their introductions to assert the great efforts with which they had sought and incorporated all older evidence. An apology for the hagiographer's own intellectual limitations often accompanied this protestation. The rule of documentary noncontradiction was an important one. It had deep roots in the history of this literature, and the hagiographers felt obliged to express their obedience to it. Whether one judges the authors' historiographical scruples (or their absence) laxly or harshly, the unavoidable conclusion about this writing is that the increased concern expressed for documentary research was not followed by a greater reliance on the results of such investigation.[47]

Style and Structure

More common than the protestation on behalf of their researching efforts, the hagiographers often begged the readers' pardon in the preface for their own clumsy Latin style, accusing it of being unworthy for the task at hand. This expressed stylistic anxiety, while not new, anticipated certain literary features throughout the text that distinguished these lives from their antecedents and in effect offer a general signal of a text's humanist origins. The features in question include a preference for classicizing Latin diction and the use of allusions to classical Greek and Latin literature. Even when the kind of bishop described conformed more closely to older models, as in Scheckmann's *Life of Saint Basin,* aspects of the literary style indicate that these texts did not belong to the High Middle Ages. Even when the author appears at first glance only to have edited an older life, the most minor of alterations, such as the appending of a preface or a panegyric poem, give evidence that the works were composed no earlier than the late fifteenth century. Although these characteristic differences did not necessarily correspond to concrete biographical claims, they are rhetorically decisive. They bespeak a formal aspect of the vitae sanctorum that points to its new and different purposes, and they suggest that the usefulness of the new hagiographical models had as much to do with the shaping of the saints' lives as with their contents.

Comparison of Emser's *Life of Holy Benno* and its monastic antecedent in Hildesheim again offers insight into the stylistic concerns inspired by humanist training. Whereas the monk's diction and orthography included frequent medieval corruptions and peculiarities,[48] Emser strove for an impression of elegance and erudition by means of complicated and classicizing Latin usages. The humanist priest, canonist, biblical exegete, and court secretary decorated his prose with rhetorical devices such as tricolon and chiasm, used Greek words, and favored classicizing phraseologies such as *toga virilis* for the attainment of adulthood, *dii tutelares* for patron saints, and *divus* as Benno's saintly honorific.[49] Even the use of æ instead of the more usual *e* in the 1512 printing gives evidence of the classicizing tendency of Emser's printer, Melchior Lotter the Elder of Leipzig. Classicizing like this is found in the other episcopal legends: Scheckmann displayed a predilection for turning classicizing phrases and using Greek words, as when he wrote *metropoleos* instead of *metropolis* and *mysticon* instead of *misticum,* as well as when he described monastic life as a *gymnasium sancte religionis* and Basin's death as *scandit ethera,* called the sun *Phebus,* and addressed the Blessed Virgin as *Theotocos.* Classicizing aspirations can of course be identified in saints' lives throughout the Middle Ages. What sets the saints' lives of this period apart is the programmatic way in which the classicizing was undertaken. An examination of patrons' attraction to the classicizing style in the following chapter reinforces our appreciation of this aspect of the humanist vitae.

Literary allusions also distinguished the humanists' lives from the older ones. The use of scriptural imagery was common in the humanist authors' works. The lives of holy men and women found in the Bible, most obviously that of Christ, had long been a defining measure by which to judge holiness. Both Emser and the Hildesheim monk drew amply from the Old and New Testaments for supportive comparison.[50] Although both authors used extrascriptural literature, Emser's use of nonscriptural sources was more extensive.[51] In addition to the chronicles such as Lampert's, Emser also referred to two prominent Quattrocento Italian historians, Bartolomeo Platina and Flavio Biondo, citing the latter to explain the background of the Investiture Controversy, which had brought Benno in conflict with the emperor. Emser similarly sprinkled his vita with classical references, for example, from Juvenal, Pliny, Plutarch, Suetonius, and Virgil. Such literary allusions can be found throughout the remaining episcopal saints' lives. The saints were being placed in settings constructed not only out of Holy Writ, as is to be expected, but out of pagan Greece and Rome as well. [52]

A final stylistic distinction evident between the new lives by humanists and their medieval antecedents has to do with the various parts making up the narrative whole and impinging on the structure of the vitae. Again using the lives of Benno as an example: Emser composed new speeches for Benno and other characters in the vita at important moments, such as the deathbed orations given by Bernward (a tenth-century bishop of Hildesheim, renowned patron of the arts, and, according to the vitae, Benno's mentor) and Benno himself. Emser shaped Benno and fit him into a literary world that neither the eleventh-century bishop nor the fifteenth-century monk could possibly have recognized. In doing so, Emser adroitly inserted Benno into the very humanist milieu—one in which the classical *verba* was paramount—in which Emser himself felt most at home.

New Life: Humanist Refashioning

But did the new verba point to a new res, or were Emser and his colleagues merely decorating the bishops' hagiographical vestments without adjusting the figures that wore them? Investigation of this question inevitably brings us to a much disputed historiographical problem about the Renaissance humanists, namely, whether anything united them other than their stance toward the

Latin language, its classical sources, and a pedagogical program giving pre-cedence to rhetoric over dialectic. This larger problem must be kept in mind as we analyze the kinds of bishops being written about and the concrete markers of holiness the authors used to justify their status as saints. In fact, the vitae indicate that the humanist authors were turning to a particular kind of holy bishop, making their subjects holy in a particular way, and using these novel portrayals to inspire new critical attitudes toward the contemporary church and society.

Childhood, Education, and Monastic Background

A medieval practice followed by the fifteenth and early-sixteenth-century au-thors was to begin explaining a saint's adult holiness with reference either to a moment of radical conversion or, more commonly, to well-established holiness in childhood. At the same time, the authors had no compunction about ex-panding on and diverging from the older narratives. Charting how the hu-manist authors did this helps bring into focus the strategies of revision they were using. Emser, for example, followed the Hildesheim vita by opening his vita with a description of Benno's infancy and childhood in Hildesheim. No evidence for Benno's youth antedates the Hildesheim vita, which recounts Benno's childhood piety and his wardship under the renowned eleventh-century bishop of Hildesheim, Saint Bernward. When he recounted Benno's family origins, however, Emser's assertions implicitly contributed to a dis-agreement among Benno's early sixteenth-century advocates: Although he included a new claim that Benno was the son and brother of counts in Saxony, he passed over in silence a specific family name recommended by colleagues but absent from older sources, including the Hildesheim vita.[53]

The pursuit of "good letters" was another claim that authors frequently added to their accounts of the saints' youth. Emser lauded Benno's training in the ancient authors and humanist studies. Benno's poetic skills merited, Emser chattily remarked, some critique for their youthful immaturity but above all else admiration. As soon as Benno was of age he took on more advanced studies, "ruminating day and night over the Prophets, both Testaments, and the commentaries of the fathers."[54] The emphasis on the Scriptures was an aspect of monastic learning that humanists, especially in Northern Europe much appreciated, and we find it in most of the episcopal vitae. By the same token, the authors rarely mention any formal training the bishops may have had in philosophy and theology, the hallmark of a scholastic education. This generality admits of exceptions, as, for example, Emser's reiteration of Benno's improbable studies in Paris, which had exactly these scholastic connotations.[55]

From Monk to Bishop

Continuing to follow the monastic hagiographer, Emser described Benno's entrance into monastic life at Hildesheim upon reaching young adulthood and his early devotion to prayers, vigils, and fasts.[56] Emser further reported that Benno served for three months as the abbot of Saint Michael in Hildesheim before the emperor, Henry III, called him to serve as a teacher at the royal canonry in Goslar.[57] On this point, Emser contradicted the Hildesheim vita, which asserted that Benno had turned down his election as abbot.[58] Emser dedicated several paragraphs to Benno's practice of contemplation and asceticism in words close to those in the vita prima.[59] When Emser's Benno received his assignment to the see of Meissen, Emser paused to reflect on the conflict between the contemplative and active lives, using the Old Testament figures of Rachel and Leah allegorically.

Other characteristics of a holy youth appeared in contemporaneous episcopal vitae, often for the first time. Scheckmann, for example, included a reference to Basin's noble lineage, although there was no evidence for this claim.[60] He described Basin's entrance into a monastery in Trier to escape the falsity of the world and to learn "virtues and letters."[61] Trithemius's Maximus began life "born to honorable and Christian parents in the city of Mainz. The boy was sent to study letters in the custom of his people. He excelled in these things and with time surpassed nearly all his peers."[62] Maximus was subsequently ordained a secular priest, making him the only bishop in this study not to have been a monk. This peculiarity provided Trithemius the opportunity to remark, "The custom in those days was that the clerics and priests were free from the usual worldly obligations so as to devote themselves to God alone, and to the sacred ministries of prayer and meditation; . . . they reviled the honors of the world, all riches and voluptuousness of the flesh that dies."[63] With the temporal qualifier "in those days," the abbot played to a presumption in the minds of his readership that secular clergy were not outstandingly moral, thereby amplifying Maximus's accomplishment.

Even though most of the bishops in the humanist vitae spent their early lives in monastic settings, their vowed life and the pursuit of monastic perfection were never portrayed as the fundamental causes of their holiness. The monastic periods in the bishops' lives were conceived, rather, as preparation for other, more decisive occupations associated with their episcopacy. Emser, for example, synthesized multiple influences on Benno at Hildesheim and Goslar—familial, educational, and monastic—always with an eye to illuminating skills that the earnest monk could later bring to Meissen as its bishop.

In the case of Benno, this emphasis on his significance as a bishop was new. Even though he held the see of Meissen for forty years, medieval chroniclers referred to him infrequently. His coevals did not record any special pastoral talents or activities. For Emser these years were of central importance, and he reworked the data to give the episcopacy a dignified character. In the earlier vita, Benno led his life as a bishop in much the same way he had lived as a monk. He continued his ascetic practices, habits of prayer, and monastic common life.[64] In contrast, Emser portrayed Benno's elevation to the episcopacy as a transforming promotion. The erstwhile monk's virtuous character, tested in the cloister, justified the promotion, but what made Benno's new status truly important was the way it inserted him into a world that was, to Emser's mind, of greater significance.[65]

Emser added details not in the Hildesheim vita, opening up the range of Benno's activities to include those specifically proper to him as bishop. His first episcopal activity, for example, was to set about improving liturgical practices in the diocese.[66] Bishop Benno made regular visitations to churches and monasteries.[67] He worked to ensure the priests' doctrinal competence, especially in preaching.[68] He took special care of the poor and widows. Emser used Benno's triumphant return to Meissen after an exile imposed by the emperor as an opportunity to show the affection of a needy flock for its pastor,[69] and a scene of clergy mourning as Benno lay in extremis suggests a similar relation between the bishop and his priests.[70] In *The Life of Holy Benno* the episcopacy introduced Benno and his talents to a far wider world than ever imagined in the Hildesheim vita. As Emser portrayed Benno's life, what had germinated among monks and canons in Hildesheim and Goslar finally blossomed within a church of clergy and laity in Meissen.

Similar emphases can be found in the other lives. Trithemius was especially conscious to blend monastic virtue with episcopal activity—both pastoral and administrative—into a seamless whole. His Maximus was expressly sustained by his learning in divine and secular knowledge, an orthodox and moral way of life, the practice of abstinence and vigils, a lack of interest in worldly gain, a desire only for the honor and glory of God, and a fervent love of Christ. In turn, the bishop directed these skills beyond his palace's walls: He preached eloquently, he traveled throughout his diocese "following the example of the apostles with bare feet" and meeting conscientiously with clergy and laity alike.[71]

Taken together, these alterations represent ways in which the humanists established continuity without slavishly reiterating the textual antecedents. The construal of noble backgrounds, rigorous (if anachronistic) educations, and a revulsion at "the world" in the humanist lives made the new portrayals of bishop saints similar to their antecedents. The favorable reference to monasticism, the coenobitic beginnings of nearly all of the bishop-saints' adult lives, and their mastery of the monastic way of life were likewise characteristic of holy bishops in vitae throughout Christian history, especially the most ancient. Nonetheless, in the fulfillment of their office these holy bishops were not simply monks in miters and in this respect distinguished themselves in the vitae from other, earlier conventions of episcopal holiness. They fulfilled the duties proper to the principal shepherd of a diocese. Mastery of monastic virtues, sound learning, eloquent preaching, and effective service in lower office (and in that order of decreasing importance) brought the holy men into the episcopal office. In all instances, the men came into office with the support of the local clergy and were usually elected by the cathedral chapter. The bishop's careful attention to his clergy, his visitation of parishes and other ecclesiastical establishments, and his encouragement and exemplification of eloquent preaching—these had been hallmarks of a holy bishop from time immemorial. They were certainly mandated continuously in ecclesiastical legislation and theological treatises. What is significant here, however, is their appearance as a complex of episcopal virtues, expressed in a particular classicizing literary style and with sudden recurrence at the end of the fifteenth and the beginning of the sixteenth centuries.

Lessons for the Present from the Past: Episcopal Challenges

Two points at which the Hildesheim vita and The Life of Holy Benno conflicted draw attention to perennially important episcopal tasks: how to deal with secular authority and how to deal with pagans. Both tasks gave the authors an opportunity to assert the proper extent of ecclesiastical authority, in the first instance vis-à-vis those who exercised temporal authority unjustly, in the second when it came into contact with unbelief. In both instances, a bishop's successful response could, by the hagiographer's reckoning, make Christian society more authentic and, quite simply, larger.

BISHOPS AND THE LIBERTY OF THE CHURCH. Two conflicts involving temporal authority that Emser elaborated in his vita were the Saxon rebellion and the Gregorian reform. The eleventh-century chronicler Lampert of Hersfeld sparingly but reliably reported Benno's opposition to the emperor in both conflicts.[72] Emser began there and embellished. In a tactic deferential to the emperor, Emser nodded first to a negative interpretation of Benno's opposition to Henry IV, acknowledging that the bishop's noble Saxon ancestry may have rendered him "inwardly indisposed to the king." Still, the anger of the king and the truculence, first, of the royal henchmen, who waged the war with the Saxons, and, later, of a dissolute higher clergy who had no interest in Gregory VII's program for church reform, were ultimately to blame for Benno's misfortunes.[73] From a spiritual perspective, the events served as a test of Benno's fidelity to God. When Benno—finding himself *inter saxum et sacrum*, between a rock and a frock—was forced out of Meissen into exile, he suffered the injustice patiently. Conjuring up the perennial issue of absentee bishops (an object of censure, as Sigismund's "Reformatio" shows, in the fifteenth century no less than in the eleventh), Emser remarked that the punishment of exile bothered Benno "not personally . . . but inconsolably for the sake of his church alone."[74] Emser thus navigated his way through treacherous shoals: He established Benno among the most prominent insurgents, exculpated him from malice toward the crown, affirmed his holiness under persecution, and still deflected responsibility from the emperor.[75]

A third conflict between secular and ecclesiastical authorities in Emser's vita included the sudden death of the secular antagonist, the margrave of Meissen. Emser drew the story, otherwise unverifiable and likely prominent as a late medieval oral tradition, from the Hildesheim legend. The conflict was "over property once stolen by the king from the church of Meissen." Which king was never specified, but by the very early twelfth century the land lay enfeoffed to the margrave of Meissen. In both the monk's and the humanist's versions, the margrave struck Benno in the course of an argument over the land. Benno responded with the prediction that "in the following year on the same day, [the margrave] would be given the penalty for the guilt he had incurred." Benno died in the meantime, and the margrave visited the tomb one year to the day after the prediction. "Not mindful that the day had arrived but not yet concluded," he mocked the dead Benno, whose ghost promptly rose from the grave. Here, the stories diverged: According to the Hildesheim legend, Benno, in ghostly form, struck the margrave;[76] according to Emser, the margrave fell over dead, but out of fear. It was a death deserved, Emser noted, "not so much for the violent hands laid against the Lord's saint, but because he approached [holy Benno] . . . as the oppressor of the poor and the desecrator of ecclesiastical things."[77]

Besides the obvious problem—noted later by Luther—that the commission of homicide rarely suggests Christian holiness, the story put the margrave in a bad light and implicitly lauded Benno for punishing a secular authority, whose successor, in this case, happened to be none other than Emser's employer, Duke George. At the same time, the fanciful story left a clear and unique impression of Benno's assertiveness on behalf of the church's rights. For Emser, the story showed that Benno had striven to protect his church close to home as he had in exile and in Rome. As told by the Hildesheim monk, who never situated Bishop Benno, once consecrated, outside his see, this was the only episode in which a secular lord appears in the vita. The earlier life's scope was, here as throughout, local. In Emser's vita, Benno's placement differed: Benno's work had an effect on all levels of Saxon society, and his activities brought him to all corners of the empire and beyond. As to *where* Benno was holy, the monk and Emser placed their protagonist in quite different worlds.

The world into which Emser inserted Benno also distinguished Emser's vita from the lives of saintly bishops composed in earlier centuries. In the Ottonian and Salian periods, for example, authors of bishops' vitae generally limited the literary settings to the milieu of the monastic or capitulary institution sponsoring the writings. Secular authorities rarely appeared.[78] Moreover, aspects of the other humanist authors' vitae suggest that Emser's alternative strategy was not anomalous in this regard. Trithemius's life of Maximus, for example, portrayed its protagonist and his episcopal colleagues as they fought for the integrity of their sees against Arians and their unscrupulous political allies.[79] In Scheckmann's vita of Saint Basin, the struggles of the Arian Milo to usurp the Trier See provide an opportunity to show Basin defending his rights against the regional authorities who supported Milo's false claims.[80] These vitae stressed the bishops' absolute obligation to govern and protect their sees against all opponents, be they the local clergy, heretics, or temporal authority. Irreducible principles of maintaining order included the bishop's right to teach the faithful all matter of doctrine and his duty to protect the temporalities and legal privileges of the bishopric. Likewise absolute was the obligation imposed upon the secular authority to remain orthodox and to support the bishop in his exercise of office. A well-ordered Christian society, these new episcopal saints' lives make clear, rested on the office of bishop.

CONVERTING PAGANS, COMBATING HERETICS. A third threat to well-ordered Christian society emerges to join the corrupt clergy and ambitious secular lords that Emser and the other authors address in the episcopal vitae: heathens and heretics. This is reflected in the emphasis the authors put on their episcopal subjects' missionary activities, even when there is little documentary precedent for the assertion. There is, for example, no eleventh-century evidence that Benno participated in the Imperial effort to convert the Slavs to Christianity. Yet as a result of Emser's description of this activity, Benno has been widely known since the sixteenth century as "the Apostle to the Wends." Emser's inspiration may well have came from Trithemius, who had described Benno in this way to Julius II in 1506; both men may have derived their stories from an oral tradition.[81]

Emser proved himself an especially sophisticated author when he worked the missionary significance of Benno's life into the vita. He prepared his reader in the work's earliest chapters, where he casually mentioned the Slavic tribes settled around Meissen to provide additional points of geographical reference.[82] Moving from geography to ethnography, Emser later elaborated his descriptions of the tribes, taking care to explain linguistic and religious variations among them.[83] His sources for these descriptions—including horrifying but also surely titillating descriptions of human sacrifice—included Helmold's *Saxon Chronicles*, Lampert's chronicle, and Saxo Grammaticus's *Gesta Danorum*. German humanists especially admired the Latinity of the last of these authors, whose Danish history was first printed in 1471.[84] Once Emser had made the pagan world sufficiently imminent, abutting Christendom not far from Meissen indeed, Emser then turned to recount Benno's crucial work in converting the Wends.[85] This missionary activity embellished the saint's image in several ways: First, it expanded the range and import of his pastoral activities well beyond the clerical and monastic environments within which the Hildesheim monk's account had been restricted. Second, it enhanced the geographical and historical prestige of Saxony and Benno's see by putting them at the forefront of the new eleventh-century efforts to expand Christendom. Third, it contributed further to the impression that Benno was a leading Imperial churchman who not only tended the flock he had received but expanded it through the conversion of pagans as well.

Other bishops were also praised for their evangelizing efforts, among them some of Germany's most famous missionary bishops:[86] The anonymous *Thuringian Legend of Saint Boniface* emphasized Boniface's missionary work in Thuringia.[87] Indeed, a key theme of the entire work is showing Boniface as the apostle to the Thuringians.[88] Scheckmann set Basin's life and episcopal career in front of a background of invading barbarians *(nortmanni)* wreaking havoc on the church. Trithemius developed a variation on this theme: Saint Maximus's opponents were Arian Christians and thus heretics rather than pagans. Trithemius described the threat Arians posed to society and Maximus's successful evangelization of them in ways similar to the humanists' addressing the pagan danger. As the oft-told tale made irrefutably true, the tribes that felled Rome were Arian. The humanist authors, enchanted as they were by the glories of ancient Rome, were no different from earlier medieval authors in their conviction that the Arians were as needful of conversion as the unbaptized.

Even in instances where a humanist minimally edited earlier works, a similar concern for evangelization and orthodoxy was frequently worked into the revised lives. Pseudo-Marcellinus's Swithbert evangelized Friesland along with Lower Saxony in the company of Saints Wigbert, Wilfried, and Willibrord.[89]

Cincinnius reiterated the significance of Ludger's evangelization of Friesland from the older vitae, adding episodes of his own invention and from other sources (including Kaiserwerth's rival *Life of Saint Swithbert*).[90] One of Andrew Lang's challenges in compiling, editing, and revising two medieval lives of Saint Otto was reconciling the difference between them on the matter of Otto's status as a missionary apostle. Ebo's earlier vita stressed Otto's wide-ranging missionary activity, which had brought him as far away from Bamberg as the region of the Pomeranians. Herbord, in contrast, stressed Otto's role as a domestic bishop, abstained from applying the theretofore common honorific title *apostolus Pomeranorum* to Otto, and favored an apostolic association with the governing Saint Peter over one with the traveling Saint Paul. Lang's first redaction, dedicated to the duke of Pomerania, reemphasized Otto's missionary activities. Lang's version may have told a story that drew, line for line, more from Herbord's; nonetheless, Lang showed no hesitation in reincorporating a strong, laudatory emphasis on Otto's missionary accomplishments.[91]

In short, the humanist authors made missionary activity a hallmark of holy bishops' success. Whether a matter of copying sources or embellishing the record, these authors were universally interested in the missionary activity and success of their holy bishops. Saintly bishops spread the faith to people who otherwise believed untrue and ugly things. A century later, another generation of authors would draw parallels between ancient pagans and contemporary Protestants. The urgency in the earlier, pre-Reformation accounts and in those of the later Counter-Reformation is similar. We will return to the connections between early and late sixteenth-century hagiography in the Conclusion. At this point, however, it is important to not that even before Catholic reformers had Protestants to oppose, many humanists, including Emser, were highlighting reforming figures who worked to correct unbelief, irreligion, and religious corruption. The analogy they found persuasive was between the religious laxity and corruption they saw around them, on the one hand, and ancient heretics and pagans, on the other. The analogy gave the authors and their readers a way of understanding religious crisis and imagining its resolution well before they also had Protestants to oppose.[92]

Developing Episcopal Holiness

Early Medieval Consensus

Missionary activity is only one of several new themes appearing in the episcopal vita of the fifteenth and early sixteenth centuries. Two other challenges in particular had consistently confronted episcopal life writers and get to the heart of how a bishop as bishop was holy. Those challenges were how to reconcile a bishop's exercise of spiritual and secular authority, and how to distinguish episcopal sanctity from the standards of monastic holiness that predominated in the medieval imagination. Two prominent bishop saints illustrate well the earliest medieval responses to these challenges. The first is Saint Martin of Tours, the onetime Roman soldier who shared his cape with a beggar, gave up his soldiering for a monastic calling, and was acclaimed bishop by the people of Tours. In his extremely influential fifth-century vita sancti, Sulpicius Severus blended the bishop's seamless exercise of both temporal and ecclesiastical authority with spiritual tendencies that were monastic. As Sulpicius wrote, Saint Martin "fully sustained the dignity of the episcopate without forsaking the life or the virtues of the monk."[93] Sulpicius's balance became the hagiographical standard for centuries, even as Imperial bishops acquired greater secular responsibility.

The notion that the bishop could be true to his spiritual duties and still exercise secular responsibilities never went unchallenged, but the level of its acceptance ran especially high from the eighth-century Merovingian to the eleventh-century Salian periods. It was axiomatic in the life-writing of these three centuries that a holy bishop could faithfully wield secular authority. The veneration of Saint Ulrich of Augsburg, our second early medieval case, exemplifies this confidence. Ulrich was a tenth-century bishop of Augsburg who led troops into battle in defense of the empire and who was also widely admired for his monastic asceticism and religious devotion. Shortly after he died, he was added to liturgical calendars for veneration not only by local bishops in Germany but also by the pope. This papal ratification of a saint who had no immediate connection to the diocese of Rome makes Saint Ulrich the first *canonized* saint. For our purposes, what is important to note is the range of skills and virtues, temporal and monastic, that inspired his veneration from Augsburg to Rome. Even if from our perspective this range seems to differ remarkably from that of Saint Martin, who abandoned the sword to follow Christ more fervently, from that of those who canonized him, both bishops did the same thing very well: they sustained the dignity of the episcopate, as Sulpicius put it, without forsaking the virtues of the monk.[94]

The High Medieval Crisis

The very eleventh-century Gregorian reform that Emser had tendentiously described in *The Life of Holy Benno* precipitated the collapse of this harmonious configuration both in fact and in literary representation. The Gregorian reform became a catalyst for both a vigorous discussion of *libertas ecclesiae* and the desacralization of Imperial authority. The resolution of the ensuing Investiture Controversy, the concordat of Worms (1122), had the effect of bifurcating the bishop's official persona. The distinction between his spiritual authority (received from the pope) and his temporal authority (received from the emperor) was suddenly sharpened in law and in ritual. The pieces might still fit together, but the seam could no longer be disguised: the susceptibility of bishops, who in fact wielded temporal authority, to arrogance and vainglory—*iactantia et vana gloria*—was too great. Authors needed a new way to evaluate and justify a bishop's exercise of temporal authority if they also wished to prove his sanctity, and one was not easily found.[95]

In fact, the later medieval solution was to avoid depicting bishop saints altogether. From the Salian period (1024–1125) onward, for example, two different ecclesiastical institutions became responsible for the composition of nearly all episcopal vitae, monasteries and cathedral chapters. Each had its motivation: Monastic authors most commonly wrote the lives of their monasteries' founders who had become bishops. The cathedral canons, generally taking more recently deceased bishops of their own dioceses as their subjects, composed the lives in anticipation of conflicts between subsequent bishops and themselves in which the vitae could serve as a kind of evidence. In contrast to the humanist writings, these lives relied almost exclusively on biblical references and precedent in their praise of the good bishops and censure of the bad. Classical references and allusions were secondary. Furthermore, the vita writers were minimalists when describing the historical context for the bishops' lives and rarely addressed issues outside the boundaries of the diocese itself. As we have seen, these characteristics contrast sharply with the episcopal vitae being composed in the German lands of the late fifteenth and early sixteenth centuries: Canons were never the principal authors of a vita, later hagiographers used classical materials as readily as biblical ones, and the connection of the bishop-saints' activities to events of broad significance was of key importance.[96]

When authors of saints' lives after the twelfth century did write about bishops, the holy bishop's spiritual comportment had less to do with the traditionally monastic ideal, as exemplified by Saint Martin, than with ideals of religious life characteristic of the high medieval reformed cloisters and the new mendicant orders that emphasized the pastorally active apostolic life and the imitation of Christ's preaching and teaching. Moreover, no longer after the twelfth century were the surrounding characters in the vitae political and military advisors, allies, or even adversaries. Rather, the bishop was depicted among the secular clergy who advised his spiritual governance of the diocese. The great bishop saint of the later Middle Ages, venerated across Europe, was

Saint Thomas Becket. Representing an episcopal holiness shaped by the two challenges we also saw active in the lives of Saint Martin and Saint Ulrich, Saint Thomas had no monastic background and was murdered for his defense of the libertas ecclesiae against royal incursions. Saint Thomas's acclaim was the response of yet another medieval generation in the search for holy bishops. [97]

The Renaissance Reality

A touchstone for humanists searching for holy bishops to write about might well have been contemporary bishops who were humanists. Some real bishops at the time were, in fact, humanists. One can identify them by a knowledge and cultivation of ancient languages and literature; significant travels, especially in Italy; love of books; participation in communication networks; sponsorship of or even participation in circles of learned persons (sodalitas); some authorship; and a characteristic presentation of self.[98] Even though such prelates did not predominate in the Imperial church by the early sixteenth century, a comparison of the bishop saints depicted in the vitae with these actual humanist bishops reveals forces guiding the hand of the authors. Emser fashioned Benno along these lines; for example, his poetic and other linguistic skills, his love of learning, his travels, and his oratory are skills, experiences, or virtues that can scarcely be found in references to Benno before Emser. Furthermore, Benno, once bishop, led a fundamentally public life. His virtues radiated outward through words and deeds, like those of a good Ciceronian orator, redounding to the benefit of the community.

The license taken by Emser and the other authors considered here has an analogy in humanist history writing. An examination of episcopal historiography (Bistumsgeschichtsschreibung) as it was developing in the later Middle Ages and as it was shaped by humanists suggests that writers engaged with historical matter differently for different sorts of patrons. Increasingly through the later Middle Ages and into the sixteenth century, diocesan chronicles delved into their dioceses' past. Their investigations had a genealogical structure. The works were aimed at telling the history of an institution; nonetheless, that history was in the first instance constituted by the lives of individual bishops in succession. As those composing these histories became increasingly humanist, they adopted this genealogical structure because it offered them a pattern with which to conduct their search for the ancient origins of German society and then to fashion their findings narratively.[99]

This late medieval interest in the German past was shaping the writing of saints' lives as well. Some of Emser's lengthiest and most elaborate excursus have to do with the ancient history of the places where Benno had lived and worked. Trithemius quarreled with the received ordinal placement of Maximus in the sequence of Mainz bishops. By situating Maximus later in the sequence, he hinted at even more ancient origins for the see itself.[100] Scheckmann selected a bishop who lived in the very epoch when fierce Germanic tribes were pushing out and replacing the Romans. Historiographical principles and patriotic motivations guided the fashioning of the chronicles and the vitae in similar ways: the bishops reigning in this past provided the life writers personages with whom they could investigate, shape, and eulogize the German past, just as the traditional chronographical subjects provided to history writers.

A second similarity between the history writing and the saints' lives regards the diminishing insertion of juridical claims coupled with an increasing inclusion of historical and topographical excursus. The later the histories of episcopal cities were composed in the Middle Ages, the more likely they would include panegyrical passages in honor of the cities. This development, which does not appear to have a parallel south of the Alps, points to a new concern for the *civitas sancta,* an idea that humanists in the empire fostered. In fact, this shift—from the juridical to the historical and topographical—is stronger when the author was a humanist than when not, and when he was invited from outside the diocese to write the history than when he was from the bishop's own curia.[101]

Similar changes were made to the lives of holy bishops. In fact, this kind of addition—the chorographical—appears so consistently in the life writing of this period that chapter three is devoted to analyzing it as a hallmark of humanist hagiography. Examples include the background to Emser's vivid descriptions of the Slavic tribes and the thorough descriptions of the geographical features in and around Hildesheim.[102] Emser also made elaborate reference to the Saxon dynasty through time, including flattering reference to Duke George's cousin Frederick the Wise, the elector of Ernestine Saxony. In the body of the vita, he included a list of canons from Goslar who had been consecrated bishops, emphasizing how widely they were spread out across the empire, and he pointed to several of the more prominent bishops of Meissen. *The Thuringian Legend of Saint Boniface* includes a splendid description of Thuringia. The description drew from earlier fifteenth-century works, Latin and vernacular, describing the Carolingian settlement of the region, various privileges extended to the Thuringians, their cities, and rulers by the emperor. The anonymous author carefully named the churches of Carolingian foundation as evidence of the dignity already enjoyed by Thuringia in the eighth century. His description of the ecclesiastical landscape is accompanied by descriptions of the geographical landscape as well, including the region's natural features and urban centers.[103] Similarly, Scheckmann, in imaginatively pointing out the Lotharingian origins of Basin's nobility, waved a hand

toward the "cosmographs" and digressed to offer his readers a brief chorographical description of the region.[104]

What enabled—or even encouraged—the authors to invest such creative
energy in these wide-ranging digressions? For an answer we can look again to a
similar phenomenon in late medieval episcopal historiography. What we find is
a development—beginning in the late Middle Ages and continuing as humanists became involved in this kind of writing—that returns us to the relationship between author, patron, and text. Up to the fifteenth century the most
common authors of episcopal historiography, as we have earlier seen, were
found in the cathedral chapters, an institution typically involved in the administration and politics of a diocese and out of which new bishops often came.
In contrast, the increasing proportion of humanists invited to contribute to
these chronicles and other historiographical texts was as commonly not bound
to the bishopric about which they were writing. That is, patrons sought out a
certain kind of literary competence first, and then assumed loyalty would follow
from the commission. The distancing between the history writers and the
dioceses about which they were writing had the effect of the decreasing the
juridical significance of the writings, in part because the outside writers were
less familiar with the intricacies of particular dioceses' legal conflicts and in part
because the patrons were decreasingly interested in having the history written
for juridical purposes. This development likewise reflects changes in the legal
system itself. Moreover, the humanist chronicles, like the humanist vitae, were
often printed and in numbers that anticipated a readership beyond the diocesan
boundaries. Distant readers as a group would be less concerned with the particular struggles between canons and bishops, to which earlier historical writings had instrumentally provided judicial precedent.[105] As such local interests
attenuated, new concerns could be brought to the writing of regional ecclesiastical history. One new purpose proved itself irresistible to the early German
humanists, namely, to craft diocesan histories so as to turn the best of bishops
into the best of church reformers. The writers of diocesan history provided these
reformers with reforming agenda, and, regardless of when these bishops lived,
programs, as it turned out, were the most apt of all for the sixteenth century.
The same development occurred in the vitae sanctorum.[106]

Reforming Bishops

Church Reform: Late Medieval and Early Humanist

The humanist authors of saints' lives took up the task of making saintly
bishops saintly reformers as well. The support for Benno's canonization in

Saxony is a case in point. Emser was a humanist whose exposure to the humanist movement and ideas of church reform stretched back to his contact with the Rhineland humanists, especially Jacob Wimpfeling. Wimpfeling had himself prepared an episcopal vita, *The Life of Saint Adelph, Bishop of Metz,* which appeared in print in 1506. Duke George of Saxony likewise manifested a sustained concern with church reform. The reform programs of regional princes, late medieval theologians, and Christian humanists are not easy to differentiate. They do not entirely need to be. What many agreed upon was that reforming the bishops was essential to reforming the church. For the prince, the goal was to reform the church as it was functioning within his jurisdiction. From there the program would spread to the rest of the empire. For the humanist, the hope was that the bishops would then be the point of emanation for the rechristianization of Germany, just as they had been the agents of christianization in ancient days. Far from rivaling each other, these tendencies complemented and supported one another: Remarkably, about half of the episcopal vitae were dedicated to or commissioned by secular princes.[107]

The connection is nowhere more obvious than in the promotion of Benno's canonization, on behalf of which the distinct reforming impulses merged. Emser was exposed to the struggles of ecclesiastical reform in the 1490s in Basel, where the reforming churchman Christopher von Utenheim was fighting to improve the secular clergy and monastic establishments. In 1495 von Utenheim had implemented a reform at the priory of Saint Alban at the request of the abbot of Cluny. After 1499 von Utenheim held important offices in the diocese under the more conservative rule of Bishop Caspar zu Rhein (r. 1479–1502).[108] Von Utenheim was himself elected bishop of Basel in December 1502. He was, like Emser, a friend of Wimpfeling, in consultation with whom he began to invoke diocesan synods, which both Wimpfeling and he considered a promising way to implement reform within a diocese.[109]

Persuading bishops, however, that reform—by whatever means—was first and foremost their responsibility was no easy task. The reformers' axiom in the fifteenth century "in head and members" meant starting reform with the prelates. Wimpfeling agreed: To effect reform, bishops themselves needed to be reformed. Wimpfeling insisted that bishops reside in their dioceses and recommended the use of diocesan synods and parochial visitations. Out of his humanist conviction that history offers the best lessons of how virtue was to be pursued and vice avoided, Wimpfeling sketched numerous examples of past bishops who illustrated the good exercise of their office, most famously in the episcopal catalogue he prepared for Albert of Brandenburg, archbishop of Mainz.[110]

Wimpfeling could also be as reproachful as he could be encouraging, leading one recent historian to remark that he made himself "the good bishop's delight and the wicked bishop's bane."[111] As a reformer, he was not unusual in inspiring resistance, and "wicked bishops" were not his only opponents. Wimpfeling also criticized the religious orders, suggesting that their exemption from the local bishop's supervision had caused their decline and weakened the bishops' just authority to the detriment of the Imperial church. This earned him the ill will of many monks and mendicants as well. It was in the search for a solution to this kind of resistance to reform that led Wimpfeling to turn to the secular princes as a collaborator in the reform of the church. Dedicating his edition of the *Life of Saint Adelph, Bishop of Metz* to Count Philip of Hanau-Lichtenberg, Wimpfeling put forward Frederick the Victorious, duke of Bavaria and count palatine, as the model of a reforming prince: "Frederick . . . cherished the bishops and supported the clerics. He avidly attended sermons, and when confronted with arduous matters, especially in war, he procured suffrages and supplications to be made devoutly by priests. He erected a new house for preachers in which studies and religion flourished. He reformed the houses of monks and friars. . . . And at the end of his days, he departed life joyously, admitted by our Lord God to Heaven in the company of his theologians and curates." Wimpfeling argued from the example of Frederick to the general principal: good princes ought to use their authority and resources to effect reform; and in return they would be rewarded in heaven.[112]

Humanists like Wimpfeling dearly valued princes such as George the Bearded. George and Wimpfeling recognized a common set of ills besetting the church, and the duke adopted a course of action that made him much like Wimpfeling's ideal reforming prince, Frederick the Victorious. George's education had been shaped by the expectation that he would enter the clergy. It included training in Latin and theology. This training gave George an intimate familiarity with the ecclesiastical problems and possibilities of the day. The division of Saxony in 1485 necessitated his succession to the throne of the Albertine Saxon duchy while his cousin Frederick became elector of Ernestine Saxony. Exhibiting an interest in humanist educational ideas, he sponsored a curricular reform at the University of Leipzig, and with his cousin Frederick he participated in founding the university at Wittenberg, where he endowed chairs for Greek and poetry. He was in regular contact with Erasmus. He supported humanists financially, and he replaced his first humanist secretary, Emser, with a second, Joannes Cochlaeus (1479–1552), when the former died in 1527.[113]

As is well known, the cousins took opposing paths in response to Luther; however, just as Frederick's affinity for Luther's theology did not lead him to dispose of his enormous relic collection, neither did George's loyalty to Rome distract him from his clear-eyed and long-standing concern to cure the Imperial church of its ills. He began in Saxony. He used his temporal authority and financial resources to support the reforming of monasteries, the training of secular priests, and the preaching of benefices. He petitioned Rome for the right to make monastic visitations in 1503. When permission was refused, he undertook the visitations anyway. Beyond Saxony, he participated in drafting the *Gravamina* at Worms in 1521. Typical for this period, George regarded the proper veneration of the saints as an outstanding means for reforming the church at all levels. From 1496, for example, he sponsored the chapel of Mount Saint Ann at Schreckenberg, endowing it with relics and acquiring indulgences for it. In this same period, George turned to Benno as a promising candidate for canonization. Though still at the time uncanonized, Benno enjoyed an active cult in Meissen, the duchy's most important diocese.[114]

Wimpfeling and George were thus the characters who looked over Emser's shoulder as he turned to the task of writing Benno's life anew. The humanist hallmarks of the text are those that today appear most obvious: the classicizing Latin, the citation of historical sources, the invention of speeches and composition of poetry, and the historical and topographical excursus. Yet the complexities of Emser's audience necessitated more changes to the sources he was working with than a few linguistic decorations, and even those were applied with strategic precision. For devotees of Benno's cult in Saxony, he stressed Benno's holiness, following the lead set in the Hildesheim vita. For the Dresden court, he emphasized local Saxon color, particularly in the opening dedication to Duke George. For the papal court, he highlighted Benno's consistent loyalty to the true popes. For papal and ducal courts alike, he used innumerable rhetorical flourishes to turn Benno anachronistically into an impassioned humanist. The resulting figure had a complexity in style and content that represents an attempt to accommodate the sensibilities of readers whose interest in Benno varied widely. These marks of their own religious and cultural interests are what would engage them with the saint and make him for them a persuasive agent of the reform that Emser wanted to effect shoulder to shoulder with Wimpfeling and Duke George. Benno represented the way in which an ethical, eloquent, and erudite humanist could govern his see. In the vita of 1512 Benno had been transformed into exactly the kind of reforming humanist bishop that, by Emser and Duke George's reckoning, Saxony needed in the early sixteenth century, and so too the empire.

Local Bishops; Imperial Aspirations

The Life of Holy Benno—its composition and use, its author, and its contents—offers a vivid example of intersecting concerns. The reform of the church, the latest learned perspectives on the use of the past, and religious idealizations of human action met in vitae sanctorum, most particularly in the lives of bishop saints, at the very end of the Middle Ages. Emser's work, though exceptional in many respects, was no hagiographical hapax legomenon. The subject that Emser was assigned and the way he fashioned his sources and then styled his own text are typical of much hagiographical production at the end of the fifteenth and the beginning of the sixteenth centuries in Germany.

The complex set of personal relationships within which Emser composed his work, most importantly his relationship to his patron, likewise attests to the significance of what was happening even beyond Emser's single contribution. These episcopal lives were being composed in a diversity of political and ecclesiastical milieus: reforming monasteries, Imperial principalities, universities, and learned urban communities. The characteristics of the studia humanitatis and the participation of individual humanists and their circles are visible in each instance: Humanists were writing episcopal vitae, diverse patrons were turning to these learned men with hagiographical commissions, and humanist style came to shape these devotional writings.

If we compare aspects of this new episcopal hagiography to developments in episcopal and diocesan historiography—the chronicles and other historical writings that took bishops as their subject but whose goals were not devotional—we find parallels of another sort, suggestions of common rules that guided composition. The most striking of these parallels has to do with the reconfigured relationship between the hagiographer and chronicler, on the one hand, and the bishop and diocese for whom the works were being written, on the other. The authors' dependence on the patron-institutions, which was critical in the production of high medieval writing about the past, was disintegrating. The writers in the later period were less likely to be in a long-standing, formal relationship with the bishopric about which they were writing. The increasing occurrence of digressions of all sorts, including chorographical in both the episcopal hagiography and historiography, indicates the decreasing necessity to embed in these writings the territorial interests of the ecclesiastical patrons. It also reveals the imaginative new topographical interests of the hagiographers, so many of whom, like their patrons, were humanistically inclined.

Freed from one set of interests, the authors and their patrons pursued another, namely, church reform, which could mean many things in the late

Middle Ages. So it is again important to remember that, among the vitae sanctorum of German saints written in Germany between 1470 and 1520, the largest number were of bishop saints. The lives and works of these bishops in their dioceses take the central role. Their precise and peculiar nature comes into sharp relief when these vitae are compared to the documentary and narrative artifacts the hagiographers used, as well as when one examines the texts added to the vitae by and at the direction of the author, such as Wimpfeling's dedicatory letter to Count Philip or the epigrams and poetry added to Engentinus's metrical vita.

A critique of the immorality and incompetence of the clergy and the bishops was by no means new to the late fifteenth century. It was rather a novel variation on venerable themes. The further calls for ecclesiastical reform in this period, opening with the councils of Constance and Basel and lasting into the sixteenth century, designated the individual diocesan bishop as the catalyst of a reform that, it was envisioned, would begin from the bottom of the ecclesiastical structure and work its way up with the helpful intervention of temporal authorities. Many early German humanists were firmly committed to the idea that modification of the episcopacy was the surest way to reform the church in the empire, and the general humanist conviction that the past provided examples of how life ought to be led pointed them to the saint's vita as a means of transforming the episcopate. Given this appreciation of the past, as well as the passionate desire for a reformed church among the humanists, the particular prominence of missionary bishops makes tremendous sense. The missionary saints were to call Germany to christianize itself, a task as necessary at the end of the Middle Ages as it had been at the end of the humanists' beloved antiquity.

The suitability of writing about bishops (or more exactly the conviction of their suitability as models of this reform) was possible only because of a larger shift occurring in the way that history writing was produced, particularly in dioceses. Local history was being written more and more with an eye cast toward its "universal" implications (e.g., the newest histories of the archdiocese of Mainz had more to do with establishing the dignity of Germany than juridically aiding the archbishop in his conflicts with the emperor). "Universal" concerns, like ecclesiastical corruption and solutions, like the rise of the reforming diocesan bishop, could inspire and then be inserted into episcopal hagiography as never before. The objects of local cults were being transformed into spokesmen for national ecclesiastical politics.

2

Legends Pleasing and Brightly Polished

The Holy Recluses

Venerable father, you have recently asked me to translate the life of
holy Ida, illustrious countess of Toggenburg and a most blessed
resident of your monastery, from the worn-out German language
into Latin. I have tried to do that although you could have found
many of your brothers, mainly in the abbey of Saint Gall, who could
have arranged such a work much more elegantly, for they are
practiced in such things. Because of the spirit of the place where they
live, they, deriving the Notkerian source from the copious river of
Bede, could write this life in a laconic style, agreeable and proper.
They could make a legend pleasing and brightly polished, fitting for
this purpose. The poetic is by no means one of my native gifts. Most
truly, however, father, I chose not to resist, but rather to comply with
your will on account of your favors to me. . . . Nor did I think a
subject worthy of the Hebrew, Greek, or Latin should be long put off.
I turned therefore to Latin for the glory of her sacred name as well
as I am able. With a racing pen, I return not word for word, but
capture instead the sense lest the exposition become too long. God
has ordained that I inspire with my works something of a celestial
delight in the readers, entice something from this black gem, and
kindle the fire of devotion.

> —Albert von Bonstetten, *The Life of Holy Ida* (1481)

The common purpose uniting authors and patrons such as Emser
and Duke George behind the lives of bishop saints is less apparent in

the lives of other saintly types. Identifying the divergent purposes, misunderstandings, and disagreements of authors, patrons, and devotees, however, illuminates another point central to this study. Revising writings about the saints, in content and in style, to whatever purpose, moved authors and patrons onto a minefield. Precedent was powerful in the cult of the saints, and deviations from it were readily recognized and evaluated skeptically. The desire to innovate had to be tempered by respect for the devotion's conservative nature, which shaped the imagination even of the humanist authors. Measuring the extent of revisions to an older vita, however limited they appear, can shed light on overarching strategies to bring new perspectives to old narratives.[1]

This chapter examines two cases of humanists' revising their own works. In the first we consider the two editions of Sigismund Meisterlin's vita of Saint Sebald (1484, 1488). Into the second of these Meisterlin reinserted a set of assertions that he had, in fact, knowingly excluded from the first edition. In the second we consider the two editions of Albert von Bonstetten's vita of Ida of Toggenberg (1481, 1485), the latter of which this early Swiss humanist made yet more classicizing. Both instances illustrate ways that patrons and humanist authors interacted in the process of composing saints' lives. That these authors made revisions of their own works in opposite directions—Meisterlin making his work less innovative and less humanist; Bonstetten, more so—obviously complicates the task of identifying a common humanist strategy. Indeed it forces us to ask whether there was such a strategy. Given certain contextual complexities that this chapter addresses, the two cases also point to how multiform the relationships between the humanist authors and broader German society were. For all the solidarity they aspired to among themselves, humanists were not isolated from other cultural strains that shaped late medieval and early modern German society. Because both cases have as their saintly subjects religious recluses, they also provide an opportunity to consider why humanists frequently composed vitae sanctorum about holy solitaries, who at first glance do not seem to represent a model of holiness that would be attractive to civically engaged humanists.

Humanists and Holy Reclusion

A life of solitude, freely chosen for religious reasons, was the principal means to holiness for eight saints in twelve vitae by seven authors. Though fewer in number than the bishops, the diversity within the set is noteworthy. There was, for example, no chronological preference for saints drawn from late antiquity or the early Middle Ages, as there had been among the episcopal saints. At one

extreme was Beat of Bern, who according to author Daniel Agricola had been
baptized by the apostle Bartholomew and evangelized the Helvetians at the
behest of Saint Peter before settling as a hermit in a cave outside Bern (see
figure 2.1).[2] At the other chronological extreme was Nicholas of Flue, a Swiss
hermit contemporary with his fifteenth-century hagiographers.[3]

These saints also came to their reclusion by diverse paths. Some had been
pursuing perfection from an early age, such as Saint Meinrad, who in the
seventh century entered the celebrated monastery of Reichenau as a youth and
after several years advanced from coenobitism—the monastic ideal lived in
community—to eremitism, taken up at the then secluded spot where followers
later founded the abbey of Einsiedeln.[4] Others, such as the tenth-century duke
of Saxony, Gerold, set aside his ducal crown in full adulthood, left his family,
and established a hermitage in the Tyrol.[5] Also, women were taken up as
subjects in this period primarily in association with monastic life: Some, like
Ida of Toggenburg and Ida of Herzfeld,[6] adopted the solitary life proper;
others, such as Adelaide,[7] the wife of the emperor Otto I, and Hildegard,[8] the
second wife of Charlemagne, spent parts of their widowhood in monasteries
but were principally venerated as monastic foundresses.[9]

The consensus that holiness could be cultivated in vowed life was of course
firmly in place in the later Middle Ages. Whether living alone in the desert or as
members of large and prestigious monasteries, participants in "religious life"
had been hagiographical subjects since Christianity's earliest days as the lifelong commitment to asceticism became analogous to martyrdom.[10] Regardless
of the critical voices recurrently raised in condemnation and ridicule of "bad
monks," acknowledgment of monasticism's spiritual value was surely also
more sustained than that of episcopal holiness, which, as we saw in chapter
one, had been contested since the eleventh century. The expansion of religious
life in the high Middle Ages to include newly reformed monastic orders such
as the Premonstratensians, newly founded mendicant orders such as the
Dominicans and Franciscans, and even new forms of so-called semireligious
life reflected and reinforced the notion that perfection was more easily attained
in religious than lay Christian life.[11] Interest in holy religious remained high
through the fifteenth century.

Just as the German humanists were beginning to write about the saints,
however, the literary evidence suggests a shift in how holiness in religious life
was understood. Saintly monks and mendicants rather suddenly ceased to
receive much attention. In these late decades of the Middle Ages there appeared, for example, no new equivalents to such high medieval masterpieces as
Jordan of Saxony's and Dietrich of Apolda's lives of Saint Dominic and Julian
of Spire's life of Saint Francis of Assisi.[12] There were no new vitae sanctorum

¶ Decimum Capitulum De dra-
conis expulsione animosa.

Orantes quicquid petimus de pectore fiet:
Si salus est animæ:si ratione petis.
Celsum deuotæq; preces scanduntiper olimpum.
Ditis virtutes rabidaq; bruta domant.

FIGURE 2.I. Urs Graf, *On the Expulsion of the Dragon*, from Daniel Agricola, *Almi confessoris et anachorete Beati, Helveciorum primi evangeliste et apostoli a sancto Petro missi vita iam pridem exarata* (Basel: Adam Peter von Langendorff, 1511). Call number: Z Gal II 157 m. Reproduced by permission of the Zentralbibliothek, Zurich.

Urs Graf (1485–1527/1529), a gifted artist active in Basel, created the illustrations for Agricola's *Life of the Gracious Confessor and Anchorite Beat*. The same set of woodcuts also appears in the vernacular edition of the life. Typical of illustrations in the printed vitae of this era, the image quietly synthesizes traditional and humanist elements: Having spent several years of itinerant preaching in the Swiss Alps at the behest of the pope, Beat, himself a Briton, drives a dragon from the cave outside Bern where he will subsequently live as a hermit. Behind him stands his trusted assistant, whose name Agricola reported as Achates, the name also of Aeneas's companion in Virgil's epic. Beneath the image Agricola has placed two elegiac couplets as a caption: *Whatever we ask from the heart in prayer will come to be if it is a matter of the soul's salvation and you ask within reason. Devout prayers ascend by way of lofty Olympus. They conquer the powers of Dis and wild beasts.*

of canons, coenobites, or abbesses.[13] Exceptions include vita about Albertus Magnus, the thirteenth-century natural philosopher, Dominican friar, and bishop of Regensburg, who was the subject of two vitae and some poetry;[14] and Joannes Trithemius wrote a life of Saint Macharius, twelfth-century abbot of the monastery of Saint James in Würzburg.[15] But no saints' lives of secular priests appeared in this period either. Replacing these common earlier saintly types in the hagiographical literature was the solitary monk. This trend is affirmed both in the number of narrative lives as well as in nonnarrative literary forms and in writings about saints. Famed humanist Sebastian Brant (1457/1458–1521) produced a large corpus of poetry in praise of the desert fathers. He even named his son, Onuphrius, after one of them.[16] Another hermit, the fifteenth-century Swiss Nicholas of Flue, attracted attention from all corners of Europe before and after his death in 1487, including from humanists, who were the first to memorialize him in vitae.[17]

The humanist interest in the cult of the saints runs most contrary to our expectations of what humanists ought to have been interested in when we confront their writings about holy recluses. Renaissance humanists, it bears reiterating, are more conventionally associated with an activist, lay Christianity. Indeed, bringing the holy bishops out of the more exclusively monastic milieus was, as we have seen, a key part of the humanist rewriting of the older episcopal lives and implicitly justifies, in this regard, humanists' treatment of them. But activist emphases could not, prima facie, be the transformative revision brought to holy recluses since a hermit brought out of his isolation would no longer be a recluse. Our discerning of how humanists made sense of eremitical subjects points in the final analysis to a new understanding of how humanists were integrated into broader contemporary religious culture. The apparent problem of these vitae from a humanist perspective is most easily analyzed in parts, examining first the interest of German humanists in the monastic life in general, then in the solitary life per se, and finally in eremitical holiness. Many early humanist writings made a sharp distinction between eremitism and coenobitism, the latter of which they widely considered opprobrious. The relationship between humanists and monasticism must be appreciated in all its complexity, of course. The monasteries were the single-most important avenue for humanist education in Germany. Many humanists were situated at monasteries, Trithemius being the most prominent.[18] However, humanists in Germany and across Europe never lauded the communal monastic life with the vigor with which they expressed the religious appeal of the solitary life as a means to attain deep philosophical and spiritual insight. These goals became prominently associated in humanist circles with Saint

Jerome, the linguist of the Holy Land, and explain his increasingly eremitical portrayal in Renaissance writing and iconography.[19]

The German humanists had a first powerful justification for the solitary life in the writings of Francesco Petrarch, the renowned fourteenth-century "father of humanism" in Italy His works on the topic included *On Contemning the World, On the Solitary Life,* and *On Religious Leisure.* The first two of these works were in print in Germany in the 1470s, and the third was dedicated to his brother, a monk.[20] Moreover, *Recommending the Hermit's Cell,* printed in Leipzig in 1488/1490 and in Cologne in 1492/1497 and exuberantly received in humanist circles, was ascribed at the time to Petrarch and only later discovered to be an excerpt from an eleventh-century tract popular among reform-minded monks in the later Middle Ages.[21] Several regionally prominent humanists also adopted seclusion, such as Joannes de Lapide (ca. 1430–1496). After a distinguished career that included establishing the first press in Paris and serving as rector at the universities of Paris and Tübingen, he withdrew in 1487 to the charterhouse in Basel.[22] The appeal of the solitary life to humanists thus appears to have two aspects. First, seclusion morally protected one from worldly distractions. Second, it facilitated deepest learning. The latter can be found among humanists across Europe; the former ran somewhat more strongly among Germans. The two aspects were not mutually exclusive, but each manifestation of interest in the solitary life favored one over the other. The vitae of recluses, as the coming pages make clear, were of the former sort. Moreover, quite aside from the degree of humanist styling to the vitae, these compositions share a characteristic with much medieval writing about the saints and in some contrast to the humanist writing about bishop saints: These lives were written in direct support of local cults. It is this set of nuances that we will examine in the vitae by Meisterlin and Bonstetten.

A Monk, a Hermit, and the City of Nuremberg: Meisterlin's Vitae of Saint Sebald

Sigismund Meisterlin and Nuremberg's Patron Saint

When Sigismund Meisterlin sent his new *Life of Saint Sebald* to the city council of Nuremberg in 1484, he included a cover letter, called the "Apologia." In it he explained why he had undertaken the project of writing a new life for this old patron saint of the city. He suggested that the abundant older writing about Sebald would normally argue against the composition of a new vita. In this case, however, the request of Nuremberg's leading citizens for a new life was reasonable because the most recent vernacular life and certain persistent fables

about Sebald were making the city's patron saint the object of regional scorn.[23]
Sebald was the city's proudest patron saint, its founder according to some. His
relics were housed there in a parish church that bears his name to this day.
Shortly after the emperor dignified the city by sending the imperial insignia
there in 1424, the pope canonized Sebald. These two events together indicate a
sharp elevation in the city's prestige. The "Apologia," however, reflected the
city's feelings of inadequacy six decades later. Nuremberg smarted in its relation to its urban archrival, Bamberg, "where [one] frequently hears jokes
being made about the new, simpleminded, and strikingly self-contradictory
legend [of Sebald]," wrote Meisterlin. He complained that the jokes "ascribe a
rustic character both to the saint" and, by implication, to the residents of
Nuremberg.[24]

Meisterlin explained that his vita resolved these problems. It fixed certain
inaccuracies and contradictions in the older legends, correcting, for example,
the claims that Sebald had, on the one hand, worked under the eighth-century
missionary Saint Willibald and, on the other, lived during the reign of the
eleventh-century emperor Henry III. Recognizing that his corrections might
offend popular sensibilities, Meisterlin remarked that he "rectified [these
problems] silently, making use of circumlocutions."[25] He also suggested that
the work be printed and sold only in small quantities, in Latin and the vernacular, and that copies be placed in the libraries of Nuremberg's principal
churches, Saint Sebald and Saint Lawrence, as well as in their naves, but
discreetly so as to minimize the chance of provoking controversy over the
changes.[26] He requested that the accompanying text, conceived of as a draft, be
corrected by the city fathers and returned to him.[27] Moreover, he asked that the
cover letter, given its delicate subject matter, be "handed over to Vulcan," that
is, burned.[28] Finally, Meisterlin subtly signaled the grand tradition in which he
wanted to place both Sebald as subject and himself as author, concluding the
"Apologia" with an unidentified epigram from Sulpicius Severus's *Life of Saint
Martin of Tours*: "May the material tell the story, not the story-teller."[29]

Meisterlin's concern about the changes he had made indicates his familiarity with Sebald's rich hagiographical tradition. The city fathers sought a new
life of Sebald apparently because the earlier ones were not inspiring the reverence for Sebald outside of Nuremberg in the diocese of Bamberg, within
whose ecclesiastical jurisdiction Nuremberg fell, that the city fathers believed
he (and, derivatively, they themselves) deserved.[30] Moreover, the frustration at
this indifference and scorn was complex: Veneration was growing at the
popular level in Nuremberg itself, yet the elite levels of society in Nuremberg,
Bamberg, and surrounding Franconia seemed unmoved.[31] To solve these
problems, the city fathers turned to Meisterlin for a new legend.[32] They seem

to have chosen Meisterlin because of the high regard in which the city's active humanist circle held Meisterlin's first historical works, the *Cronographia Augustensium* (1456/1457) and the *Chronicon ecclesiasticum* (1483). A prominent nineteenth-century historian would consequently judge him Germany's first modern historian.[33] Meisterlin had begun religious life as a monk at the monastery of St. Ulrich and Afra in Augsburg, professing in 1456. The celebrated early humanist and city mayor Sigismund Gossembrot (1417–1493) tutored him in the humanistic studies. He studied the arts and canon law in Padua in the late 1450s and traveled two other times to Italy for Gossembrot to copy manuscripts. His service in several administrative posts, including novice master at the monastery of St. Gall, suggests that he was regarded highly by his fellow monks and that he was sympathetic to the monastic reforms being implemented across Europe in the fifteenth century. Meisterlin arrived in Nuremberg in 1478 to take up a preaching post at the church of Saint Sebald. His writings and surely also his expansion of the parish library brought him in contact with the city's vibrant community of humanists. In addition to his two lives of Saint Sebald, Meisterlin also compiled a book of miracles for Saint Simpert, bishop of Augsburg, whose vita, as we have already seen, another humanist monk of the Augsburg monastery, Veit Bild, amended and published.[34]

Sebald's Lives

Meisterlin sent his new vita to the Nuremberg city council in 1484. As indicated in the "Apologia," he considered this version a draft and requested corrections. Although neither the response to Meisterlin nor an annotated copy of the 1484 vita are known to exist today, a revised vita, datable to about 1488, is.[35] On many points, the 1488 vita corresponds more closely to the older lives than to the 1484 vita. In particular, it reincorporates several problematic claims of the traditional accounts. Meisterlin's literary sensibilities and strategies had apparently proven themselves to be too radical, and the council requested that Meisterlin recast Sebald closer to his old self. Meisterlin's two vitae of Saint Sebald offer the historian today a chance to see how humanists' work could be shaped by their patrons' religious, political, social, and historical sensibilities (see figure 2.2).[36]

THE 1484 VITA. The story Meisterlin told was rooted in the written and oral traditions about Sebald that were accessible in Nuremberg. As he recounted in the 1484 vita, Sebald was an eighth-century Danish prince, who from his earliest years felt a strong desire to serve God. Because of his good judgment, intellectual talents, and other virtues, his parents looked forward to passing on the reins of government to him. His own yearnings, however, pushed him to follow Christ more radically, a desire that he prudently decided to keep secret in his youth. When he reached adulthood, his parents arranged a marriage for him, which he tried in vain to avoid. On his wedding night he persuaded his new wife to celibacy within the marriage. Shortly thereafter, he left Denmark and joined the three offspring of the king of Brittany, Richard, in Eichstätt: Willibald (700–787), Wunibald (701–761), and Walpurgis (710–779/790). Together they committed themselves to a life of religious asceticism and placed themselves under the authority of the eldest, Willibald. Meisterlin designated Sebald as the novice, emphasizing how much he learned from the words and example of Willibald. Rather than enter a monastery or form a hermitage, the foursome decided to serve Christ itinerantly. Together they vowed to make a pilgrimage to Rome. During these travels they scavenged for their food, and Meisterlin recounted that they found themselves fed "with bread from heaven."

In Rome the pope consecrated Willibald bishop and sent all four back to Germany to assist Boniface (672/675–754). On the way they preached and near Milan confronted non-Catholics, whom Meisterlin identified as Arians. A particularly obstinate one found himself being swallowed up in the earth, but Sebald's generous prayers saved him. Shortly after the group arrived back in Germany, Willibald became bishop in the newly erected diocese of Eichstätt, Wunibald established the monastery of Haidenhaim, and Walpurgis entered the convent. Now on his own, Sebald recalled an earlier hermitage near Regensburg that he had briefly occupied and decided to return there. Shortly thereafter he moved to the area that Meisterlin identified as near where Nuremberg was later founded. Sebald's life of solitude in these woods was spent in vigils and fasting. Meisterlin recounted one miracle during this period: Sebald restored the vision of a fellow forest dweller, who had been blinded as punishment for poaching.

Sebald eventually died, exhausted by his fasting and vigils. Local peasants, whom for years he had instructed and edified, discovered his body, laid it on a bier, and yoked it to untamed oxen. Their reins relaxed, the oxen led the funeral procession out of the forest and to a deserted place, once the site of a Roman encampment, later Nuremberg.[37] A series of miracle accounts from older records concluded the work, such as, for example, the story of a woman who wore a locked iron collar as a sign of and penance for past sinfulness. At Sebald's grave she was forgiven, and the collar miraculously loosened. Some of the stranger miracle accounts from the earlier hagiographer—such as the story of a Scottish monk plucking at the beard of Sebald's corpse only to have dead

FIGURE 2.2. Albrecht Dürer, *Saint Sebald on the Column*, ca. 1501. Inv. DG1930/176. Reproduced by permission of the Albertina, Vienna.

Conrad Celtis's sapphic ode to Saint Sebald surrounds Dürer's *Saint Sebald on the Column*. The ode concludes with praise to the city of Nuremberg and to Emperor Maximilian. The woodcut features the saint holding the Nuremberg parish church that still bears his name and houses the sixteenth-century shrine by Peter Vischer. Sebald's dress is that of a pilgrim. The crests above the saint are those of Denmark and France, representing the supposed origins of the saint and his wife, respectively; below him, of church dean Sebald "Clamosus" Schreyer and poet laureate Celtis. Dürer created many images of Saint Sebald. Rainer Schoch remarks that "the assumption is not unreasonable that Dürer spent a fifth of his life in and around the church of Saint Sebald." Kurth 169; Strauss 65; Schoch 129.

Sebald's suddenly animated right hand reach up and poke his eye out—were absent from the vita.

Meisterlin's 1484 *Vita s. Sebaldi* diverged from the earlier hagiography on four key points: First, Meisterlin resolved contradictions between the older vitae and other sources as well as those internal to the older vitae. He omitted references to the eleventh-century emperor from the rhyming office to leave unchallenged the idea that Sebald was an eighth-century figure (although it seems more likely that the historical Sebald had indeed lived in the eleventh century). According to another legend, Sebald had cured a Scottish monk (not the one whose eye his corpse would later poke out). The Scottish monks, however, did not live in or around Nuremberg until the eleventh century. Meisterlin eliminated the story. He also did away with an older claim that Sebald had studied in eighth-century Paris, and he avoided suggesting that Sebald lived in or founded Nuremberg, a settlement datable only as early as the eleventh century. Lawyer that he was, Meisterlin carefully explained the legal canons, unjust as they were, that led a certain count's henchmen to blind Sebald's fellow woodsman, who had poached from the forest.[38]

Second, Meisterlin shifted the regional and political focus, de-emphasizing or removing the vita's most international and most local aspects. This change was as much a matter of replacing one set of dubious claims with another as eliminating them altogether. Thus, Meisterlin eliminated the French origins of Sebald's mother and bride and did not repeat the claim that Sebald had been present at Nuremberg's foundation. At the same time, Meisterlin retained the detail that the place where Nuremberg stood was first settled by Romans, and he added an unlikely German etymology to his consideration of the meaning of Sebald's name.[39] Meisterlin also ornamented this earlier life with frequent topographical descriptions of the places in Germany that Sebald had passed through and historiographical asides that brought into the story Saint Boniface and the Carolingians Charles Martel, Pippin, and Carlomann.[40]

Third, Meisterlin reduced the miracle accounts. He recounted Sebald's generous rescue of a Milanese Arian from the Jaws of Hell and Sebald's turning of water into wine. By sympathetic magic Sebald took icicles that a neighbor had offered him as firewood—whether out of poverty or contempt Meisterlin left to the reader's judgment—and successfully ignited them for warmth. Meisterlin returned to Regensburg a story of Sebald repairing broken glass through prayer, correcting a mistaken reference to the yet-unfounded Nuremberg, and linking the story to a legend crediting the invention of unbreakable glass to Tiberius Caesar, founder of Regensburg. Few posthumous miracles were recounted. They were striking only in their conventionality, and thus unlikely to attract the scorn of Nuremberg's more sophisticated Bamberg neighbors.[41]

Fourth, Meisterlin carefully pointed to scriptural parallels in elucidating Sebald's dispositions and actions, a strategy he explained in the "Apologia" as enhancing the life with the "spice of Scriptures" (*condimentum Scripturarum*). Thus, Sebald's escape from the Danish court echoed that of Moses from Pharaoh; his crossing of the Regnitz River using his cape as a raft, numerous successfully dry water crossings in the Bible; his travels as a pilgrim, Tobias's guidance by the Archangel Raphael; and the heavenly nourishment he received in the Alps, the manna received in the desert by the Israelites. Moreover, to this last episode he added fragments of a Eucharistic poem by Saint Bonaventure, perhaps as a celebratory recognition of the Franciscan cardinal's own recent canonization in 1482.

Taken as a set, this ornamentation points in the direction of a particular ecclesiastical milieu into which Meisterlin was placing Sebald. It was of course beyond question to all participants that Sebald had been a hermit. In a time, however, when monasteries were undergoing controversial reforms and eremitism remained both highly regarded and highly suspect, Sebald's life as a solitary apparently required additional justification. Meisterlin's new emphasis on the communal aspects of Sebald's early life after his conversion with the monastic-missionary siblings Willibald, Wunibald, and Walpurgis responded to this need. As a solution, it betrays the hagiographer's own monastic background and sensibilities. By designating Willibald as the group's quasi-abbot and describing the rigors of its asceticism and missionary zeal, he effectively distinguished its life from that of the sarabaites and gyrovagues–wandering, begging monks without any abbot. Only after this tutorial under Willibald, in which he had appropriated the skills and virtues of a good monk, gained experience laboring in the apostolic vineyard, and demonstrated his loyalty to Christ's vicar the pope, did Sebald cross the Regnitz—like the Israelites crossing the Jordan into the Promised Land—and establish his hermitage in woods.

Meisterlin thus balanced Sebald's sanctity on three points: First and most important was his life as a hermit, which Meisterlin prepared by emphasizing the ascetical, coenobitic, and obedient life that Sebald led from his departure from the Danish court to Willibald's appointment as bishop of Eichstätt. Second, Meisterlin placed Sebald in a world where the orthodox and the heterodox were in conflict, and Sebald—in the manner of a missionary and thematically distinct from his eremitical achievements—fought for orthodoxy. Third, Meisterlin reinforced the authenticity of both Sebald's religious life and his orthodoxy by giving them the pope's explicit sanction in the narrative: As the touchstone of Catholic institutional affiliation, one pope guided Sebald in the legend so that another, some eight centuries later, would be able to canonize him.

Some of these details—the missionary dimension and the papal loyalty—reiterate aspects of the episcopal vitae. These assertions also happen to support Sebald's sanctity precisely at the points where eremitism could find itself uninspiring in a humanist context. The suspicions against eremitism that Meisterlin implicitly acknowledged have their roots in early Christianity. The sixth-century Benedictine Rule emphasized, for example, that only the most advanced monks were to be permitted to take up the eremitical life and condemned outright the sarabaites and gyrovagues. In fifteenth-century Germany there were a number of controversies over eremitism—its legitimacy as a form of monastic life and the institutional relationship between coenobites and hermits at particular monasteries—that Meisterlin was likely aware of. The idea that there could be good hermits had not been ruled out, but it was a way of monastic life, many argued, especially susceptible to abuse.[42] Exactly these concerns shaped the complex of virtues and meritorious experiences that Meisterlin ascribed to Sebald.

REVISING THE REVISION, 1484–1488. Meisterlin had another chance to distribute his revised portrayal of Nuremberg's patron in the new chronicle of the city that he composed between 1484 and 1488. The inclusion of highly abbreviated vitae of prominent personalities taken from the past was customary in such historical works. Unsurprisingly, Meisterlin included a description of Saint Sebald. Surprisingly, this portrayal diverges from the 1484 vita and follows the traditional narrative at several points where Meisterlin had pointedly altered it in the 1484 vita. Meisterlin reinserted the claims, for example, that Sebald's family had royal French roots and that Nuremberg had already been settled in Sebald's lifetime. One explanation for the reversed revisions is that the city fathers had rejected Meisterlin's first work as "too abstract and too unpolitical."[43] Meisterlin had, in other words, attenuated the strongest associations between the hermit and the city, as well as removed the awe- and devotion-inspiring details of the story. As a result, the new Sebald appealed neither to the elites who desired a saintly patron about whom they could boast to their neighbors nor to the population who put great stock in the received tradition and its saint's miraculous powers. Meisterlin's historiographical sophistication had given Sebald a case of devotional anemia.

The appearance of Meisterlin's second full-length vita in or shortly after 1488 confirms Nuremberg's dissatisfaction.[44] Reincorporating stories from the older tradition into the 1488 version that he had excised from the 1484 version,

Meisterlin's revised vita reflects the concern inferred from the chronicle that the first vita was too abstract and apolitical. One kind of amendment has to do with the increased significance of the city of Nuremberg. Meisterlin granted now that Nuremberg had already been settled as Sebald arrived and made explicit its unbroken roots back to the fall of Rome. He also included an excursus on Germany's greatest cities, including Nuremberg, and in describing the ecclesiastical history of the principal provinces of Germany placed Nuremberg under the jurisdiction of Wurzburg without describing the later foundation of Bamberg at all.[45] In another kind of revision, Meisterlin restored to Sebald some of the grander aspects of his background. Sebald's mother, for example, had her royal French heritage restored, as did his princess bride.[46] A priest visited him on his deathbed, and his day of death was redesignated in the year of Charlemagne's imperial crowning. The list of posthumous miracles was expanded.

Meisterlin did not reverse all of his changes. He did not reinsert the chronological inconsistencies and contradictory details. Sebald stayed rooted in the eighth century. Meisterlin kept his original elaboration on the *vita communis* Sebald experienced under Saint Willibald with its implicit acknowledgment that the solitary life was a form of religion suitable only for the advanced monk. Meisterlin sustained his tendency to neaten up the miracles, even though more of them were recounted. Finally, the Latin remained lightly classicizing, and the scriptural references and allusions, abundant.

Meisterlin's vitae of Saint Sebald represent, with the other eremitical vitae treated in this chapter, an affirmation of eremitical sanctity, transformed by complex interactions between several participants in the composition. The participants included Meisterlin, as we have seen, a fifteenth-century monk, among the earliest tutored in humanist studies in Augsburg, trained in the schools and libraries of Italy, and an experienced and successful writer of histories. Meisterlin was prepared to refashion the hagiography of his adopted city's patron to refute the scornful charges of its rivals, make Sebald an exemplary monk, tidy up historical infelicities in the narrative, and raise its literary niveau. This mix of concerns on his part—part monastic sensibilities, part civic loyalties, part humanistic learning—resulted, however, in a vita that did not meet its patrons' expectations. For those who received the fruits of Meisterlin's efforts and who had indeed hired him precisely for the ways that his mix of talents and concerns had already made him an accomplished writer about the past, traditional ways of representing the dignity of the saint and his city, including colorful miracle stories, could not be sacrificed purely for the sake of stylistic and historiographical sensibilities. The revised life of 1488, in several respects less humanist than the vita of 1484, was the result of a compromise between Meisterlin's scholarly standards and the values of those who hired him.

Ida of Toggenburg: More Brightly Polished

Albert von Bonstetten

An author's own revisions did not always follow this pattern, as the writing of Albert von Bonstetten about Saint Ida of Toggenburg clearly shows. Ida was a countess-turned-anchoress venerated in the later Middle Ages in Thurgau, a region in the Swiss Confederation near Lake Constance. Like Sebald, she became the subject of multiple vitae by a single humanist author. In contrast to Meisterlin's revising of his own work, acute dissatisfaction on the part of the patron was not the impetus. Moreover, the revising had nearly the opposite effect on the narrative. Rather than making the story more like the older vitae in content, the second vita of Ida was more classicizing in style. The author in question, Albert von Bonstetten (ca. 1442–ca. 1504),[47] entered the monastery of Einsiedeln at about the age of twenty, studied the liberal arts in Freiburg and Basel and canon law in Pavia, and became the dean of the monastery in 1474. His studies, his early travels in Germany and Italy, and the higher offices he held within the monastery community were similar to those of his contemporary Sigismund Meisterlin. Bonstetten was also a prolific writer of history. His historical writing includes *The German Wars of Charles, Duke of Burgundy, and His Death* (1477), *A Description of the Upper German Confederation* (1479), and *The History of the House of Austria* (1491, and its German translation 1492).[48] He addressed contemporary secular questions in political treatises, as in *Prospects for the Vacant Duchy of Burgundy* (1479).[49] A large number of his letters are extant, making him an accessible example of humanism's reception in the fifteenth-century Swiss Confederation.[50]

He was also one of the most active writers about saints in the period. All of his vita subjects are monastic saints: He wrote vitae of the duke-turned-hermit Gerold of Saxony (Latin and German, 1484) and the countess-turned-anchorite Ida of Toggenburg (1481 and 1485 in Latin, 1486 in German), a biographical report about his visit to the fifteenth-century hermit Nicholas of Flue (1479), and a revision of the medieval "Passion of Saint Meinrad" (1480).[51] He also composed the "Prayer of Blessed Bernhard of Baden" (1480), a hagiographical poem about a German margrave buried and venerated in Italy,[52] and an office of the Virgin Mary for the emperor Frederick III (1493).[53] In a similar vein he wrote the *Miscellany on the Origin, Indulgences, and History of the Distinguished Monastery of Holy Mary of the Hermitage* (1480, German translation printed in 1494).[54]

Bonstetten wrote a Latin life of Saint Ida, countess of Toggenburg, in 1481 (*Vita divae Iddae*, that is, *The Life of Holy Ida*), revised it in 1485 (*Legenda beate*

Ite, that is, *The Legend of Blessed Ida*), and translated the revision into German in 1486.[55] The Latin versions include a dedicatory letter to the abbot of Fischingen, the monastery that Ida had frequented as a recluse. In his Latin lives, Bonstetten referred to an older legend in the worn-out *(obsoleta)* German tongue as his principal source.[56] He claimed, however, not to be copying it but "with a swift pen" to be summarizing and reworking it.[57] He explained that the worthiness of his subject warranted her life's translation into a sacred language, and because of these his least weak was Latin, he used it.[58] Finally, he explained in the letter that he had undertaken the project as a favor to Henry Schüchti, abbot of Fischingen, who had helped him on many previous occasions, to inspire devotion to Saint Ida and, in the best humanist form, to delight his readers.[59]

The abbot and abbey's connection to Saint Ida and her cult had to do with her remains, which were buried at the abbey. Although a regional cult can be documented from the thirteenth century onward, the Toggenburg family had not fostered it since they had lost control over the region in the early fifteenth century. Participating in the trend of increasing activity surrounding saints' cults in the fifteenth century, the abbey had already commissioned a new reliquary for Ida's skull in 1440. A new abbot had arrived at Fischingen from St. Gall through the intervention of the reforming bishop of Constance, in whose diocese the abbey lay. He continued to foster Ida's cult. While keeping Bonstetten's Latin vitae for his abbey, he forwarded a new German translation, also prepared by Bonstetten, to a women's monastery in Magdenau. Moreover, he directed the renovation of Saint Ida's burial chapel in 1496. From this point into the sixteenth century, the number of pilgrimages and endowed Masses in Ida's honor at the monastery continuously increased.[60]

Ida's Lives

A FIRST EDITION, 1481. Bonstetten recounted Ida's life in 1481 as follows. The noble woman Ida of the line of Kirchenberg in Swabia married a count of Toggenburg named Henry, who lived in a fortress in the mountains near Fischingen. Henry presented her with a golden wedding ring. One day, after finishing the laundry, Ida left the ring to dry in the sun. While she was distracted, reflections of the sun off the ring attracted a raven, which stole it and put it in its nest. Several days later a hunter in the count's entourage heard the cawing of ravens, climbed the tree where their nest was, and discovered the ring. Rejoicing at his good luck, he put the ring "on his finger as if it were his own, unaware of its history."

A servant of the count recognized the ring and reported to him, " 'I have seen the nuptial ring of your wife on the finger of the hunter, and it leads me to believe that she gratified his desires and he engaged in obscene fleshly delights with her.' " The servant showed the count the hunter wearing the ring, and the count ordered him "to be arrested and tied to the tail of a wild and unrestrained horse. He then drove the horse over the precipice of the mountains so that, thus torn apart, [the hunter] ended his life in agony." The count then seized his own wife and threw her down from the fortress's highest point into a ravine some two hundred yards deep. As she fell, however, Ida promised God that, should she survive, she would never return to the marriage chamber of her husband or anyone else but instead love God with a vow of chastity. God heard Ida's prayer; and as "she reached the ground, she was set, whole and uninjured, upon the earth." She found a cave to live in and survived on various roots, as well as "holy prayers and the love of God."

Sometime later another hunter in the count's service was out with his dog, which suddenly picked up Ida's scent and followed it into the abyss. First the dog and then the hunter discovered Ida in her cave. The hunter quickly returned to the count, announcing, " 'Praise be to God and the saints above that your wife still enjoys the light of this world.' " The skeptical count followed his servant-hunter down into the abyss. When he discovered her, he took her survival as a sign of his own impudence. He threw himself down on the ground and begged forgiveness for his sins against her. She responded that God did indeed forgive him. He pleaded with her to return home, promising that he would condemn her accuser to death. Ida turned down his offer, asked that no one be executed on her account, and then asserted, " 'I will not at all assent to your request that I inhabit our former home; for the yoke with which I was once joined to you in matrimony is invalid and non-binding.' " Against his pleading, she insisted that her spouse was now Jesus Christ and asked only that he prepare a place for her where she could live for God separated from the world. The count obliged.

She continued to live in the forest, traveling daily to Fischingen for matins at the monastery, accompanied in the morning darkness by a stag with twelve candles in its antlers. Her pious reputation spread, and local inhabitants supported her with alms. A convent of consecrated virgins in Fischingen requested that she reside with them because of her holy manner of living. She consented on condition that they provide her with her own cell that could be neither entered nor exited. Noticing her piety, a demon began disturbing her in the fashion of a poltergeist. On one particularly troubled night she prayed for the help of an unnamed, deceased count of Toggenburg, who came bearing a light that made her immune from the attacks of the demon. Bonstetten's story ended with the attestation that she died on the feast of All Souls (November 2) and was interred at the altar of St. Nicholas of Myra in the monastery church in Fischingen, where she had so regularly traveled to pray before her immure- ment. Bonstetten remarked in conclusion that through the favor of God her prayers protect those pestered by evil spirits, as well as suffering from "sick- nesses of the body, infestations of the head, and especially hysteria." The 1481 vita did not include a more specific recounting of miracles.

This account follows the German life of 1470 closely. There does not ap- pear to be an alternate source. From earlier fragmentary documents we can reconstruct slightly differently that Ida was a countess of Homberg and of Habsburg descent. She became countess of Toggenburg by marrying Count Diethelm IV. Married and widowed twice, she became an anchorite and had herself immured at a convent chapel near Fischingen, a town in regions gov- erned by her son, Diethelm V.[61] When she died, she was buried at an altar endowed by her son and dedicated to Saint Nicholas in the Fischingen abbey in an uncertain year.[62] The fifteenth-century legends of Saint Ida themselves, however, are remarkably similar to older legends of Saint Genevieve of Bra- bant.[63] She was accused of adultery by a rejected would-be paramour while her husband was away fighting the Moors. Upon his return, her husband sen- tenced her to death along with their child, whom he assumed to be the fruit of the illicit union. His servants took pity on Genevieve, however, and left her and the child deep in the woods, where the Virgin Mary protected them. On a hunting trip some six years later, the husband stumbled across his wife in the forest, they were reconciled, and she returned to the castle, where they lived happily ever after.[64]

The Genevieve story did not include a stolen ring, but the more significant differences between the legends of Genevieve and Ida had to do precisely with the latter's adoption of a recluse's life. Unlike Genevieve Ida saved her accuser from execution. Ida also refused to return to the castle with her husband; she then lived in her cell, which her husband built for her, in the last years allowing herself to be immured by a monastery of nuns. These variations were not Bonstetten's inventions, appearing, as they do, in the 1470 German *Life of Ida of Toggenburg*. Hippolyte Delehaye, the first to exploit the connection between the two women, argued that the association between a certain Ida buried at the abbey of Fischingen and the story of the countess falsely accused of adultery probably had more to do with confusion over the abbreviations for *conversa* and *comitessa* on the gravestone in Fischingen than with historical documen- tation used or misused. Furthermore, a fifteenth-century miracle book at Einsiedeln—one surely accessible to the author of the 1470 German life of

Saint Ida—included the story of Genevieve's rescue in the woods by the Virgin Mary.[65]

The differences between the 1470 German life and Bonstetten's earlier vita are more subtle. Three aspects warrant mentioning. First, Bonstetten added details, such as personal names, specific dates, and geographical reference points, as for example in the opening paragraph (the 1470 life appears on the left; Bonstetten's 1481 life, on the right):[66]

We read concerning the holy woman Saint Ida that she was a countess of Kirchberg in Swabia and was given in marriage to a count who lived in the old Toggenburg castle. He gave her a ring made of gold, as was the custom among great lords.	Blessed Ida was descended from the noble line of the counts of Kirchberg, whose dominion, family, and name shine to this very day with great honor among the Swabians. She was joined in matrimony to a count from Toggenburg named Henry, who inhabited a high and mighty fortress, surrounded by the woods of the monastery of Fischingen and sitting amid the mountain peaks, which divide along a river coming forth from Thurgau into two parts. Moreover, she accepted a wedding ring from Henry made out of Arabian gold, as she wanted to be faithful to him according to matrimonial law.

A second tendency on Bonstetten's part—already perceptible in the passage above—was his longer, sometimes different, explanations for events, as well as a shifting of the story into a more formal register, as in Ida's renunciation of her marriage to the count:[67]

She answered him, saying, "Before God, kill no one on my account. And as for returning home with you, I do not want to do that as I am no longer your wife."	Ida responded, "Far be it that anyone should enter into danger of death because of me. Moreover, I will not assent to that request of yours that I again inhabit our former home with you. For the yoke with which once I was joined to you in matrimony is invalid and nonbinding."

Third, the most exact correlations between the German and Latin versions occurred where there were descriptions of something wondrous, such as the stag who guided Ida to matins at Fischingen every morning: "And she lived there for many years. On all days she was accustomed to attend the monastery of Fischingen for matins. A stag always went before her with twelve lights hanging from its antlers."[68] However, Bonstetten omitted the concluding chapter of the 1470 life on posthumous miracles, a frequent point of contrast between Latin and vernacular lives in this period, however close the narrative portion of the vita might be.[69]

THE REVISION OF 1485. Bonstetten's second life, *The Legend of the Blessed Ida*, was again written for Abbot Henry and appeared four years after the first edition. Rather than a direct revision of the first life, this vita was a fresh reworking of the 1470 German life.[70] The second life differed from the first in content by Bonstetten's addition and subtraction of material. Usually these changes made the second life more historically accurate, such as Bonstetten's omission of Ida's husband's name: As it was, there had never been a count of Toggenburg named Henry.

The more striking difference, however, has to do with language and style: Bonstetten gave this work a more classicizing ring and shifted its register yet further upward on a scale of formality. For example, Bonstetten specified the name of the hunter who had discovered Ida in her cave as "Achates."[71] Achates was also the name given to Saint Beat's companion in Daniel Agricola's life of that missionary turned recluse in Bern.[72] And as it happens, they share the name with a figure from classical literature: Aeneas' companion in Virgil's epic bears the name Achates. Other classicizing touches include inserting expressions such as "olympiacum Jesum Christum" and "Socraticum vultum ostendebat" in the second vita and replacing "solis radii" (which reflect off Ida's ring and attract the attention of the raven) with "Phebi radii." Classicizing is also evident in rephrasings such as the following, in which Ida requests that her new hermitage be placed in a meadow at the foot of the mountain Hürnli (1481 vita, left; 1485, right):[73]

Petit illa tabernam sub Hürnlin monte nominatissimo ad saccellum, cuius patrona est beatissima virgo Maria, exaedificatam.	In ea Augia, per quam scanditur mons ipse qui Hürenli communiter appellatur, circa basilicam, cuius virginea mater patrona existit: In his pratis locum delego, hic habitare in atriis domini cupio.

Bonstetten made such changes—classicizing and complicating—throughout his second text.

Finally, certain changes made the text more suitable for use in a cultic context, that is to say, for use by pilgrims at Ida's grave and by devotees on her feast day. For example, Bonstetten solved a specifically liturgical problem when he specified in the latter vita that her feast was celebrated on November 3 even though she died on November 2. Her feast, in course, should have been celebrated on her date of death. However, November 2 was already laden with the feast of All Souls, one of higher rank and universal popularity that would take precedence over Ida's own feast day.[74] Mindful that the attractiveness of pilgrimage sites was based on the dignity of a shrine's relics and the reputation of its miracles, Bonstetten also restored and revised an account of miracles worked through Ida's intercession at her grave site from the 1470 life that he had left out of the 1481 life. He wrote: "She was given great grace and favor from almighty God. For the tricks of the devil deceived no one who commended themselves to her prayers. To put it simply: if we call upon her from our souls, she can easily repel all sicknesses of the body, infestations of the head, and especially hysteria, with her prayers to God."[75]

IDA'S TWICE-TOLD TALE. Bonstetten's two hagiographical vitae offer the reader a glimpse into how humanists took on hagiographical projects. Many compositional factors remained unchanged between the two lives: Author, patron, saintly subject, and language were the same; a single monastery was the venue for both vitae; neither vita was printed; and both were kept in proximity to the relics that were constitutive parts of the cult. Four years and textual differences in style and content separate the two lives. The revisions allow for easy summarization. Bonstetten raised the register to let the life of Ida speak to an audience more familiar with and favorably disposed to ancient Latin and classical literature, and he reinforced the connection of the life to the same saints' cult by reinserting the miracle accounts and small variations in dating and place naming.

The textual alterations cannot be part of a consistent strategy of revision if one assumes the opposition of classicizing linguistic tastes and confidence in miracles. The reinvigorated world of classical references and allusions, of Athens and Rome, played to one audience; the enchanted world of saintly invocations and miraculous interventions in fifteenth-century Thurgau played to another. The dilemma so constructed perplexed the two Swiss historians who researched Ida's cult most closely in the twentieth century. One solved the problem by asserting that, in fact, the earlier life was the better suited for liturgical use. The other overlooked the tension and called the changes suitable to a "thin, upper echelon of intellectuals throughout the world." This latter solution, however, overestimates the geographic scope of Bonstetten's readership, while underestimating the social variety of those who would be exposed to it.[76] Bonstetten's vita never circulated widely and was overtaken in popularity in Switzerland a century later by the Jesuit Peter Canisius's writings about Saint Ida.[77] The concern of both historians, however, calls to mind Peter Brown's rejection of any two-tiered treatment of the cult of the saints, which would categorize the cult's components into elite and vulgar according to anachronistic presumptions about the sophisticated and the superstitious.[78]

Humanist Authors and Unlikely Lives

A real solution avoids these constructions altogether and looks to Nuremberg for inspiration by contrast. It begins with the proposition that one and the same audience could enjoy allusions both to ancient Rome and Athens and to the most traditional elements of the cult of the saints. Bonstetten, a monk of Einsiedeln, was brought to the project by an abbot of Fischingen, erstwhile monk of St. Gall, after Bonstetten had established himself as one of the leading historians and devotional writers in the late fifteenth-century Imperial southwest. That the cult of the saints might be incompatible with his intellectual background or literary interests is a presumption we might make. Bonstetten's contemporaries, including the abbot, did not. Bonstetten's intellectual background and literary renown, in fact, recommended him to the Benedictine abbot and ensured his suitability as an author of vitae sanctorum. Bonstetten then did just what was expected. He started with the limited resources at his disposal and produced a new life by classicizing the Latin and improving its cultic usefulness. A similar dynamic between patron and author was at work in the same years in Nuremberg between Meisterlin and the city fathers.

Bonstetten's and Meisterlin's works show how malformed the argument is for a humanist antipathy for the traditional cult of the saints. Once the presumption is discarded, Meisterlin's and Bonstetten's vita pairs exemplify the complexity of the concept "humanist hagiography." Meisterlin's revising sacrificed historiographical precision for the sake of devotional loyalties and political usages. This was a direction of revising that corresponded to the modern, faulty intuition about the relationship between hagiographical writing, on the one hand, and humanist style and religious sensibilities, on the other: "Better" hagiography must be "less humanistic." Bonstetten's revising moved the text in a different direction. The humanist flavor of the work increased according to the wishes of its patron, who was to use the text in quite conventional ways. In

light of these different trajectories, resistance to the idea of humanist commitment to and engagement in the cult of the saints appears doctrinaire. There
was not an inherent or a pragmatic incompatibility between the two—the
"humanist" and the "hagiographic"—and certainly not to the humanist authors themselves.

Meisterlin's and Bonstetten's vitae also highlight forces outside humanist
circles that shaped the authors' literary production and show a vigorous level of
interaction between humanists and broader society.[79] The patrons were key to
making sense of the humanists' writing. Many patrons were not formally
trained in the studia humanitatis. At the same time, they were sympathetic and
attracted to the learned culture and so sought out authors expert in it. Nothing,
for example, indicates that Bonstetten's patron was of particularly refined
humanist tastes. Yet he received, had translated into German, and distributed
the later, more stylistically "humanist" vitae. In contrast, Nuremberg was renowned as a home and home-away-from-home for many of Germany's most
active humanists. The city and citizenry patronized leading humanist intellectuals and Renaissance artists throughout the late fifteenth and sixteenth centuries. Yet Nuremberg rejected the vita that was ostensibly "more humanist"—
more classicizing and less miracle-laden—in favor of one closer to the medieval
models.

Like the authors of episcopal vitae, many authors of these eremitical vitae
had already achieved renown for historical writings, both secular and ecclesiastical. For this very reason, they were approached with these projects. As in the
episcopal vitae, there was a range of humanistic characteristics in the Latin
that the authors could self-consciously apply to their texts and so distinguish
these eremitical vitae from their antecedents. Indeed, it was nearly defining
of the humanist authors that they command a range of Latinity and could
apply it as they judged suitable. It was only necessary that the hagiographical
subjects have an established cult—a specific place of veneration, a tradition of
oral legends and pilgrimages—and a patron interested in fostering that cult.
These localized emphases are even more evident in the eremitical vitae than
the episcopal vitae since the composition and reception of the latter, as we have
seen, were far more likely to encompass trans- or multiregional concerns.

Working to portray the holiness of the recluse in ways convincing and
persuasive to a new generation of potential devotees, these authors were faced
with an old challenge: What justified the solitary life? The intellectual and
spiritual elitism that appear in Petrarch's writings or in the Renaissance iconography of Saint Jerome were assuredly not prominent in these vitae. As a
group the vitae did not recommend the hermit's life for general imitation. They
did not assert the claim that the recluse's commitment was superior to other

monastic forms of life either. And they did not propose it for the young. Indeed, the usual conversion to the eremitical life followed many years of experience in some other way of life, be it coenobitic as in the case of Meinrad, wandering coenobitism as in the case of Sebald, or marriage and family as in the very different examples of Ida of Toggenburg and Gerold of Saxony. Furthermore, none of these hermits led a life of absolute seclusion; those who were not associated with a larger monastery—such as Beat, Nicholas of Flue, and Sebald—found spiritual companionship in and around their hermitages.

As we also saw in the episcopal vitae, eremitical saints from the earlier centuries of Christianity in Germany are the most common saintly subjects about whom the humanist authors wrote. By the late fifteenth century most of these saints had already established hagiographical traditions, sometimes even thick dossiers of written materials. Some authors worked to please patrons who had sought them out because of their established reputations as writers on historical and religious topics. Even more striking, and distinguishing this set of compositions from the episcopal vitae, the authors of eremitical vitae were working for local cults in their own vicinity. The authors' scholarly reputations were of course part of the attraction that brought the patrons to them in the first place, but direct connections between the authors and the cults are more in evidence in the cases of hermit saints: Agricola, a friar in Bern, wrote the life of Saint Beat, a hermit from outside of Bern; just as Bonstetten had written the lives of Ida for a fellow Benedictine, his life of Saint Gerold had as its subject a saint whose hermitage afterward became a dependency on Bonstetten's own Einsiedeln; Meisterlin worked in the parish in Nuremberg that bore Saint Sebald's name. As authors turned to hermits, they engaged in a project nearly as old as Christianity itself, invigorating local cults. While this dimension of the humanist activity distinguished these projects from most of the episcopal vitae, humanist composition of eremitical vitae reinforced what we have seen already in the episcopal vitae: The authors were not inventing something new. Rather, with considerable rhetorical finesse, they drew sacred artifacts from the past; arrived at a balance of the complex religious sensibilities—their own, their patrons', and their audiences'—often after a few failures; and put these holy figures—now as Bonstetten put it in his vita of Saint Ida "brightly polished"—in the service of contemporary devotion.

3

Situating the Saints

Germania illustrata *and Saints' Lives*

Celebrated men and well-born youths,...take away the infamy of
the Germans according to the Greek, Latin, and Hebrew writers
who ascribe to us drunkenness, savageness, severity, and whatever is
brutish and deranged. Consider it shameful for yourselves to be
unfamiliar with the histories of the Greeks and Latins. Consider it
beyond all shame to be unfamiliar with the situation, the stars, the
rivers, the mountains, the antiquities, and the nations of our region
and land.

> —Conrad Celtis, "Oration Delivered Publicly in the University
> in Ingolstadt" (1492)

Interest in the ancient and medieval history of Germany began increasing among German writers in the late fifteenth century. Among
humanists the quest for an illustrious German past was stimulated
in part by two very different forces: One was the humanist confidence in the ethical utility of historical investigations; the other, a
new humanist pride in regional cultures. Germans learned this latter sentiment in two ways from their Italian counterparts, who were
both proud of their ancient Roman heritage and condescending toward the culture north of the Alps. A common reverence for ancient Rome united humanists in Italy and Germany. But in the humanist appropriation of this ancient past, the Italians were able to
claim a privileged relationship to that history. The literature and

culture of ancient Rome belonged to the Italian patrimony, and the Germans benefited from it only as stepchildren whose own lineage was far less noble. In these circumstances, that certain Italians could be condescending and that certain Germans were troubled by this was a particularly *humanist* problem: German humanists precisely as humanists were susceptible to the Italian haughtiness because both German and Italian humanists agreed that the ancient Greco-Roman cultures marked a high point in human civilization and because the Germans granted that these ancient cultures belonged more to the fifteenth-century Italians than to themselves. Only given these acknowledgments—common to German and Italian humanists—could the scarcity of descriptions of German lands and tribes in the ancient writings of Livy, Pliny, and Ptolemy stimulate Italian superciliousness and embarrass Germans.

At the same time, Italian writers, ancient and contemporary, pointed the way to a solution. Ancient writers had written several works that, in fact, hinted at an ancient German greatness. Contemporary writers were among the first to discover these texts and to excite the Germans into exploiting them. Aeneas Silvius Piccolomini (1405–1464), later Pope Pius II, was among the first in this latter category. His *Germania* (1457/1458) was an early, influential tract portraying Germany in a positive light from the perspective of an Italian humanist. Written as a response to the complaint of a church official in Mainz that taxes and tributes to the Holy See had driven Germany into poverty, Aeneas Silvius argued that the clearest evidence against such a claim was the evident richness of Germany—its cities and peoples. The leading churchman and future pope's argument may well have been shaped by considerable self-interest, but coming as it did from such a prominent humanist, the tract lent credence to the idea that Germany indeed had a praiseworthy history and culture.[1]

Aeneas Silvius's insistence, "Your nation is greater than any other!,"[2] soon became the German humanists' own rallying cry, and at last they began exploiting a series of classical texts for a more positive judgment of German history. The most studied of these new old sources was the first-century Roman historian Tacitus's *Germania*, which Poggio Bracciolini (1380–1459), a humanist with a knack for finding long-neglected ancient manuscripts, had discovered by late 1425. German humanists found in Tacitus not only an ancient writer with impeccable credentials praising their ancestors but also the warrant that they needed to write flatteringly about their own peoples, land, and history in imitation of his panegyric style.[3]

Germania illustrata and Chorography

The most concerted attempt to redress the literary imbalance was the *Germania illustrata* project.[4] The name echoed the title of Florentine humanist Flavio Biondo's history of the Italian peninsula, the *Italia illustrata*, written by 1453 and printed in 1474. Biondo's work was a fourteen-part review of settlements on the Italian peninsula in the mid-fifteenth century, written to link the individual regions into a coherent whole, as well as to establish the connections between his contemporary Italy and the ancient one.[5] The project's most vocal and energetic supporter was the Imperial poet laureate Conrad Celtis (1459–1508): His inaugural address as professor at Ingolstadt in 1472, quoted in the opening epigraph, is taken as its instigation.[6] He labored for many years on his own contribution and encouraged similar efforts in the humanist circles in which he traveled.[7] Nonetheless, the attempt to compose a national history yielded mixed results. It successfully inspired learned Germans to investigate Germany's past for great men and events (and even the occasional woman as, for example, Celtis's own editing of writings by the tenth-century nun and poet Hrotsvitha of Gandersheim[8]) and to write about their discoveries panegyrically and patriotically. Yet the attempt failed to achieve a synthesized national overview. Several wide-angle German histories did appear in this context: Jacob Wimpfeling's *Epitome of Things German* and Beatus Rhenanus's *On German Matters*, for example. Most results, however, were only regional in scope: Joannes Aventinus's *Bavarian Chronicle*, Jacob Unrest's *Carinthian Chronicle*, and Hartmann Schedel's *Nuremberg Chronicle*, to name just a few.[9] The successful balance Biondo struck between the regions and the overarching cultural whole, *Italia*, eluded the early German humanists.

Despite this ultimate shortcoming, the genre of writing undertaken by the German humanists in imitation of their Italian confreres warrants closer investigation, if only because they produced so much of it, and as we shall see, the interest shaped their writing about the saints. This kind of writing—the "illustrata" of Biondo and the early German humanists—can be designated as "chorography." Chorography was a form of scholarly writing and, by ancient and medieval reckoning, a subfield of geography. It was part historical chronicle and part descriptive geography, typically regional in scope rather than global, blending anecdotally local legend, genealogy, and topography.[10] The term chorography dates from the sixth century B.C. and was initially used to distinguish the study of identity and difference across space from chronography, the study of continuity and change through time.[11] Ptolemy's *Geography*, a second-century Greek work that in Latin translation became increasingly popular in Europe through the later Middle Ages, introduced Europeans to the concept.

It is not possible to point to an unequivocal definition of chorography in antiquity. Even Ptolemy described it ambiguously, sometimes as narrative cartography, sometimes as a subdiscipline of astrology.[12] Late medieval and early modern authors gravitated toward the former of these understandings and adopted two points from Ptolemy to distinguish chorography from geography: First, chorography was the description of individual regions and their most important characteristics, such as rivers, ports, and villages. Geography, in contrast, was concerned with larger land masses and the relation of whole regions to one another. Second, chorography and geography distinguished themselves according to the particular branches of knowledge that undergirded them: Geography was considered a mathematical project; chorography, a literary, even poetic one. Ptolemy, whose *Geography* was a listing of cities and regions with their astronomical coordinates, expressed a preference for mathematical geography over narrative chorography. The latter, he lamented, was too dependent on the unreliable reports of strangers, travelers, and sailors. Fifteenth- and sixteenth-century writers understood chorography to include a narrative historical dimension. For the German humanists chorography turned out to be especially useful: Even given his preference for mathematical geography, Ptolemy, simply by writing about it, made chorography a way, sanctioned by the ancients, for German humanists to express themselves enthusiastically about German lands and peoples and so to compensate for the paucity of edifying descriptions of German culture in the ancient Roman writings.[13]

Chorographical additions and alterations to their sources were among the most common changes humanists made in their new vitae. The markers of chorography in the vitae, as in other kinds of writing, were of several sorts. First and most simply, the setting could be established with reference to geographical features: For example, the hagiographers pointed out that Saint Beat lived in a cave in the mountains outside Bern and that Saint Ida of Herzfeld lived her adult life between the Rhine and Weser rivers. Second, the setting could be defined according to established political and ecclesiastical jurisdictions. At times the hagiographers referred to jurisdictions valid in the time of the saint, at times those contemporary to the hagiographer, at times both. Thus Sigismund Meisterlin told his readers that Saint Sebald lay buried where there had once been a Roman settlement and where now the city of Nuremberg stood, and Albert von Bonstetten told his readers that Saint Gerold had left the duchy of Saxony and founded a hermitage in a deserted place that as he wrote fell under the jurisdiction of the abbey of Einsiedeln.

Third, this placement could be ethnographical insofar as saints could be located with reference to the tribes whom they Christianized. Thus Saint Swithbert was situated among the Frisians, and Saint Otto, among the Pomeranians. Tribes could of course relocate, making this kind of reference geographically more fluid than the preceding two, but specific geographical regions could usually be inferred, and the authors who used ethnographic settings often referred to other, more stable geographical features as well.

A fourth and final sort of placement, the genealogical and social, was more fluid yet. This placement most commonly established the saints' noble backgrounds by reference to relatives, social circles, and dynasties. It also usually supplemented other, more concrete geopolitical references. For example, in Emser's vita of Benno, the references to the Salian and Wettin dynasties sharpen the geopolitical setting by focusing the readers' attention on the particular conflicts shaping Saxony during Benno's eleventh-century episcopate and Emser's own day. This kind of setting, like the other three, had been a popular hagiographical technique since the early Middle Ages to be sure; it was every bit as important to the late medieval and humanist hagiographers. Whatever the particulars of a saint's setting were, in the humanist writings under investigation here, some amendment to the setting as it was portrayed in the antecedent vitae always appears. This claim holds true even for the vitae that were minimally edited in preparation for printing. In short, the most consistent insertions have to do with chorography.

Furthermore, the hagiographers could associate setting with the saints in degrees of bearing. More direct associations encompass those where the place provides the setting for events related directly to the saint's life. Such is the case when Emser identified Hildesheim as the place of Saint Benno's birth and then described where Hildesheim was, relative to other towns and prominent geographical features. Sometimes, however, chorographical passages are more excursive: Emser's exposition of Saxony's terrain, flora, and fauna, for example, bears hardly at all on the biographical narrative narrowly construed since Benno never mined, tilled, gathered, or hunted.

These changes occurred in the saints' lives with a frequency, however, that precludes dismissing them as ephemeral or arbitrary. Closer inspection of the ways the authors established their saints' settings, in fact, indicates that the authors brought to their writings some of the same inspiration that motivated other writings that are more conventionally understood to contribute to the *Germania illustrata*. This link between the writing about saints and Celtis's historical plan brings into focus a new usefulness for the vitae. To show this, we will examine two salient instances of vitae crafted with new chorographical intent. First, we will consider two early sixteenth-century lives of Saint Bruno of Cologne—in one Cologne appeared prominently; in the other, not at all—to show how regional loyalties mattered in telling the story of a saint venerated across regions. Then we will turn to an early sixteenth-century revision of the tenth-century *Life of Saint Ida of Herzfeld* that demonstrates the subtlety with which an author could rewrite a saint's life in the service of the new German regional patriotism.

The City of Cologne and the Chorography of Saint Bruno

The association of saints with particular social, political, and ecclesiastical communities in the fifteenth and sixteenth centuries was nothing new. Authors of saints' lives had long played a role in legitimizing devotees' claims of association with saints. A principal way in which writers affirmed, adjusted, or denied these associations was through the geographical and social setting constructed for the saints in the vitae. A saint's geographical placement and social and institutional affiliations were often a matter of controversy. Over the centuries these elements could become the object of continuous adjustment, reflecting with each variation the shifting balance of power within a city, region, or set of competing institutions.[14]

The range of political and ecclesiastical entities that might seek the associative benefits of a saint was quite broad. The identity of the hagiographer's patron usually gives a strong indication of what person or institution sought these benefits. Knowing that Meisterlin was writing for the city council of Nuremberg, for example, is essential to understanding why Meisterlin made the changes he did in his second life of Saint Sebald. The differences between Meisterlin's first vita and its revision, as well as the Nuremberg city council's insistence on these revisions, likewise illustrate that a humanist author, even one of Meisterlin's renown, did not have the only, the first, or even the last word on how that relationship was cast.

Whereas patrons forced Meisterlin to reassert a relationship between city and saint that could already be found in the antecedent vitae, the prior of the Saint Barbara Charterhouse in Cologne, Peter Blomevenna of Leiden (1466–1536), developed the hagiographical relationship between Saint Bruno, the founder of his order, and the city of Cologne in his 1516 *Life of Saint Bruno*.[15] Blomevenna's emphasis is all the more notable because he otherwise relied on a vita of Bruno written only a year earlier by another Carthusian superior, the prior of the Grande Chartreuse, François Dupuy (Franciscus Puteus, 1450–1521). Dupuy's work included barely a mention of the reputed city of Bruno's birth and was silent on his noble family background.[16] Blomevenna's emphasis on Bruno's origins in Cologne is thus a divergence from both Dupuy's work and the anonymous late thirteenth-century Parisian vita, which both Carthusian priors had used as their principal source.[17]

These hagiographical efforts in the 1510s occurred in conjunction with attempts by the Carthusian order to have Bruno canonized.[18] Carthusians had been venerating Bruno as a saint since the fifteenth century, particularly in Cologne. The Cologne Carthusians built a chapel in honor of Bruno in 1489 that featured a cycle of eleven paintings portraying Bruno as a saint.[19] In the same year Sebastian Brant included a poem on Bruno in a larger collection of religious verse.[20] Outside of Carthusian circles the *Koelhoff Chronicle*, printed in 1499, reinforced the city's association with the proto-Carthusian when it compared the Blessed Virgin with Cologne: The one was mother of the Savior, and the other, of Bruno (see figure 3.1).[21]

By the early sixteenth century, such devotional interest in Bruno had inspired members of his order to hope for his canonization. Such a hope was behind the preparation of Bruno's writing for publication in Paris by the humanist printer Jodocus Badius Ascencius in 1509.[22] A strategy for canonization was also behind the reaffiliation of the monastery of Saint Stephen in Calabria with the Carthusians in 1513. Founded by Bruno at the request of the Norman king of Sicily, Roger, the monastery had subsequently affiliated with the Cistercians. The monastery also housed Bruno's remains, which were promptly exhumed and authenticated once it had returned to the order of its founding. Finally, in July 1514 at the request of four priors delegated by the order's general chapter, Pope Leo X verbally authorized the recitation of an office in honor of Bruno within the houses of the order. The authorization fell short of the delegated priors' hopes (Bruno was not canonized until 1623). Nonetheless, the order interpreted the papal consent as permission to encourage the veneration of Bruno. In May 1515 the general chapter ordered the inclusion of Bruno's name in the order's liturgical calendar and books. The head of the order, François Dupuy, wrote a new vita of Bruno, which was printed in Basel in 1515. The chapter then invited Blomevenna, as prior of the charterhouse in Bruno's native city, to deliver a sermon on the order's founder at its next meeting. Shortly afterward, the Carthusian press in Cologne published the sermon and at the same time another vita, also by Blomevenna.[23]

The chorographical adjustments in Blomevenna's work are noteworthy precisely because this composition and that of Dupuy have so much in common: Both were written by superiors of the same religious order as part of concerted efforts to invigorate the veneration and inspire the canonization of the order's founder. Geography distinguishes the two lives, in terms of both

FIGURE 3.1. Albrecht Dürer, *The Virgin with Saint Bruno*, 1515. Inv. nr. 1960:492 D. Reproduced by permission of the Staatliche Graphische Sammlung, Munich.

Saint Bruno, the proto-Carthusian, stands to the Madonna's left; Saint John the Baptist, a patron of the monastic life in general and the Carthusian order in particular, to her right. She holds the Christ child and stands on a crescent moon, an image taken from the Book of the Apocalypse. Other monks kneel in prayer around her as Saints John and Bruno extend the Madonna's cape over them in protection. A miter and crozier at the bottom of the woodcut likely represent Bruno's rejection of episcopal office in Reims and Reggio. Dürer's Bruno is the first printed image of the holy man. Kurth 301; Strauss 177; Schoch 240.

where they were written and what was written about. One was composed at the order's mother house in Savoy, the other at a monastery founded some centuries after Bruno's death but nonetheless in the city of the saint's birth. From the very first sentences, the Carthusian authors distinguished their chorographical perspectives and thereby established distinct aims in shaping Bruno's life.

Dupuy, after setting the chronological framework in an unsurprising fashion with reference to reigning popes and emperors, followed the thirteenth-century Parisian vita prima, passed over any stories of Bruno's early youth, and began with the story of Bruno's conversion. The experience took place in Paris, where Bruno was studying theology, and was animated by startling revelations from the corpse of a deceased Parisian professor, highly celebrated in life but theologically heterodox. Laid out in church and awaiting burial, the corpse began announcing to assembled mourners (in stages over several days) first, his indictment before the Divine Court, then the court's verdict of guilty, and finally, his damnation. The event so upset Bruno that he recommitted himself to the Christian faith and, Dupuy continued, gradually adopted a hermit's life, attracted a band of followers, and founded a series of monasteries.[24]

In contrast, Blomevenna, while recounting the story of the doomed professor, established a different framework at the outset by passing over grand references to reigning princes and prelates and first addressing Bruno's origins in Cologne and his German nationality.[25] Blomevenna spent several lines describing Bruno's youth in Cologne and remarked on the adult Bruno's occasional visits to Cologne, otherwise not attested to in the earlier writings.[26] At the end of the vita Blomevenna, who had throughout his work applied the title "saint" to Bruno and designated him "of Cologne," recounted how the saint's head had been brought as a relic to Cologne, an honor that uniquely befitted the city of Bruno's birth.[27]

Blomevenna made numerous digressions in the vita to describe Cologne—its Roman origins and dignity; its foundation by Agrippa, Octavius's son-in-law; and the Roman origins of Cologne's leading families, from one of which Bruno himself had supposedly descended. Some of these claims were accurate, others spurious or at best unverifiable—unlike the claim about the city, which the Romans had indeed founded, no evidence before this vita attested to Bruno's noble origins.[28] That the Roman origins of a German city would intrigue a learned monk in the Lower Rhineland at the beginning of the sixteenth century is hardly surprising. The *Germania illustrata* project was fostering exactly this fascination.

Blomevenna's chorographical agenda—his desire to extol Cologne, its environs, and Bruno and thereby to establish a mutualism between city and cult beneficial to the Carthusian order as well—are even more evident in his sermon to the general chapter of the order in 1515. This sermon became the foundation of the vita composed and published with it.[29] Blomevenna preached a Latin sermon that was medieval in structure but classicizing in imagery and diction. Reflecting on the Gospel parable of the wise man who built his house on rock, Blomevenna first described Bruno's religious virtues—his holiness, his wisdom and knowledge, his humility, his love of God—with reference to patristic and scholastic writers.[30] In the latter part he spoke more generally about Cologne and its sacred topography. He sketched a panoply of saints protecting the city, including the three Magi and the martyred Saint Ursula and her companions. These saints surround Bruno. As Blomevenna addressed his fellow Carthusians, he referred to a print of the Cologne cityscape he had apparently brought with him and concluded by presenting the print to the monks of the Grande Chartreuse. This portion of the sermon allowed Blomevenna to emphasize, as he also did in the vita, the Roman origins of the city, its leading families, and, of course, Bruno himself.

Mutually to Be Praised: Ida and Westphalia

Joannes Cincinnius (ca. 1485–1555) composed *The Life and Holy Conduct of the Blessed Widow Ida*, a revision of the tenth-century life written by the monk Uffing.[31] Cincinnius accomplished his chorographical revisions less by amending the geographical coordinates of Ida's life than by situating her in a new social, political, and cultural milieu. Cincinnius was particularly attentive to emphasizing Ida's regional significance to the place where she had spent her last years in seclusion, namely, Westphalia. There had been, however, no such entity in Ida's day. References to the "Westfalai" as a people first appeared in Franconian chronicles in the late eighth century.[32] Herzfeld, where Ida settled as an anchoress, was indeed a town in the vaguely bounded region of the Westfalai. Still, the monk Uffing made no mention of Westphalians or Westphalia in his tenth-century composition. No document located a town, let alone a person, "in Westphalia" until the mid-eleventh century.

Before turning to the differences in greater depth, however, a set of similarities needs to be noted. Although neither author resided in Herzfeld, both Uffing and Cincinnius wrote from a monastery that, though some sixty miles distant, had long-standing ties to the shrine.[33] Monks sometimes staffed the shrine and coordinated regional pilgrimages to it. Indeed, both men wrote their lives with an eye to the pilgrims in Herzfeld. The tenth century had been a prolific literary period for Werden.[34] Monks had composed numerous important saints' lives—such as several vitae of the regional missionary bishop Saint Ludger—at about the same time Uffing wrote the life of Saint Ida (around 980) on the occasion of a translation of Ida's relics.[35] As Cincinnius wrote his own *Life of Blessed Ida,* the monastery was recuperating from a decline that at its nadir had left the abbey with a mere four monks. The abbot Adam Eschweiler had affiliated the monastery with the reformist Bursfeld Congregation in 1474, an action that reinvigorated monastic life in Werden into the sixteenth century.[36]

A first evaluation of Cincinnius's *Life of Blessed Ida* does not suggest significant originality on Cincinnius's part. The vita appears to be nothing more than an abbreviation of the early medieval work. This was the opinion of the Bollandists, who dismissed Cincinnius's vita as "a small book in the monastery at Werden...ascribed to the priest Joannes Cincinnius, director of the monastery archives at the beginning of the sixteenth century....Given that the author lived some five centuries after Uffing, it cannot hold anything not already in Uffing's vita other than new miracles."[37] In the nineteenth century, historian Roger Wilmans, whose history of Westphalia included an edition of Uffing's *Life of Saint Ida,*[38] and Augustin Hüsing, a historian of the diocese of Münster in Westphalia,[39] were of a similar opinion.

Closer examination of Cincinnius's work indicates, however, that the librarian liberally omitted and added materials even as he depended on Uffing's vita for most of his narrative. The additional materials usually came from sources that we can identify today. These changes are numerous enough to justify closer inspection. The most significant had to do with his treatment of the political and ecclesiastical figures that made up Ida's social circle, as well as his rearrangement of the regional and historical setting in which Ida lived. In these regards, Cincinnius's work added two new elements to the legends of Ida, one having to do with the Carolingian dynasty during which she lived, the other to Westphalia, where she lived. In both instances the association is suggested to the common advantage of Ida, the dynasty, and the region. In highlighting Westphalia as the place where Ida was her most saintly, however, Cincinnius defined the region beyond what it was conventionally understood to be, particularly in terms of its geographical and political frontiers. Moreover, Cincinnius's description of Germany's western boundary for eighth-century Saint Ida anticipated that region "between the rivers Rhine and Weser," which did not become recognized until the sixteenth century.

A Humanist Hagiographer: Joannes Cincinnius

John Kruyshaer von Lippstadt, who latinized his name to Joannes Cincinnius, belonged to the first generation of literate northern European who could readily receive a humanist education. He attended the Schola Paulina in Münster, which was in the final stages of a humanist reform in those years (up to 1502). There he fell under the influence of its leading humanist teacher, Rudolph von Langen. He continued his studies in Cologne, where he received the baccalaureate in 1504. The more exact contents of his studies are difficult to ascertain: A prize won in 1504 indicates a talent in classical languages, and various annotations in his own hand in a book of Ovid indicate an interest in mathematics and geography.[40] His office of librarian at the Imperial abbey of Werden, where he was employed from 1505 till his death in 1555, placed him in a position especially suitable for humanists.[41] And thanks to extant correspondence between Cincinnius and other humanists, his own literary compositions, and records of his librarious acquisitions we have uncommonly rich sources with which to reconstruct the intellectual development and broader interests of a humanist who achieved regional notoriety.[42]

Cincinnius's book dealing reinforces the impression of one vibrantly attached to the latest trends in both learning and Christian devotion. His shelves were graced with copies of secular historical and geographical works, such as Schedel's chronicle and the Waldseemüller edition of Ptolemy's *Geography*.[43] His most revealing devotional acquisitions include several works of Joannes Baptista Mantuanus (1448–1516), a Carmelite humanist and devotional writer active in Mantua, as well as a widely read touchstone for German humanists looking for appropriate forms of devotional literature.[44] The prominence of his works in Cincinnius's library suggests the Werden humanist's own confidence in the synthesis of religious devotion and humanist style.[45] Similarly, Cincinnius received a copy of Erasmus's *Life of Saint Jerome* in 1519.[46] And his ownership of sermons by John Tauler and *The Passion of Our Lord Jesus Christ* by Daniel Agricola (author of the *Life of Saint Beat;* see chapter two) links Cincinnius to a Christocentric mysticism and devotion to the Passion popular in the late Middle Ages.[47]

Cincinnius's own writings reveal his interests as well. In *The Book of 400 Questions regarding Divine and Natural Matters* (Cologne, 1527), Cincinnius drew from classical works such as Ptolemy's *Geography* and Aristotle's *On the Soul,* as well as medieval works of natural philosophy, to produce a miscellany on natural philosophy touching on themes as diverse as cartography and alchemy.[48] *On the Defeat of Varus's Three Legions* (1539) consisted of excerpts from and translations of ancient Roman authors—Livy, Tacitus, and Suetonius among others—on the battle between Germans warriors and Roman legionaries in A.D. 9.[49] As fifteenth- and sixteenth-century Germans, especially humanists, investigated their past in search of greatness, the battle of the Teutoberg Forest, as it is commonly called, became a historical watershed in the formation of a

German cultural identity. Nearly all histories of ancient Germany included reference to the battle (as they still do), in which the Germanic tribal chieftain and former Roman soldier Arminius dealt a devastating blow to the three Roman legions led by the regional governor Quinctilius Varus, ensuring that area east of the Rhine and north of the Danube remain independent of Roman control. The humanist historians could hardly contain themselves as they proudly recounted the agonized cry of Caesar Augustus upon hearing of the loss, "Varus, give me back my legions," rendered by some, "Give me back Germany."[50] Cincinnius's excerpts from the classical accounts of the battle demonstrate his classical and patriotic interests that in turn reveal his ties to humanist culture.

Notably, three of Cincinnius's compositions at Werden were lives of holy persons: *The Life of Saint Ludger* (1512/1515),[51] *The Life of Blessed Ida* (1517), and *The Agonies of the Maccabees* (1518/1524).[52] Cincinnius prepared Latin versions of all three and an additional vernacular version of the first. He had only *The Life of Saint Ludger* printed (Cologne, 1515). The saints chosen as subjects also indicate an orientation toward local cults that we have seen in the earlier chapters as well. Saint Ludger had founded the Werden abbey, which took his name and possessed his relics. Saint Ida was venerated at the monastery and in the region.

Despite its exotic topic the *Agonies of the Maccabees*—a reworking of the Old Testament story (2 Maccabees 7: 1–42) in which a Syrian king tortured and killed seven Israelite brothers and their mother for refusing to violate Jewish dietary codes—was no less locally connected. A twelfth-century archbishop of Cologne had reputedly imported Maccabee relics for a Benedictine monastery in Cologne dedicated to the Maccabees. The monastery church had burned down in 1462. In the early sixteenth century it was being rebuilt. Between 1520 and 1527 goldsmiths crafted a new shrine for the relics. At the same time Cincinnius composed his legend.[53]

Cincinnius's Revisions of Medieval Lives

In contrast to the retelling of the biblical Maccabee story, Cincinnius's *Life of Blessed Ida* and *Life of Holy Ludger* are undisguised revisions of older works, accessible to Cincinnius at the abbey. Historians have disparaged Cincinnius's *Life of Holy Ludger* as the merest revision to Altfrid's ninth-century vita.[54] Given this repeated accusation, measuring the significance of Cincinnius's revisions to the *Life of Blessed Ida* will concern us for the remainder of the chapter. Cincinnius never had the life printed, nor does it seem that he intended to. In fact, only two manuscripts are known today.[55] In a dedicatory letter to the pastor of the pilgrimage church at Herzfeld on the Lippe River he wrote the following:

> O venerable pastor, a short time ago you requested that I compose for you in intelligible and succinct prose the life and remarkable conduct of the blessed Ida, wife and widow. . . . I was able in my own small way to do both and have prepared this little book about the life of holy Ida in a form more intelligible and at the same time more expansive, even if also more succinct in terms of words, than the one that Uffing is known to have composed. I have added a little more about our homeland (*patria*) and the place of Herzfeld and also about the times in which the holy wife, pleasing to God, shone bright. I was able to collect these things out of histories and similar conjecture (*ex historiis et verisimili coniectura*).[56]

In addition to indicating that his goal was a "shorter," "more intelligible" life that was also to be more descriptive of their patria, the dedicatory letter provides evidence of the attempt to invigorate the cult taking place at both Herzfeld and Werden. There had been a new translation of Ida's relics in Herzfeld in 1496, as well as an expansion of the church.[57] At Werden Cincinnius himself compiled an inventory of sacred objects at Werden in 1512 that included reference to a newly smithed reliquary for Ida's remains.[58] Between Werden and Herzfeld a vibrant devotion to Ida can be documented from the translation in Herzfeld in 1496 until 1522, when copies of the two lives of Ida, Uffing's and Cincinnius's, were bound together in the volume now preserved in the parish archives in Herzfeld.[59]

The work's full title in both manuscripts—*Liber sermocinalis atque succinctus de vita et sancta conversatione beatae Idae viduae* [A Short Book for Preaching on the Life and Holy Conduct of the Blessed Widow Ida]—reinforces the purposes that Cincinnius expressed in his dedicatory letter.[60] The text is intentionally short and structured to be read aloud, most likely to pilgrims at the sites where her relics were held, Werden and Herzfeld.[61] Ida was not the only saint gaining such attention in Werden. The Imperial abbey appears to have been engaged in a broader campaign to increase devotion to the regional saints. This context helps explain Cincinnius's *Life of Saint Ludger*, a reworking of several medieval lives of Saint Ludger, composed in 1512 and printed in 1515.[62]

Cincinnius admitted his reliance on Uffing's earlier life of Saint Ida in his dedicatory letter. In the vita itself he introduced quotations from Uffing several times with the expression "as we read" (*ut legimus*). A comparison of the texts verifies Cincinnius's undisguised reliance on the older text. He directly copied more than half of Uffing's work, and altogether three-quarters of Cincinnius's work quotes and paraphrases Uffing's. Variations in vocabulary were due perhaps to peculiarities in the Uffing text at Cincinnius's disposal but may also have been inspired by Cincinnius's desire to make the vita more idiosyncratically his own. In fact, even when the smaller linguistic changes are mildly classicizing, they do not suggest a systematic attempt to classicize or otherwise improve Uffing's Latin.[63]

Cincinnius also consistently omitted passages from the older work that drew out the spiritual implications of events in Ida's life and at her tomb. For example, both hagiographers recounted the same story of a woman who stole the clothes of a fellow pilgrim in Herzfeld but tripped and died as she made her escape. Both versions concurred that her death had been the appropriate consequence of her violation of the Seventh Commandment.[64] Cincinnius, however, left out Uffing's elaboration that "this was a double retribution for the crime itself and for the desecration of the place. It left a great impression on thoughtful people, but confusion and fear overcame the indecisive and sinful."[65] Such abbreviations were not uncommon in vitae prepared for legendaries and preaching.[66] At the same time, these changes may be indicative of a humanist tendency—evident even in the miracle accounts of a saint's vita—to de-emphasize such divine intrusions into the secular world.

Chorographical Revisions

At three points Cincinnius added to Uffing's narrative and altered several of Uffing's assertions. First, Cincinnius replaced the early medieval preface almost completely. Uffing had used his preface to address several general points: He affirmed the importance of the cult of the saints in general, arguing "that the innumerable saintly protectors of the peoples should be held in honor and that no part of the earth should be neglected." He stressed the noteworthiness and impeccability of the miracle accounts as evidence for Ida's holiness. He touched upon the problem of her marital status and defended her love of Christ, the "Eternal Groom." He pointed out her noble origin and sketched her genealogical relationship to the Carolingians. And he defended the historical accuracy of his presentation. He then began his account of Ida's life by introducing her future husband, Egbert.[67]

Cincinnius, in contrast, took up from Uffing's preface only the matter of Ida's relationship to the Carolingians and expanded on it throughout the vita. An emphasis on genealogical links between a saint and important dynasties and personages was a common hagiographical strategy. The higher quantity of such references suggests Cincinnius was more mindful of this potential use of Ida's life in the sixteenth century than Uffing had been in the tenth. He added new references to Saint Ludger and thereby created new connections between the monastery that was employing him and the saint about whom he was writing. He wrote, for example, that Ida was Saint Ludger's godmother and that Ida's and Ludger's families were business associates and friends. The kernel of documentary precedent to these claims is found not in the historical or hagiographical sources for Ida but rather in those for Saint Ludger, especially in the ninth-century vita of Ludger by the Werden monk Altfrid, Cincinnius's principal source for his own *Life of Saint Ludger*. These changes reveal a strategy of making Ida holy "by association," which we have already encountered in many humanist vitae and which hagiographers used throughout the Middle Ages and early modern period.[68] In his first chapter, Cincinnius added references to a relative, Adelhard, and to the regions of Burgundy and Francia. His inclusion of reference to "Francia," the western portion of Charlemagne's kingdom, was his own innovation.[69] Cincinnius likewise introduced Westphalia—the place most intimately linked to Ida's sanctity in Cincinius's vita, but unmentioned in Uffing's—giving it historical orientation in connection with ancient Saxony.[70]

The authors also diverged on the matter of Ida's marital status. Although married saints and writings about them were hardly without precedent in the Middle Ages, the author of a married saint's life was generally under greater pressure to explain how one's marital status, and in particular conjugal activity, had not impeded the attainment of saintly holiness.[71] Uffing addressed the issue directly: "She was, nonetheless, always aware during carnal relations to give to God what is God's and thus to regulate conjugal love so that no shadow of insincerity was able to darken her disciplined heart."[72] Cincinnius removed these lines altogether and replaced them with his first chorographical addition. He first located Egbert as "a count of eastern France (*Francia*)." Then, having located Ida's family origins in Brabant, a lowlands region straddling France and Germany, Cincinnius took the opportunity to describe Roman France (*Gallia*): "It is to be noted that the entire tribe or region of Gaul (*tota natio sive regio Gallie*) was divided in three parts up to the time of Charlemagne. One part, reaching down to Italy, was called *Gallia Narbonensis*. Another part, bordering Spain, was called *Gallia Lugdunensis*. And the third part was called *Gallia Belgica*, extending to the east up to this side of the Rhine and upward into the kingdom of Friesland."[73]

The classical allusion is immediately obvious; however, Cincinnius's division of Gaul is more complex than it at first seems. Although *Gallia est omnis divisa in partes tres*, Julius Caesar did not include *Gallia Narbonensis* among them, which Augustus first established as an administrative part of Gaul in its own right in 27 B.C., about a quarter century after Julius Caesar had penned his "On the Gallic War." Also, there was no point in time when Narbonne numbered among the *Tres Galliae* or when Aquitania, the part of Julian Gaul missing from Cincinnius's description, did not. Finally, *Gallia Lugdunensis* (Lyon) did not border Spain.[74]

Cincinnius's variant is unusual, perhaps even anomalous. It might be explained as an infelicitous conflation of Aquitania and Narbonne.[75] Given the significance of Gall for humanists and, in particular, its eastern frontier along the Rhine, derived from ancient Roman imperial history and separating the empire from barbary, it is hard to imagine the description as a slip on Cincinnius's part. As it happens, the provinces that Cincinnius referred to correspond to the three of four Gallic provinces that bordered Germany by Ptolemaic reckoning: *Celtogalatia in quattuor divisa est partes,* namely, Aquitania, Lugdunenses, Belgica, and Narbonenses. Ptolemy's *Geography* was the single most important geography book in late medieval and early modern Europe.[76] Beginning in the sixteenth century, editors regularly added new maps and commentaries. Among the most important editions in the empire were the Pirckheimer translation with the commentary of Regiomontanus (Strassburg, 1525)[77] and the exquisitely illustrated Waldseemüller edition (Strassburg, 1513) (see figure 3.2). Cincinnius acquired a copy of the Waldseemüller edition in 1515.[78] Two years later he finished *The Life of Blessed Ida.*

Cincinnius's references to the region of Westphalia and the people called Westphalian indicate a third addition to Uffing's text. As mentioned earlier, written reference to the "Westfalai" began appearing in the eighth century. But evidence for a transference of the people's name to a region first appeared only in the eleventh century.[79] In Cincinnius's day, "Westphalia" had several common referents: a duchy of Westphalia that dated from the twelfth century and fell under the jurisdiction of electoral Cologne; a league of cities affiliated with the Hansa; one of the twelve Imperial counties instituted as part of an Imperial reform between 1512 and 1522; and finally, a larger and ambiguous cultural region.[80]

From the lively fifteenth- and early sixteenth-century discussions over the extent of this last designation, Cincinnius derived his own notion of the Westphalia where Ida had been a saint. This region took its territorial limits from the writings of the thirteenth-century encyclopedist Bartholomaeus Anglicus, who described it as bounded by the River Weser to the west and the Rhine to the East and further bordered by Saxony on the east, Thuringia and Hessen on the south, Cologne (and the Rhine) on the west, and Friesland and the sea on the north. Subsequent authors into the early modern period built on and amended this definition, with the western border proving the most in need of adjustment. Contested was the extent to which the Rhine was Westphalia's border and the inclusion of the county Berg, which lay on the east of the Rhine just north of

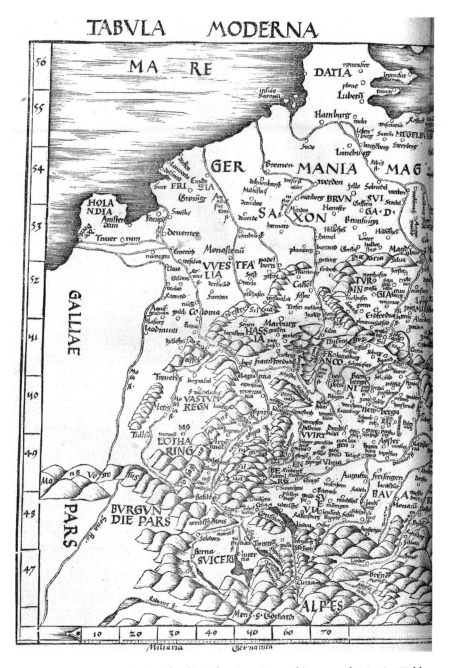

TABVLA MODERNA

FIGURE 3.2. "Germania," in *Claudii Ptolemei . . . Geographie opus*, ed. Martin Waldseemüller and Matthias Ringmann (Strassburg: Schott, 1513), tabula 46. Call number:
2 Phil. V, 36. Reproduced by permission of the Thüringer Universitäts- und Landesbibliothek, Jena, Germany.

Martin "Hylocomylus" Waldseemüller (ca. 1472–1522) and Matthias "Philesius"
Ringmann (ca. 1482-1511) collaborated on several important cartographical works in
the early sixteenth century. The richly illustrated edition of Ptolemy's *Geographia*,

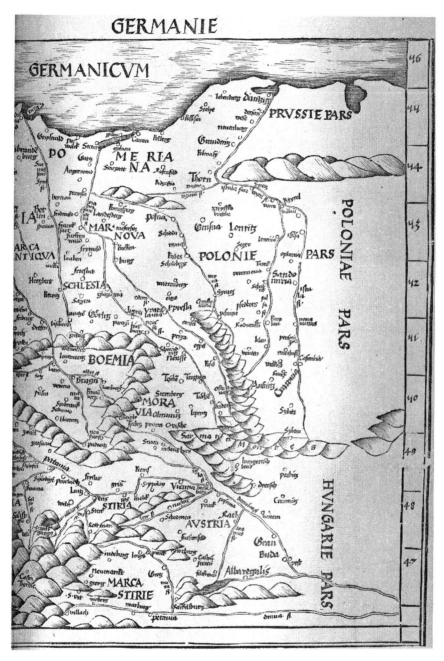

printed in Strassburg by Johannes Schott in 1513, is among their most famous. Waldseemüller prepared the maps; Ringmann, the Latin text. A substantial appendix supplements Ptolemy's own work with maps of "modern" areas, such as this image of Germany. Werden librarian Joannes Cincinnius owned a much-annotated copy of the Waldseemüller *Geographia*.

Cologne, in Westphalia. In the fifteenth century no less than Aeneas Silvius cast a literary glance on Westphalia. In his mid-fifteenth-century geographical work, *History of Europe,* he reiterated the significance of the Weser as Westphalia's "wet boundary" to the west, the political boundary with Hessian Berg to the southwest, and the regional boundary with Friesland to the north. He added a reference to the Hochstift Utrecht to the northwest but remained vague about the extent of the Rhine as a border and the inclusion of Berg.[81] *The History of Europe* suggested regional boundaries that influenced German geographical writers for decades. Cincinnius was, no doubt, responding to it as well.

Cincinnius's principal source for the history and character of Westphalia was Werner Rolevinck's *Book in Praise of Westphalia* (1474).[82] Rolevinck was born in Westphalia and wrote prolifically as a Carthusian monk in Cologne. *The Book in Praise of Westphalia* was, in its day, among the most widely disseminated texts of its kind.[83] Rolevinck was not a humanist by training or profession and represents a side of the Modern Devotion (of which he was much a part) that did not commit itself with great vigor to the studia humanitatis. Still, he numbered among the active early participants in the search for Germany's glorious past.[84] By Rolevinck's reckoning, Westphalia extended from the Weser to the Rhine and into the lowlands. Although excluding Berg, he identified Weser and Rhine as the usual "wet" boundaries of Westphalia. In style and content, the book is a chorographical tour de force: part history and church history, part ethnography and linguistic survey, part botany, geology, and zoology. His sources included Cicero, Horace, Livy, Sallust, and Suetonius among others. He quoted the Sacred Scriptures and many church fathers. Among his medieval sources he cited Gregory of Tours, John of Essen, Henry of Herford, the Venerable Bede, and Jacobus de Voragine.[85] The book was replete with inspiring descriptions of the great deeds performed by ancient Westphalians, of Westphalia's natural beauty, and the achievement of Westphalia's political and social institutions and customs. In so doing, Rolevinck worked to mobilize his Westphalian readers to make their present situation as glorious as their historical one: The work is nothing less than a panegyric to Westphalia for the Westphalians.

Cincinnius followed Rolevinck's delineation of Westphalia's boundaries, excluding Berg but otherwise following the Rhine northwestward into the lowlands. His references to the archdiocese of Münster, the province of Cologne, and the duchies of Berg and Cleves parallel those in Rolevinck. Cincinnius's reliance on Rolevinck elsewhere was similarly loose, such as the mix of cities and geographical landmarks that Cincinnius used to mark out Westphalia and the Rhineland.[86] His own, however, is the insistence that the most important length of Westphalia's western border was shared with Francia. The defense of such a claim is hard to follow. Cincinnius's efforts to raise Westphalia's own dignity by reference to such dignified neighbors as France and to turn it into the German bulwark to the west, however, are easier to understand.[87]

Cincinnius likewise relied on Rolevinck in referring to the early medieval legal organization of Westphalia. He indicated that Westphalia was "divided into numerous, distinct *Gaue,* and that each *Gau* was a district, whose name ended in *-goa,* formed from numerous neighboring settlements and placed under the direction of a prefect or judge, in much the same fashion as Friesland."[88] At the same time, this was a fairly free use of Rolevinck's work, which refers only to the Saxon use of "satraps" and "princes," not kings.[89] Cincinnius did not let himself be held captive by political and historical definitions and precedents in defining "Westphalia." Rather, he reached beyond past concepts, as had indeed Rolevinck, in defining the land blessed by holy Ida's presence.

A third set of texts informing Cincinnius's own work comprised sources he had also used for his *Life of Saint Ludger.* For example, Cincinnius offered a description of Münster that is found in Altfrid's tenth-century life of Saint Ludger: "And so we read that Münster is situated in the Nordgau and Alna in the Südergau. So it is that from these individual parts of the Münster region that their names come to this very day: [For example,] one calls those near the Stiburna River Stiburners" and so on.[90] These texts came out of the life of Saint Lebuin, a ninth-century text composed at Werden, and—as one of few sources that report that the area was governed by "satraps"—an important source for Rolevinck too.[91]

Trends and Syntheses

The question remains why Cincinnius made these alterations in a saint's vita. The impression he gave later historians was perhaps not so unfounded. So much of what he did can indeed appear at first as mere quibbling. However, the closer one looks at the words, sentences, and paragraphs from Uffing's vita that Cincinnius omitted, altered, and replaced, the less sure–footed the dismissal of these revisions is. In seeking an explanation for the changes, a new answer emerges when Cincinnius and his work are situated at the intersection of two cultural currents coursing their way across Europe in the fifteenth and sixteenth centuries and nowhere more so than in monasteries like Werden. The first was the interest in regional history that began occupying many German writers in the same period. The second was the interest in the cult of the saints that had been newly animated at the end of the fifteenth century in certain ecclesiastical circles in the German lands.

Cincinnius's *Life of Blessed Ida* exemplifies how these forces could interact in the mind of a monastery librarian, who, on the one hand, was rather unremarkably requested by an abbot to pen a new life of a local saint but who, on the other, participated in the latest learned fashions and concerns. *The Life of Blessed Ida* exemplifies a dimension of the conceptual difficulties in discussing "humanist hagiography." Indeed, it would even raise the question of whether Cincinnius understood himself to be engaged in a "hagiographical" project, if by that is meant one in which the author is religiously motivated to write a life in praise of a saint and in the service of the saint's cult. Should not, in fact, Cincinnius and the several other authors in this chapter be better categorized as chorographers, direct and not ancillary contributors to Celtis's *Germania illustrata* project?

The distinction is surely more our own than Cincinnius's. Indeed, Cincinnius's work, his own several other saints' lives, the works on saints by other authors in his library, and the various works we are examining in *Reforming Saints* offer the twenty-first-century reader a glimpse into how traditional medieval devotional writing could be reworked in light of new cultural interests. Cincinnius's effort demonstrates how the clear-cut cultural worldviews that are later developed to organize the past and that in juxtaposition seem so incompatible can, in fact, peaceably amalgamate in the minds of actual historical figures. Such seemingly conflicted literature, in fact, demonstrates how new ways of making sense of the world, such as many humanists were endeavoring to develop, still must draw from the traditions and world views being left behind. Scholars like the Bollandists and Wilmans had a different target: they were foremost interested in the eighth-century saint and her times. Strictly speaking, their evaluations of Cincinnius's vita are no less correct today than when they were penned: Given the other resources available, Cincinnius's work does not help reconstruct Ida's eighth-century life, prepare critical editions of Uffing's tenth-century work, or win insight into the Carolingian imperial strategies "between the Rhine and the Weser." It is other historical insights that have been missed in consequence of these later learned judgments, insights into one group—the Renaissance humanists, their patrons, and their readers—portentously situated at the cusp of the early modern period.

In no small part was the attraction to saints' lives in the fifteenth and early sixteenth centuries due to the invigorated interest in regional and national history that the humanists broadly shared with the elite in the empire even outside of humanist circles. These decades were a watershed for regional identities in the empire. The humanists hoped, moreover, to fashion *Germania* as a cultural and political entity that spanned competing regional identities.

This effort moved them to seek out a distinctively German history, as they had seen the Italians do. That the humanists would include in their sights heroic Christian figures should come as no surprise. Indeed, this study, in tandem with recent studies of Italian humanist writings about the saints, demonstrates how readily humanists undertook these tasks. That no German patron saint in fact evolved in this period should, however, not disappoint us. This period's history writers were ultimately unsuccessful at writing a German history. Forging an inclusive German patron saint proved to be no easier.[92]

4

Turning Swiss

The Patriotism of the Holy Hermit Nicholas

For Christian teaching and living is nowhere more easily planted
than among those peoples who know least about the deceptive fraud
of this world. . . . The innocent ways [of the Appenzellers] still show
us something from the Old Confederation, toward which God's
Word will doubtless draw pious, God-fearing people, who will give
up their selfishness, which—as Brother Claus of Unterwalden
also prophesied—is so harmful. Indeed, where it is not rejected,
no dominion can survive.

> —Ulrich Zwingli, "The Shepherd" (1524)

The example of Brother Claus has been neglected until now and
only a few people are familiar with him. . . . For this reason [the
author] has, out of special love, set down for memory what this dear
pious man did, who, like Saint Beat and Saint Meinrad, lived
blessedly in this land.

> —Peter Canisius, "Ninety-two Meditations and Prayers" (1585)

Living Saints and New States

If any single figure qualifies as the fifteenth-century's saintly
superstar, it is Nicholas of Flüe (1417–1487).[1] Nicholas—or Brother
Claus, as his devotees have also called him—attracted unparalleled

attention within his native state of Unterwalden, in what is now central Switzerland, and from across Europe. Correspondence, travel reports, ecclesiastical interviews, and numerous other kinds of contemporary documentation relate stories of his asceticism, prayerfulness, and wisdom.[2] Nicholas attracted a steady stream of pilgrims beginning almost immediately after he adopted a hermit's life in 1467 in a mountain valley called the Ranft. Civil officials in Nuremberg, Milan, and Venice, among other cities, sought eyewitness verification of the astonishing rumors that circulated about his holy life, either commissioning local writers[3] or sending their own ambassadors to visit him and report their findings.[4] Archduke Sigismund of Austria and his wife furnished the hermit's chapel and requested prayers in return,[5] while high prelates granted visitors to his chapel generous indulgences.[6] A pilgrim to the Ranft dubbed Brother Claus "a living saint" in 1474,[7] and the first vita, dated a year after the hermit's death, observed that the people had already "precanonized" (*precanonizare*) him.[8]

Humanists were among the most active promoters of Nicholas's saintly cult. The learned Benedictine Joannes Trithemius traveled to the Ranft in about 1480 and consequently drafted a sermon proposing Nicholas as a model of religious perseverance.[9] Trithemius also included the hermit in his necrology for the year 1487 in the *Spanheim Chronicle* and *Hirsau Annals*.[10] Nuremberg physician Hartmann Schedel included a description and woodcut of Nicholas in his *Chronicle*.[11] Renaissance Germany's foremost woodcut artists in Nuremberg undertook the illustrating in the first printed work about the hermit, which appeared in 1488 (see figure 4.1).[12] German archhumanist Conrad Celtis and his colleagues composed epigrams on the occasion of the hermit's death,[13] and John Geiler von Kaysersberg—a leading churchman, preacher, and intellectual in Strassburg, associated with the city's humanists circle, if not a humanist himself—used Nicholas as an example of humility and faith in sermons delivered between 1500 and 1504 and published in 1505, based on his visit to the Ranft in 1471 or 1472.[14] In 1510, beyond the borders of the Swiss Confederation and the Holy Roman Empire, French linguist, mathematician, and theologian Carolus Bovillus (ca. 1470–1553 or 1567) was still clearly moved as he described his 1503 visit to the Ranft and introduction to Nicholas's life by the monks of the Engelberg monastery.[15] Moreover, devotion to Nicholas in the sixteenth century transcended hardening confessional divisions in Swiss society, as this chapter's epigraphs show: No less a reformer than Ulrich Zwingli (1484–1531) appealed from the pulpit to the example of the holy hermit several times between 1523 and 1526,[16] and no less an instigator of the Catholic renewal than Peter Canisius (1520–1597) published a collection of biographical meditations and prayers about and by Nicholas in 1585.[17]

FIGURE 4.1. Albrecht Dürer, *Brother Claus in front of His Hut*, from *Bruder Claus* (Nuremberg: Marx Ayrer, 1488). Call number: 4° Inc.c.a. 571. Reproduced by permission of the Bayerische Staatsbibliothek, Munich.

This anonymous pilgrim's tract is among the oldest printed documents about Brother Claus. Within three years of the hermit's death in 1487, it was published three times, once in Augsburg and twice in Nuremberg. Willi Kurth attributes the image to Dürer's earliest years of apprenticeship in Nuremberg or to "the new style," marking the art in Nuremberg from 1488 and of which Dürer became the leading representative. Kurth 1.

By the time Nicholas's cause for canonization was first introduced at Rome in 1591—the Holy See did not canonize him until 1947[18]—there were already five written lives, of which the oldest two were in Latin.[19] The first, *The Story of Nicholas, Hermit of Unterwalden* [*Hystoria Nicolai Undervaldensis eremitae*] (1488), came from the pen of Henry Gundelfingen, a one-time professor of poetry and rhetoric at the newly founded university in Freiburg im Breisgau.[20] Henry "Lupulus" Wölflin, a teacher of ancient languages in Bern, composed the next, *The Life of Holy Nicholas of Sachseln* [*Divi Nicolai de Saxo vita*] (ca. 1501).[21] Lupulus's work then became the basis of the three subsequent German lives. Among the longer Latin narrative sources there also numbers a report by Albert von Bonstetten, based on a 1479 visit to the Ranft.[22]

Nicholas's cult and the writing about him stands out in this study as being the only case involving a living saint. Bonstetten and Gundelfingen had met their subject, and the interest behind the earliest literature was in the living holy man. Nicholas's contemporaneity placed a challenge on the shoulders of Bonstetten, Gundelfingen, and Lupulus different from that carried by, say, Meisterlin when writing about Saint Sebald in Nuremberg. This might be thought to make their task easier, since they did not have to account for an established, textual hagiographical tradition. At the same time, even without written sources there were strong presumptions about how Brother Claus had become and was as holy as his reputation suggested. These expectations and rumors, directly associated with Brother Claus and presumed in general about holy men and women needed to be accounted for every bit as much as the increasing quantity of written materials.,[23]

Complicating the matter of collating and evaluating the authors' sources, the evidence is unclear as to the extent of authors' familiarity with earlier written materials. Indeed, there is no evidence that Gundelfingen had Bonstetten's report or that Lupulus had either predecessor's compositions. Indeed, it is more likely that the later of the three Latin-language authors composed their works without familiarity with their predecessors' works. It is certainly clear that they followed different editorial principles in fashioning their portrayals of Nicholas. The consequences of this independence emerge strongly at two points: first, the way each author contrived the holiness of Nicholas as a hermit, and second, the relationship each author construed between this holy hermit and the place where and the people to whom he belonged. We have already touched a tension relevant to the former point in chapter two, namely, that between the ascetical holiness of solitaries as represented in the medieval tradition and the scholarly advantages of the *vita solitaria* espoused by humanists. Yet the religious ascet- icism imputed to Nicholas, even while he was still alive, not only was essential to his popularity but was also an extreme form by the standards of ancient and medieval Christianity. Each of the three humanist authors discussed Nicholas's asceticism in a distinct way: Bonstetten minimized it by linking it to forms of asceticism legitimatized in writings by and about the desert fathers. Gundel- fingen described Nicholas's asceticism dramatically and made it a centerpiece of his narrative. Lupulus reported it in a distancing way through aloof and languid reference to the testimony of witnesses. The first issue this chapter thus aims to illuminate is the ways the authors linked Nicholas's asceticism to holiness and to explain the different approaches.

The humanist writings about Nicholas also take innovative stances on the matter of his being "Swiss." The previous chapter has already addressed chorographical strategies adopted in general by humanist authors and their contribution to regional identities and patriotic trends in the German territo- ries. The challenges and consequences of making Nicholas "Swiss" are, how- ever, exponentially more intriguing because Swiss identity was by all measures in a crucial period of development precisely as Nicholas lived and the humanists wrote about him.[24] Moreover, the task of determining how Nicholas was re- presented as "Swiss" in the earliest lives is made all the more complicated by the status Nicholas subsequently achieved in Switzerland (and enjoys to this day) as its foremost native-born saint, an archetype of Swiss piety and conscientiousness, and a revered national founding father.[25]

Although Nicholas appeared in his fifteenth- and early sixteenth-century hagiography in no wise as a patron saint for Switzerland—there was no such political entity by 1501—he was a figure who was chorographically associated with its antecedent components: places such as the Alps and Helvetia, peoples such as the Helvetians and the Swiss, commercial and defense alliances such as the confederation along with its constituent parts, the *Orte*.[26] What can be seen developing in the writings about the holy Nicholas was a political orientation toward the Confederation of Swiss states,[27] in the first instance on the part of the states themselves, but then of the residents of those individual states toward the confederation as a whole. Becoming more "Swiss" came at the expense of being "German," despite the linguistic similarities between the confederation states and abutting territories. Analysis of the early Nicholas dossier exposes a productive correspondence between writing about saints and writing about the past, between what is conventionally but sometimes misleadingly distinguished as hagiography from historiography, such as we saw in chapter one, as well as the new ways that humanist writing about saints was creating political and cultural identity. In the final analysis, by 1501 Nicholas was not already the first patron saint of a nation-state. Thanks to the humanist life writing, however, he was the precursor of this important saintly type. That the holy hermit Nicholas could remain such a unifying figure for the Swiss through the bitterly divided sixteenth century makes the humanist attention to him worth especially close inspection.

Nicholas's First Lives

Henry Gundelfingen and The Story of Nicholas (1488)

Henry Gundelfingen (1445–1490)[28] authored Nicholas's first full-length vita, *The Story of Nicholas, Hermit of Unterwalden*, no later than 1488, the year following Nicholas's death. Gundelfingen's familiarity with the hermit likely benefited from his visit to the Ranft in the winter of 1481–1482.[29] He sent the manuscript, along with the text and music of a liturgical office,[30] to Lucerne in 1488 from Waldkirch near Freiburg, where he enjoyed one of several benefices that supported him.[31] Gundelfingen's dedicatory letter admitted his debt to Lucerne, "for [its] generosity and kindness to [him] had always been so great."[32] This debt had concretely included, since his fourteenth year, a benefice from the collegiate church of Beromünster, which fell under the jurisdiction of the city of Lucerne and where his father had served as provost until a promotion to the chancery in Constance. By 1480 the city council had named the son a canon at Beromünster, an office he accepted likely without ever serving there in a clerical capacity.[33]

Gundelfingen's education, academic activities, correspondence, and literary corpus indicate his humanist association. Born in Constance, he had studied the ancient languages and rhetoric in Heidelberg and Freiburg. At the latter university he received his master of arts in 1465, began teaching on the arts faculty in 1471, and became dean in 1473. In the 1470s Gundelfingen offered the first lectures on poetry and rhetoric at Freiburg, a task he abandoned in 1486, possibly for lack of students. While at Freiburg he made the acquaintance of prominent contemporaries Peter Luder, Albert von Bonstetten, John Geiler von Kaysersberg, and Frederick von Zollern.[34] His writings reveal a range of familiar humanist concerns: Extant lecture notes include a commentary on Juvenal, marginalia on the works of Terence, and a grammar lecture with references to Italian humanists Francesco Filelfo and Lorenzo Valla.[35]

Regional historical interests predominated in his writing, as is evident in works such as *An Epitome in Three Parts of the Chronicle of Austria's Princes* (1476), dedicated to his principal patron, Sigismund (1427–1496), count of Tyrol and archduke of Austria; a panegyric on the Swiss Confederation (1479) that included the history of the region under the Caesars; *The Origins of the Schwyzer and Oberhaslers* (1480s); and *The Warm Springs of Baden* (1489), a compilation on the origins of the Badeners. Other works that indicate his humanist interests— whether through topic, genre, or classicizing Latin—include *Memorials of War* (before 1476), a mirror of the prince dedicated to Sigismund (compiled from Vegetius, Walter of Chatillon, and Aegidius Romanus); a panegyric to the city of Lucerne, *The Pleasures of Lucerne* (1480/1481); and *The Topography of Bern* (1486).[36]

The motive behind Gundelfingen's authorship of *The Story of Nicholas* is a question without an answer in the usual places. He did not, for example, identify a patron in the work itself. City officials in Lucerne would have been one likely source of a commission. In addition to the author's personal connections to the city, Lucerne was linked to the holy man and his cult: City officials were in direct contact with Nicholas while he was still alive,[37] there was significant pilgrimage traffic from and through Lucerne during Nicholas's life and beyond into the sixteenth century,[38] and Lucerne chroniclers wrote several early descriptions of the hermit.[39]

One may infer another possible explanation for Gundelfingen's authorship from the liturgical office appended to *The Story*. Given that offices were written to be used in churches and monasteries, one might expect to find some record of a patron or client for Gundelfingen's composition at an ecclesiastical institution in or near Unterwalden, such as the prominent abbey of Engelberg; there is none.[40] A future canonization was on Gundelfingen's mind as he wrote, as his sympathetic reference to the faithful's "precanonization" indicates; however, no other evidence exists of a petition being prepared. The archduke Sigismund of Austria was certainly interested in associating himself with Nicholas's cult and had been Gundelfingen's patron and protector at the university in Freiburg. This makes the absence of any reference to him in the manuscripts particularly glaring. The dedicatory letter merely suggests that Gundelfingen began considering to whom he might dedicate the work only after writing it.[41]

The contextual factors governing the shaping of the vita and its hagiographical object need not be limited to the patron-author relationship, of course. If we turn to comparing the set of themes given precedence in *The Story of Nicholas* to what we find in other narratives about Brother Claus, one issue comes into especially high relief: Gundelfingen devoted a significant portion of the history to extolling the superiority of the *vita contemplativa*—and specifically the eremitical life—to the *vita activa*. The venerable conflict between contemplative and active lives in ancient and medieval Christian literature played a muted role, it will be recalled, in the eremitical lives analyzed in chapter two. For Gundelfingen it was a major theme in the direct descriptions of Nicholas and in several excurses.

Casting some light on how and why this became such an important theme in Gundelfingen's work is the author's own withdrawal into a quasi-eremitical life. Less than two years before sending the completed history to Lucerne, Gundelfingen abandoned his lectures in Freiburg in 1486 and retreated to Waldkirch. He expressed religious motivations for this conversion.[42] Such a career adjustment was actually not particularly aberrant among humanists and other learned persons in this period: Gundelfingen's more renowned humanist contemporary, Joannes Heynlin de Lapide (1428/1431–1496) spent his last years as a Carthusian in Basel after spending most of his life in a successful, if nearly always embattled, academic career and several years as an itinerant preacher.[43] At the same time, Gundelfingen wrote about the adoption of the solitary life in general and with application to Nicholas's decision with a defensive tone that suggests *The Story* might be an instrument with which he made an apologia for his own decision. The personal interest in Nicholas's conversion, the general hope for Nicholas's canonization, Gundelfingen's own encounter with Nicholas in 1481 and 1482, Nicholas's recent death, and the broader public attention to Nicholas contribute to a reconstruction of Gundelfingen's motivation in composing the vita and office, even without identifying a patron. The dedication to "the senators of Lucerne" was the acknowledgment of a debt of gratitude from a man who had lived from the generosity of the city since his youth but who now felt compelled to withdraw into eremitism.

Henry "Lupulus" Wölflin and The Life of Holy Nicholas (1501)

Less is known about the early years of Henry "Lupulus" Wölflin (1470–1534). He may have earned a master of arts in Paris, and he taught Latin, Greek, and poetry from 1494 to 1498 in Bern, where Zwingli was his student. Ordained a priest in 1503, he became a canon at the collegiate church of St. Vincent in the same year. He was implicated in the Jetzer affair—a cause célèbre involving Dominicans, Franciscans, and pretended apparitions of the Virgin Mary (1506–09)—and fined.[44] Regularly finding himself in financial difficulties, he put himself at the disposal of an indulgence preacher in 1507 and served as a translator in the Bern churches in 1518.[45]

The intimate familiarity with the indulgence trade that his work in Bern brought with it may well have laid the ground work for a conversion he reported having in the Holy Land in 1520. Upon his return to Bern, he began exhibiting sympathy for the new theological ideas of his former student Zwingli. He married in 1523 and consequently lost his benefice at St. Vincent. Bern's adoption of Reformed Protestantism in 1528 allowed him to take up work again as a scribe and notary in the city until his death in 1534. In addition to his teaching activities and the latinization of his surname, indications of Lupulus's humanist sensibilities include his composition of Latin poems, panegyric in style and historical in subject, a liturgical office in a humanist style for Saint Vincent that included a vita (Basel, 1517), a travel report of his trip to Jerusalem, and his life of Brother Claus. Zwingli's biographer Oswald Myconius praised Lupulus as a teacher of the ancient languages.[46] Lupulus and Jacobus Montanus, author of a life of Saint Elizabeth of Thuringia (Münster, 1511), are the only two authors of vitae sanctorum in this study to ultimately break with Rome.

Lupulus completed The Life of Holy Nicholas of Sachseln in about 1501. An introductory letter indicates that he composed the work for officials of Unterwalden, in whose boundaries the Ranft lay, and articulates a shared hope for Nicholas's canonization: In fact, by the end of the fifteenth century local officials around Flue and the Ranft were carefully attending to the popular cult surrounding Nicholas by renovating old chapels and building new ones on sites associated with his life. They had also begun collecting funds for the expensive and lengthy process of petitioning Rome for the hermit's canonization.[47] A letter and a poem dedicating the piece to the prince-bishop of Sitten (Sion) and ruler of Wallis (Valais), Matthew Schiner (1465–1522), preceded the introduction.[48]

Schiner had for some years associated himself with the cult and financially supported the expansion of the pilgrims' chapel in the Ranft in 1501 (this then suggests the likely year of the vita's completion).[49] Although more occupied as a practitioner of ecclesiastical Realpolitik than as a great patron of the arts and letters, Schiner was aware of the growth of humanist culture in influence and prestige at courts around Europe, and he patronized it.[50] Joachim Vadian was one of several Swiss humanists he corresponded with, and through his ally Cardinal Thomas Wolsey he developed an interest in the work of Thomas More and may have met the learned statesman on a trip to England.[51]

Lupulus gave the work a classicizing ring throughout: He begged pardon for his inelegant Latin. He protested his hopes that the recipients of the vita would defend it against inevitable calumniators, that the life of the saint would become better known through the good offices of the recipients, and that the work would be a refreshment for those otherwise exhausted by secular concerns. And of course he made generous use of classical metaphor and allusion, above all to flatter the bishop.[52]

The dedicatory letter also addressed a number of issues that had little to do with Nicholas's life but that hint at principles guiding Lupulus's approach to writing a saint's life. He brought into the text classical political ideas, for example, when he cited Plato in praise of Schiner's "gentleness and kindness" in governing Wallis. Lupulus continued that good governance and princely virtues were necessary not only for the internal well-being of the community but also for "reconciliation with one's adversaries."[53] Here Lupulus also contrasted "our own land" and "foreign lands" expressed a hope that through this vita the good things of "our land" would become known "in foreign lands."[54]

In a final passage, Lupulus turned his attention to "the men of Unterwalden" for the sake of a brief reflection on the relation of historical facts to belief. The prefatory materials allow the inference that Lupulus came to compose his life of Brother Claus for a quite traditional reason: Prominent civil and ecclesiastical authorities wanted a life in order to advance the holy man's canonization and thus to enhance the dignity of the holy man, themselves, and their communities. Lupulus brought his own literary and scholarly acumen to the task, as well as a sense that hermit's holiness had political implications.

Ways of Being Holy

Conversion and Asceticism

The centerpiece of Nicholas's holy fame was his asceticism, particularly his fasting. The earliest report of it was made by chronicler Matthias Kemnat in

1473, who suggested that Nicholas's lengthy and extreme fasting demonstrated that he was either a living saint *(ein lebendig heilig)* or a devil *(ein deuffel)*.[55] Hartmann Schedel related it with awe in his *Chronicle,* calling Nicholas's life *abstinentissima.*[56] For some two decades, it was reputed, Nicholas maintained a complete fast *(qui per annos xx sine omni corporali cibo vixit).* The single exception—of three morsels of bread and a few drops of wine—was made in obedience to an investigating bishop's command, after the satisfaction of which, it was reported, the hermit could not help but vomit, to the reverent astonishment of the onlookers.[57]

This asceticism inspired much curiosity not only because of its severity but also because of its contrast with Nicholas's earlier life, during which he had been a husband and a father of ten children, as well as a soldier, a town official, and a laborer. The humanist vitae compared these phases not as bad to good but as good to better: Nicholas had been an edifyingly successful family man and civic leader who became a profoundly holy hermit. Analysis of the conversion linking these two phases reveals contrasting attitudes on the part of the humanist authors toward Nicholas's eremitical holiness. Gundelfingen's description, for example, was the more dramatic. Without suggesting anything morally ambiguous about Nicholas's earlier life, Gundelfingen emphasized the worldliness of Nicholas's successes, exaggerating (when not inventing) dignities and offices in appropriately anachronistic, classicizing terms.[58] The conversion itself, according to Gundelfingen, was brought about by "the two lights of reason and intelligence," with which Nicholas recognized that reclusion was the way to "a good and holy life based on virtue alone." For Gundelfingen the transition from family man to hermit was a conversion in a literal sense: Nicholas had led one way of life; now he led another.

Lupulus, by contrast, accentuated the continuities running throughout Nicholas's life, during which he gradually mastered select virtues. Lupulus relied for evidence on a source not at Gundelfingen's disposal, the so-called *Churchbook of Sachseln.*[59] The *Churchbook* consisted of testimony from the hermit's family members and longtime friends, testimony compiled after Nicholas's death with an eye to the hermit's canonization. It related episodes from Nicholas's childhood, as well as several portents his mother received while he was still in utero. Lupulus reported, "His devotion to God increased more and more; and the stimulus of divine grace pressed him—now called a friend of God—into seeing that the whole world was an insufficient place to dwell."[60] Lupulus's Nicholas enacted a conversion, but one in which the movement from family household to hermit's cell was accidental to the profound long term trends.

Nicholas's departure from his wife and ten children to his hermitage gave contemporaries the same pause it gives devotees today. Indeed, his case provides illuminating contrast to Cincinnius's laconic treatment of Ida's marital status (chapter three). Although early investigations affirmed that Nicholas's wife, Dorothea, had sanctioned his adoption of a hermit's life,[61] she herself left no written record of her reaction to his departure.[62] In the two vitae, however, Dorothea's consent appears discreetly and exonerates Nicholas from the charge of abandonment. Gundelfingen reported that, after she consented to his departure, Nicholas "left behind all his belongings . . . keeping nothing for himself" for her well-being.[63] In contrast, according to Lupulus, Nicholas's "most faithful advisor" accepted her husband's aspiration more in acquiescence than with approval:[64] "Because he had begged her so often, she finally consented against her will to his importunate requests."[65] Lupulus further explained that the family regularly visited Nicholas "for the sake of his salutary teaching" at his hermitage, which was in fact a mere three hundred yards away from the family homestead.[66]

Both narratives proceed from describing Nicholas's arrival in his hermitage in the Ranft to addressing the intriguing matter of his fasting. The fasting provided an obvious link between Nicholas and the desert fathers, a link both authors exploited. No wonder he "is compared with the fathers living in the desert of Egypt," Gundelfingen exclaimed.[67] In the search for precedent, Gundelfingen also turned to the *Dialogue of Miracles* of thirteenth-century Caesarius of Heisterbach, drawing out of it the story of "a devout virgin from the diocese of Tulle," who lived for twelve years "without any bodily nourishment after receiving the Eucharist for the first time."[68] More than providing a precedent for Nicholas's asceticism, reference to the ancient desert fathers and other ascetical saints allowed Gundelfingen then to use the example of Nicholas to criticize contemporary society and religious life: Nicholas's choice contributed "to the restoration of eremitical religious life, instituted by Anthony, Paul, and other fathers, but now nearly completely suppressed."[69]

Nicholas's fasting, however, was not simply the central piece of his asceticism; it approached the limits of what was believable even in a world accustomed to the miraculous. Lupulus addressed Nicholas's extreme fasting with caution. Relying again on *The Churchbook of Sachseln*, he showed a concern to situate the asceticism within the broader context of Nicholas's persistent striving after multiple virtues. He raised the matter of recurrent skepticism among some in regard to the truth of these fantastic claims and the motives behind Nicholas's withdrawal,[70] and defended the possibility of these ascetical feats with reference to historical precedents.[71] Just like his gradual growth in the virtuous, Nicholas made a smooth transition to complete abstinence, beginning by fasting Fridays in his youth, increasing steadily to four times weekly, then daily with the exception of "a small bite of bread and a few dried pears," and so on until he stopped eating altogether some time after moving into his hermitage.[72]

In point of fact, the extremes of Nicholas's fasting do not have an obvious precedent. There had been of course numerous fasting saints in ancient and medieval hagiography—Saint Macarius of Alexandria, a fourth-century hermit in Lower Egypt, was much celebrated for eating only a few cabbage leaves on Sundays during Lent[73]—but Nicholas's complete abstention from food for decades has no precedent before the twelfth century. When similar extremes did begin appearing, it was in propaganda against the heretical Cathars. When it appears in literature about the orthodox, the ascetics are women.[74] Lidwina of Schiedam (1380–1433) was among the most renowned. The prominent Franciscan reforming preacher John Brugman (1400–1473) composed her vita and several revisions in the mid-fifteenth century, and Thomas à Kempis's abbreviation of Brugman's work was printed for the first time in 1498.[75] Lidwina's fasting distinguished itself from Nicholas's in two respects: First, hers was not absolute in that she occasionally received the Eucharist, whereas Lupulus reported that Nicholas needed only to watch the priest receive communion to be sated.[76] Second, fasting made Lidwina constantly ill. All reports of Nicholas's physical state, however, were positive: He was gaunt and dirty but otherwise in good health. The extremes of Nicholas's abstinence, while not contradicting the much-identified trends distinguishing late medieval male and female devotions, offer a striking exception to the rule.[77]

The question remains, however, whether there was a "humanist" approach to the asceticism that the authors ascribed to Nicholas and that had indeed caught the attention of many of their contemporaries. Canonization was certainly a hope of both authors, and asceticism was a virtue conducive to that case. At the very end of the Middle Ages, the Holy See canonized several popular ascetics such as Catherine of Siena (canonized in 1461) and Antonino of Florence (canonized in 1523—the last, along with Benno, before the Council of Trent). Other reference points against which Gundelfingen and Lupulus, along with their readers, could measure Nicholas were as diverse as fifteenth-century religious culture in toto.[78] Copied, excerpted from, translated, and printed continuously throughout the late Middle Ages, the *Vitaspatrum*—a collection of vitae, short travel reports, and apophthegmata concerning the first generations of Christian hermits and monks in the Egyptian, Syrian, and Palestinian deserts—was a popular and authoritative source of images of ascetical holiness. By the end of the thirteenth century, vernacular versions of the *Vitaspatrum* circulated in Germany. Jacobus de Voragine drew from the *Vitaspatrum* for his yet more popular *Golden Legend*, as did Caesarius of Heisterbach for his

Dialogue of Miracles, the early thirteenth-century collection of exempla quoted by Gundelfingen to suggest a precedent for Nicholas's fasting.[79]

A practice of more moderate asceticism in the Western monastic tradition owed its institutional origin to the sixth-century Rule of Saint Benedict.[80] A corresponding hagiography, however, surfaced only as early as the high Middle Ages, best exemplified by the *Vitasfratrum* of fourteenth-century Augustinian canon Jordan of Quedlinburg. The *Vitasfratrum* consists of stories about persons in religious life, just as had the *Vitaspatrum,* but unlike his predecessor, Jordan was guided by a sense of spiritual moderation (*mediocritas*) and shaped his story to better suit the medieval monk, discerning a middle way between the harsh asceticism of the desert fathers and the laxity of fourteenth-century coenobitism.

In humanist works, the more fantastic ascetical claims were often disapproved. The introduction of Erasmus's *Life of Saint Jerome* (Basel, 1516), as we have seen, included a condemnation of such claims as absurd inventions. Even though humanist authors often simply recounted the strange signs of the holy hermits, as we saw in chapter two, Erasmus's work exhibits an alternative strain of humanist fashioning of the ascetic. As in the case of Erasmus's Jerome, the justification for a life in the desert and its exemplarity was in the ascetic's scholarly pursuits. Jerome's departure for the desert, his translation of the Bible from original languages into Latin, the spiritual counsel he offered visitors and correspondents, and the humble monastic community he founded begin to sketch a Christian asceticism that the humanists could aspire to and praise.[81] Other hermits likewise attracted the attention of humanists—such as Sebastian Brant's poetic engagement with Saint Onuphrius that extended over many years. This attention moderated the penitential asceticism that had captured the imagination of the medievals and usually emphasized the hermits' dedication to study and reflection, if of no other book than the Bible.[82]

Gundelfingen and Lupulus could not avail themselves of this route: Nicholas was obviously not an intellectual, and much of his spiritual life—rich with visions and, some claimed, mystical—was foreign to the German humanists. Given certain civil offices Nicholas held before his conversion, it is unlikely that Brother Claus was completely illiterate. Still, Nicholas's hagiographers—before and after Gundelfingen and Lupulus—unanimously reported his illiteracy. To compensate for this lapse, Gundelfingen and Lupulus, as well as Bonstetten and other authors, included special reference to a certain Brother Ulrich, a holy man attracted to the Ranft by Nicholas's reputation. Brother Ulrich took the role of Nicholas's disciple, a relationship in the best tradition of the desert fathers. The two earliest life writers, along with

Bonstetten, made a special point of remarking on Ulrich's intellectual bearing and honorable social background. More to the point, both Gundelfingen and Lupulus made strong assertions that Nicholas's illiteracy was, in fact, a surer way to holiness than conventional learning: The Spirit was the source of a knowledge that the books of the academics were not. Lupulus, in a passage similar to ones found in Gundelfingen, described "learning poured into [Nicholas] from above" that gave him an insight into the spiritual life that could easily surpass that of the learned.[83]

Gundelfingen's vindication of Nicholas's search for the surer knowledge of the Gospel fits into the context of a late medieval skepticism toward the spiritual value of scholastic knowledge, a position common among humanists. This is the spirit in which Gundelfingen—himself gradually entering a life of greater isolation—contrasted those "in the world," who "will be buried only to sink into the inferno" because of their worthless accumulation of knowledge, to those like Nicholas, who in their isolation draw from the diverse canals leading to "the vineyard of the Lord according to the Gospel," from which one gains "more learning than in the golden temple of the synagogue, in the conventicles of the worldly."[84] The imagery of sustenance and refreshment gained from the Gospel is, in fact, a hallmark of the alternative proposed by this humanist spirituality,[85] and one can sense a resonance between Gundelfingen's ideas and the later ones of Erasmus that he called the "philosophy of Christ."

Gundelfingen's condemnation of worldly learning and his advocacy of solitude are leitmotifs running throughout the vita: Nicholas's life was an example of the holy choice to flee the slavery of worldly success for the good of the soul. Gundelfingen highlighted the urgency of Nicholas's decision for the solitary life by pointing to three broader personal, social, ecclesiastical, and spiritual problems. The first two have already been touched on: First, Gundelfingen criticized the moral helplessness of the learned against the wisdom that comes from the Gospel; second, he praised Nicholas for reinvigorating a form of religious life otherwise neglected by the church.

A third consideration has to do with reclusion's social utility. At one point in the vita Gundelfingen responded to an imaginary interlocutor who asked why an unlearned hermit who had withdrawn from society without contributing to its common good deserved praise. Gundelfingen first historicized the issue by accusing his interlocutor of misapprehending Nicholas's choice, which, Gundelfingen asserted, must not be compared to the ancient hermits whose life was a freely chosen, personal sacrifice, but rather with contemporary hermits, whose way of life was a cause of scandal. Gundelfingen's insinuation ran thus: The eremitical life as practiced in his day failed because it was attractive not in the spirit of the ancient desert fathers but only as an alternative to the legalistic, desiccated religion practiced in contemporary Christianity. Freely chosen solitude, as the church had not seen since ancient days and as Gundelfingen's interlocutor had never seen until Nicholas, was for that same reason an edifying choice. By fostering true religion throughout the church, it was not antisocial at all.[86] Arguments such as these further suggest that one of Gundelfingen's goals in the vita was to defend his own intimately personal choice to leave the academy and adopt a reclusive life. As unusual as Gundelfingen's periphrastic explanation of Nicholas's social conscience was, his disappointment with monastic life in his own day was not peculiar at all. Erasmus echoed the sentiment nearly three decades later in his own vita of Saint Jerome, when he wrote, "I must say, on the chance that the reader may labor under a misapprehension, that the life of a monk was far different at that time from what we see today, trammeled as it is by ceremonial formality."[87]

A Pater Patriae?

A second dimension of Nicholas's hagiography that sharply distinguishes it from the vitae we have examined in the preceding chapters has to do with how the authors associated the saint with the political society of which he was a part. Humanists consistently identified the native and adopted homelands (patriae) of their saints, as we have seen—Sebald, from Nuremberg; Benno, from Saxony; Ida from Westphalia. If the authors had limited their regional interest to a few political references to Unterwalden and then waxed eloquently about the Alps' snowy peaks and wooded valleys, the vitae would have fit neatly into chapter three. But, quite frankly, no saint was associated with a political society and culture in any other vita the way that Nicholas and his holiness was linked to "the Swiss Confederation." The singularity begins with the very ambiguity of what his patria was at the moment when he lived and at the moment when the humanist authors penned their lives of him. Later Swiss generations identified that patria as Switzerland. In the fifteenth century the vita authors did not— indeed could not—make such an identification because no such entity as Switzerland existed at the time.

The late medieval Swiss Confederation was a union of Alpine cities and rural territories that joined for mutual economic advantage and defense (see figure 4.2). How the member states understood themselves in relation to the confederation and its status within the Holy Roman Empire was ambiguous throughout the late Middle Ages. As the earliest reports of Nicholas's holiness were circulating in the last quarter of the fifteenth century, the confederation's legal status and its members' own sense of identification with it were undergoing profound change. Traces of these developments appear in the writings

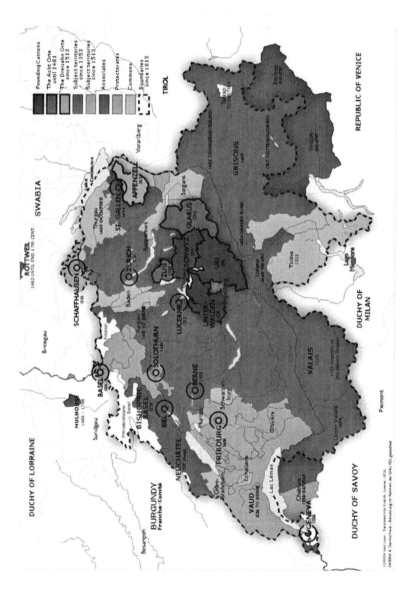

FIGURE 4.2. Map of the late medieval Swiss Confederation. 2004, A. Darmochwal. Translated in English by Lupo.

about Nicholas. In fact, the portrayals of Nicholas made him increasingly representative of an idealized Swiss personality. Such social and political association was not new to the cult of the saints: Saints had long come to stand for dynasties, crowns, cities, and so forth. The object of this saintly patronage, however, was new: What the Swiss Confederation was and was becoming in the very decades that authors were first penning lives of Nicholas had no equivalent. Although the path the confederation followed did not end in a nation-state like that of other, larger powers in Europe, the Swiss developments do indicate a transformation into a political entity unlike the medieval monarchies, principalities, and free towns that until then had developed sophisticated ways of using saints. The humanist authors, as we shall see, allowed Nicholas to be shaped by and to shape developing Swiss political and cultural identity.

THE LATE MEDIEVAL SWISS CONFEDERATION. In order to draw related political, social, and cultural implications from the Nicholas texts for our understanding of Swiss identity and humanist participation in the formation of both, we must sketch the late medieval history of the Swiss Confederation. Two aspects of late medieval Swiss political history require review: One concerns the confederation's conflicts with outside powers, especially Burgundy and the Habsburgs; the other, conflicts among member states.[88] The historical roots of the confederation (the *Eidgenossenschaft*) can be found in numerous pacts of mutual defense and evolving protocols for resolving disputes among signatories developed in the late thirteenth century and expanded through the fifteenth century.[89] Most of the signatories were free imperial cities within the Holy Roman Empire. The confederation thus existed within the empire analogously to other moral communities formed for commercial or military advantage, such as the Hanseatic League. For ambitious German noble families and the imperial court, however, the confederation had the particular advantage of being a limited but well-situated threat to the Habsburgs. The Habsburgs did not acquire consistent headship of the empire until the mid-fifteenth century. Their familial origins were in the southwestern part of the empire, in and around the territories of the confederation, and their political base in the later Middle Ages was the duchy of Austria. Any disruption—real, perceived, or anticipated—of the Habsburg enterprise in the southwest worked to the advantage of those who opposed Habsburg ambitions within the empire.

As the confederation increased its membership in the early fifteenth century, a weak earlier consensus against the Habsburgs diminished yet further. Swiss cities increasingly appreciated friendly relations with the Habsburgs, who controlled some trading routes and had agricultural interests within the confederation, as politically and economically advantageous. Following a vicious war between Schwyz and Zurich over the Toggenburg inheritance, the Peace of Ensisheim (1444) temporarily resolved the newly increasing ambivalence over the confederates' relationship with the Habsburgs: Austria abandoned territorial ambitions inside the confederation, and the French granted the confederation its first international diplomatic recognition. Conflict with Burgundy, however, quickly replaced the clash with Austria. A new set of wars ended in 1477, when Swiss forces defeated the Burgundians at Nancy and killed Duke Charles the Bold of Burgundy.[90]

Although Charles's death brought the immediate Burgundian threat to a close, it reinvigorated the Habsburg one by augmenting its new imperial dimension: In 1477 Mary of Burgundy, Charles's only heir, married the emperor, now a Habsburg, Frederick III.[91] The confederation reacted by holding itself aloof from imperial political activity. In international matters France became its ally. In 1488 the confederates refused to join the Swabian League, a compact of imperial states to the northeast of the Swiss, formed in defense against the Wittelsbachs of Bavaria. In addition, the confederates refused to participate in the imperial reform program legislated at Worms in 1495, which included a court reform and new imperial taxes.[92] The cold war turned hot in 1499, when the Tyrolese invaded confederation territories. The conflict—still distinguished by name as the Swabian War in Switzerland and as the Swiss War in Germany—lasted only a year but astonished contemporaries for its savagery.[93] In the resulting Peace of Basel (1499), Emperor Maximilian acknowledged the confederation's rejection of his reforms and recognized a new degree of Swiss autonomy.[94]

External conflicts had proceeded hand in hand with internal ones. Economic rivalries between states, as well as disagreements over the admission of new member states, often erupted in military violence. The admission of Fribourg and Solothurn into the confederation in 1481 and the consequent shift of the majority from rural to urban states inspired one such debate. By many accounts the conference to settle the dispute would have failed were it not for the intervention of Brother Claus. The resulting Compact of Stans had both constitutional and social consequences. Constitutionally, the states affirmed previous constitutional agreements and foreswore interference in the domestic affairs of the other confederates. Socially, it affirmed the dominance of elites in the states over the loosely disciplined communal forces.[95]

NICHOLAS AT STANS. This violent and convoluted history plays an important part in the earliest writings about Nicholas of Flue. The most obvious place of intersection is at the Council of Stans (1481), where despite limited direct evidence even the most skeptical historical reconstructions include some sort of consultation between Nicholas and the frustrated delegates.[96] Following his participation at Stans, two ways of asserting Nicholas's contributions to Swiss political society emerged in writings about him in the ensuing decades. One strain explicitly emphasized Nicholas's participation at Stans. In 1507 Lucerne chronicler Petermann Etterlin put this position in its earliest narrative form: a report on Swiss civil conflict that characterized Nicholas as having rescued the confederation from nothing less than self-destruction.[97] The other interpretive tradition promoted Nicholas as a founder of Switzerland but included no mention of Stans. It asserted more generally that his political advice contributed to the civic well-being of the confederation. His political wisdom fit within the broader context of the sage counsel he dispensed to all visitors. The vitae by Gundelfingen and Lupulus as well as the German-language lives throughout the sixteenth century reiterated this latter interpretation.[98] It was not until Joachim Eichhorn's *Story of Brother Nicholas of Sachseln, the Helvetian Hermit of Unterwalden* (1608) that the two traditions—Nicholas as the rescuer at Stans and Nicholas as dispenser of practical, at times political, wisdom—were conflated.[99]

In both traditions, it could be argued, the hermit sanctified a certain social ordering established at Stans, namely, its imposition of tighter elite control over the communes. Keeping distinct the two descriptive traditions, however, attenuates the sometimes exaggerated and misplaced significance of Stans. The humanist authors found no need to refer to Stans in the earliest lives of the holy hermit even while asserting his political contributions to the social order ratified by it. Along these same lines, Nicholas was increasingly referred to in the hagiography as Brother Claus—indeed as he is most commonly known today in Switzerland: Neither Gundelfingen nor Lupulus ever referred to him this way. Hans Salat in 1537 and the authors of subsequent vernacular lives all referred to Nicholas as Brother Claus (*Bruder Klaus*), and Eichhorn used the Latin, *frater Nicolaus* throughout his early seventeenth-century work. This development corresponds, in fact, to an increasing emphasis on fraternity (*Brüderlichkeit*) within the confederation as its unifying principle, one that, in fact, compensated for the decreasing power of the communes.[100] In short, what we discover in the early Latin lives are the beginnings of an association between Nicholas and Swiss civil well-being. This association as articulated by the earliest hagiographers, contemporaneous to their subject or nearly so, is more equivocal than and different from what authors wrote even as little as a century later. What was written in the hagiography more broadly was inchoate if judged against a later vision of Switzerland and its historiography. More importantly, the first stage of the hagiography was ambivalent on the significance of a political treaty and the nature of the political entity that would become Nicholas's own.

NICHOLAS AND THE CONFEDERATION. Although the authors, joined by Bonstetten, concurred that Nicholas's political and practical wisdom had strengthened Swiss society, they differed in their descriptions of what that Swiss society was and what about his asceticism was so valuable. Although Bonstetten's travel report was based on the humanist's 1479 visit to the Ranft, some two years before the Council of Stans, the oldest autograph we have dates to 1485 in a copy he sent. By this point Bonstetten had certainly heard about Stans and might have added something about it as he readied it for the city council at Nuremberg. In fact, Bonstetten's claim was rather modest: he identified Nicholas's homeland as Unterwalden and referred to its participation in the "ancient league" *(liga)*, a common, older term for the confederation.[101] When he later made a reference to the "confederates," it was to the states in the confederation, not the people in the states.[102]

Gundelfingen, in contrast, discussed Nicholas's contribution to the commonweal more emphatically. Describing Nicholas's life before his conversion to eremitism, Gundelfingen praised Nicholas as "in war the flag bearer, a soldier, and the chief centurion" and "in peace a minister of the Underwaldensians like none other."[103] After Nicholas's conversion, Gundelfingen considered Nicholas's contribution to the well-being of the confederation as different in kind: "Of this much we are certain: The great, high, and almighty God has turned his gentle and kind eyes already upon the most strong confederates of the great league and through the intercession of the pious and blessed Nicholas has deigned to heal them of every bother, trouble, and sickness and to conserve them in their league and to grant them salvation."[104]

Like Bonstetten, Gundelfingen may have had Stans in mind as one piece of evidence among several for the claim implicit to this quotation, although we cannot be certain. Indeed, the phrase "to conserve them in their league" *(in eaque liga conservare)* suggests the hermit had provided the confederation with a solution to its internal tensions. But as Gundelfingen, continuing, emphasized the power of Nicholas's prayer—indeed, "our federation would have come to an end long ago had not the prayers of Nicholas...shone up to God"[105]—it was rather Swiss victories at Grandson and Morat during the recent Burgundian wars that he mentioned by name.[106]

Gundelfingen also rejected the interpretation of Nicholas's intercessory power as an affirmation of God's favor on the confederation. Instead, these Swiss successes introduced the way for Gundelfingen to inveigh against the greed, ambition, and warlikeness that the confederation and its leaders manifested. Such behavior stood against the example of Brother Claus, who "taught the people to fear God...and keep His commandments, and to support themselves entirely on the sermons of his priests."[107] In contrast, "we zealously prepare for war not to protect the state, but to fill our pockets. Putting our bodies and souls at great risk and disadvantage, we seek in the furthest corners of foreign lands—in Italy, France, and Germany—for profits and wealth. We all, from the smallest to the greatest, follow after Avarice."[108] Gundelfingen's criticism of the Confederation's political and economic ambitions was unrelenting. It should be remembered that as he wrote, Gundelfingen had for about two decades not lived in the confederation and that he was withdrawing from the society that he was admonishing. Not at all the insipid vita it has sometimes been judged, Gundelfingen's work was a complex manifesto—a plea for the vita solitaria over the vita activa, a personal apologia for the author's own adoption of the solitary's life, and a harsh moral appraisal of contemporary Swiss society.

Lupulus's work lacked the scornful undercurrent of the earlier one. He placed Nicholas with, rather than against, a carefully designated social mainstream. In both the dedicatory letter and the prefatory poem to Schiner, Lupulus praised the bishop's skill with the temporal and spiritual swords (utriusque gladii gubernacula).[109] In his prologue to the "men of Unterwalden," Lupulus emphasized, just as Gundelfingen had not, the Swiss aspect of Nicholas's holy life by inserting an early chorographical panegyric referring to the inherent strengths of a culture he labeled "Alemannic."[110] In the vita itself Lupulus included a detailed excursus into the confederation's recent political and military history. With many of the same chorographical topics and flourishes that we saw in the previous chapter, Lupulus achieved a goal similar to those of the other chorographers and averred the confederation's greater political autonomy and cultural prestige.[111] Where he could, Lupulus connected these events of great moment for the confederation with biographical material from Brother Claus's life, such as his military service.[112]

Lupulus also attempted to associate Nicholas with an ethnographic notion of who the Swiss were. He placed Nicholas, for example, "in Helvetia" and "among the Helvetians."[113] The terms, used in reference to the land and peoples of the confederation, have their late medieval origins with the humanists. The humanists' attraction to these terms was legitimated by references to the "Helvetii" in Julius Caesar's writings.[114] The connection was first influentially made by Conrad Türst in the Description of How the Confederates Are Placed (1496) just five years before Lupulus completed his Life of Holy Nicholas.[115] Although ancient Helvetia was not geographically identical to the confederation in 1500, the classical association was irresistible. It also had the benefit of distancing the Swiss from the Germans: Helvetians were, as any humanist knew, not Germans, but Celts. And as the more loyal advocates of the confederation also recognized, "Helvetia" and "Helvetians" were concepts that could unite people who had no particular sense of cultural solidarity or unity with the confederation except through their local states.[116] The origins of these associations in Türst and their incorporation into the vitae reiterate what we find over and over again in the humanist saints' live, namely that developments in history writing and writing about the saints proceeded hand in hand.

Lupulus developed the idea that Nicholas's practical wisdom solved local and regional problems more elaborately than Gundelfingen had proposed.[117] Lupulus outlined those larger problems elliptically and did not mention specific battles or principalities as had Gundelfingen, but nevertheless recurrently suggested that violence and greed were vices deeply imbued in the Swiss people and their confederation. As a remedy, "whenever consulted in arduous matters concerning the confederated cities, [Nicholas] always counseled tranquility in the homeland (*patria*), concord among neighbors (*vicini*), the praise of God, and the observance of His precepts."[118]

Another story told first by Lupulus reinforces the place of these negative characteristics in the Swiss persona and thus the need for a patriotic Swiss moral exemplar. Nicholas, wandering outside of Switzerland shortly after leaving his wife and family in search of an appropriately isolated spot for his hermitage, arrived at "an attractive place," probably in Alsatia. Along the way, he met a local farmer, who, "though approving of his pilgrimage as pious and just, admonished him because he was from the Swiss Confederation (*ex Helvetiorum foedere*), which was held in no little contempt in other lands (*nationibus*); and he counseled him to consider better and quieter retreats within his homeland (*inter paternas latebras*), rather than to be thought of as a refugee among strangers (*apud alienos*)."[119] Lupulus made no attempt to refute the farmer's judgments. Rather, the situation provided an opportunity, via a literary conceit, to broach the topic of Swiss identity through the eyes of an outsider. By recounting the tale Lupulus accomplished a straightforward and two-pronged goal. First, his account affirmed a simple moral and patriotic lesson: Do not wander, stay at home, and be good. That home was within the Swiss Confederation. Second, Lupulus suggested a more intimate association between individuals and the confederation than we have yet seen. He took the same Swiss violence that by Gundelfingen's reckoning deserved the severest moral obloquy and turned it into a unifying force. Withdrawn from moral censure, Swiss bellicosity turned the confederates into the Alsatian outsider's common enemy. Moreover, as Lupulus told the story, the farmer warned Nicholas as an individual on account of crimes imputed to his homeland: Nicholas, and by extension now any individual from the regions of the Swiss Confederation, would be seen as a confederate.[120]

The Saintly Nicholas and Swiss Unity

Saints had of course long represented and protected political entities like cities, monarchies, and dynasties. To that extent, humanist characterizations of Nicholas represent nothing new. He differed from the typical civic patron, however, on at least four points, each of which accommodates differences in the Swiss entity that he was gradually becoming patron of. First, he was made a model peasant and participated in the civic life of his region as such, rather than as a ruler or subject, categories of civic belonging that the Swiss would at least theoretically repudiate.[121] Second, as we saw in the episode in Alsatia, Nicholas suffered, with his compatriots, a negative reputation among foreigners. The farmer rendered an ambivalent judgment: Nicholas deserved praise for his pilgrimage but censure for his place of origin. Nicholas's holiness, it would seem, could be misapprehended from outside the confederation.

Third, all three humanist authors characterize Nicholas's prayerfulness as redounding to the benefit of his home state and the confederation. Frequently in the vitae the authors were ambiguous in distinguishing the two, betokening the ambiguous relationship between states and the confederation in precisely the decades when the vitae were written. The absence of reference to Stans in these early vitae thus does not represent any neglect on the part of the authors but rather shows that the event had not yet been elevated to the status of a historically defining moment in Swiss consciousness. Only in the writings (Protestant and Catholic) about Nicholas after 1501 did Nicholas gradually become the expressed patron of the confederation. Nicholas's patria, and all that classical term connoted, for Gundelfingen and Lupulus was still at best Unterwalden. In the fifteenth century Nicholas could be a moral exemplar for people in the confederation; he could not quite yet be the confederation's patron.

Fourth, Nicholas's vitae made the hermit a peacemaker within and for the confederation. The authors achieved this even without explicit reference to Stans. His peacemaking was accomplished through his eremitical example, as well as his wise counsel. Word and example had an effect on both society and individuals. The twist is not entirely precedented: Saints certainly delivered prophetic admonishment against individuals and societies. Patron saints could also serve as the mouthpieces of critique against the immorality of local rulers. However, for a patron saint to identify fundamental flaws in the very essence of those whose patron he was is unusual indeed.

These four saintly characteristics of Nicholas make the foundation upon which he would become a patriotic patron saint of a new order. The humanist writings reenvision the saint in a way that allowed Nicholas, unlike any other contemporary or antecedent portrayal of a saint, to weather the storms of sixteenth-century confessionalization to become saintly founding father for Switzerland. In that Nicholas as portrayed in the humanist writings could transcend confessional divisions and become a common symbol of Swiss identity into and through the sixteenth century, he stands in incisive contrast to Saint Benno of Meissen. As we saw in chapter one, Benno became a divisive symbol, embraced by Catholics and denounced by Evangelicals during the sixteenth-century in Saxony and Bavaria.[122] This contrast between Nicholas and Benno reinforces the lesson that humanists could and did instrumentalize the cult of the saints diversely and even to cross-purposes. More importantly, the contrast indicates how humanist writings contributed to hagiographical traditions. In a confessionalized sixteenth century, these stories thus brought into that controverted period both unity, as in the case of Nicholas, and division, as in the case of Benno. Renaissance hagiography was an appropriation of the past that could in turn be appropriated by future generation in equally unpredictable ways.

Conclusion

In *Saint Jerome in the Renaissance* Eugene Rice charts the titular saint's
transition in literary and artistic portrayals from "an object of awe
and devotion" in the Middle Ages to "a subject for research" in the
early modern period. Rice notes that the fifteenth and early sixteenth
centuries were especially full of Saint Jerome's devotees: They included late medieval ecclesiastics working "to reform the church by
returning it to the evangelical poverty, simplicity, and abnegation of
its beginnings"; humanist literati, most prominently Erasmus, who
gratefully appealed to him as "a model of how to reconcile [the humanists'] study of pagan literature and philosophy with Christian
piety and commitment"; and Catholic apologists who found in him
"clinching authority" for traditional doctrines against new criticisms raised by Luther, Calvin, and their followers.[1]

Rice's study differs in fundamental ways from this one. He
takes one saint and traces interest in him across an extended period
of time in a Catholic Europe without great attention to synchronic
regional and cultural variations. This study has examined a range
of saints as depicted by a chronologically more restricted set
of authors in a geographically narrower region. Nonetheless, Rice's
study makes two points that this study, mutatis mutandis, confirms; first, that humanists participated in the cult of the saints. And
second, reducing this commitment to philological and biographical accuracy does not represent the fullness of their efforts.[2]
Rice's analysis also points us in the direction of a final question,

touched upon in the Introduction: How do the writings about saints by early German humanists fit in the transition from the Middle Ages to the early modern era? The early German humanists stand at the halfway point between two looming hagiographical monuments: the earliest edition of the thirteenth-century *Golden Legend* and the first, seventeenth-century volumes of the *Acta sanctorum*. These two milestones in the history of writing about saints in Latin Christianity are often placed in stark contrast: *The Golden Legend* representing the traditional and superstitious; the *Acta sanctorum*, the modern and erudite. Consideration of how the humanists' contributions to the veneration of the saints sharpen the contrast is one task of this Conclusion; how they build less expected continuities, the other.

Continuity with the Past

Humanists and the Medieval Past

Simply ascertaining that humanists wrote devotionally about the saints is the foundation of the literature's continuity with the past. Our examination of what had once often been passed over as "mere editions" has yielded some unanticipated results. Humanists, as it turns out, must be numbered among the active participants in a resurgence of writing about the saints that began in the last quarter of the fifteenth century in German lands. While the new stylistic elements in the writing help identify the humanist origins of the works, it was not changes in style alone that made the work worth undertaking to the authors: Writing about the saints gave the first generations of humanists in Germany a stunningly rich way of accessing Germany's "medieval," Christian past and of creating a German history in keeping with a larger humanist vision.

We have seen the late fifteenth- and early sixteenth-century authors constructing their narratives about holy men and women by drawing these figures from the past with a variety of strategies. Emser engaged in a search for scattered documentary evidence, Trithemius invented them, Bild collated older vitae, Meisterlin edited medieval sources, and Gratius did the same, albeit with falsified ones. Two considerations that shaped these authors' writings were new strategies of localizing the saint and new stylistic preferences. The appeal for vitae composed along these lines appears in multiple layers and sectors of German society. Emser worked in the court of an imperial prince; Bonstetten worked from his own abbey for neighboring monastic communities (see figure C.1); and Meisterlin worked for the council of a free imperial city. Contributing to the cult of the saints, humanist authors wrote from, within, and to

FIGURE C.1. Albrecht Dürer, *The Virgin Mary with Albert von Bonstetten*, in *Septem horae canonicae virgineae matris Mariae* (Freiburg: Friedrich Riederer, 1493), 2v. Call number: 8E Inc.s.a. 45. Reproduced by permission of the Bayerische Staatsbibliothek, Munich.

This woodcut, whose creator remains disputed, decorates Bonstetten's *Seven Canonical Hours of the Virgin Mother Mary*. Kurth suggests that Dürer drew the work in Freiburg on the way to Basel. Bonstetten, a dean of the abbey at Einsiedeln, was a strong advocate and representative of humanism in the southwestern empire. He was also a prolific author of saints' lives, devotional literature, and regional history. Kurth 82; Strauss 18.

diverse sectors of contemporaneous German society. At the same time, we also saw humanist authors and their patrons struggling over the new saintly portrayals, particularly insofar as the new diverged from the traditional. Whether irenically or agonistically, however, the humanists' writing about the saints was not undertaken in isolation from general society but engaged the authors with broad segments of German society, those out of which their commissions came and those in which the saints were venerated.

Elite Texts and Common Devotion

Although hagiography was certainly the period's most popular literature, the vitae were indeed "elite texts"—heard by some, read by a few, owned by yet fewer. But perhaps less elite than one might at first imagine. The choice of Latin language by the authors does not in the first instance suggest that they wanted to popularize the material's contents. It does, however, indicate that the authors aspired to reach a readership beyond the narrow confines of those speaking the vernacular dialects where particular cults were located. Moreover, Latin religious texts such as sermons and vitae could, in fact, popularize stories and ideas, not insofar as more people could read the Latin text but because those who could read the Latin texts were in positions to spread the ideas even farther. The printing of many vitae demonstrates authors' and patrons' interest in the literature's dissemination throughout and beyond the circles in which they lived and worked, as well as beyond the local milieus in which the saints had been venerated. In this respect, writing about saints was being remolded in the hands of humanists much like writings about the past in general.

The less common printing of the hermits' vitae begins to indicate the writings' range of uses and readerships. Although a life's manuscript form does not necessarily mean that its intended use was simply local, as Bonstetten's manuscript report on his visit to the Ranft for city councilmen in Nuremberg and Nördlingen and for Louis XI in Paris shows, not all the newly written saints' lives were intended for regionally broad audiences. Moreover, some lives were not oriented to major programs of social and ecclesiastical reform like the vitae of bishops were. Even given a range of purposes eremitical and episcopal vitae do share certain literary hallmarks and a range of techniques for using sources and fashioning character. They also share a common concern for expressing the chorographical placement of the saint. What the lives of the recluses bring into more distinct relief because of the stronger local ties to the saints being written about was the diversity of ways that people could relate to concrete cults and how humanist authors had to negotiate conflicting convictions not about the cult in some theoretical, abstract sense but about the life, the biographical details, of the cult's object. The foregoing chapters have demonstrated how popular pressures could shape even elite texts, and how humanists—dependent on patrons to be sure but also part of the broader cultural context, which revered the ancient stories as such—were susceptible to these forces as they shaped and reshaped the saintly portrayals. Thus even more than the bishops' lives, the recluses' lives show the humanists working outside of an isolated humanist world and are thus invaluable markers of the beliefs and devotions that shaped the larger world of late medieval Christianity in which the humanists lived and of which they were a part.

Situating the Saints

Over and above the obvious linguistic markers of the humanist compositions, the most striking development within the set of humanist-authored lives is their chorographical refashioning. Bringing the literary backgrounds into the analytical foreground and evaluating digressions as essential parts of the authors' work exposed a subtle but definitive way that these authors worked as humanists, namely, as contributors to the *Germania illustrata* project. The research and writing of saints' lives let the authors investigate and construct a German past, find in it a greatness that was "ancient," and articulate that greatness in a classical panegyrical style. The chorographical refashioning of the hagiographical traditions in the vitae reveals how forward looking—and tendentiously so—these authors could be.

The author's fixation with the *German* past and their commerce with local hoi polloi might serve as evidence—to dredge up a boilerplate disparagement of humanism in the empire—of how German humanists were something less than their Italian counterparts. In point of fact, the vitae show the Germans behaving like many of their southern colleagues, and looking to some of them for models to follow, in creatively appropriating this religious literature. North and south of the Alps, humanists were integrated into a larger society that venerated saints. Within that larger society, it was intuitive to address pressing contemporary issues through a literature that was conceived not as "conservative" so much as ordinary. This ordinariness would prove itself perduring. Even if some humanists expressed frustration with dimensions of the medieval practice, as Erasmus did in his *Life of Saint Jerome*, literature about the saints—however transformed it would become through the sixteenth century—was as ubiquitous in early modern Catholicism as in medieval Christendom. As the vitae and other writings examined in this volume show, fifteenth- and early-sixteenth-century German humanists did not recuse themselves from participating in the cult of the saints, this fundamental component of pre-modern European culture, certainly not programmatically nor in correlation to any scale of more or less humanist.

Forward Looking

The full range of reforming interests, attachments to local cults, new regional associations, professional relationships across the empire and the Alps, and even personal devotions came together in the humanist vitae of the holy Nicholas of Flue. This case demonstrates with special poignancy the creative vigor with which the humanists could approach the task of composing new saints' lives. The writings of Bonstetten, Gundelfingen, and Lupulus are especially valuable because they antedate both the sixteenth-century Reformations and Swiss independence from the Holy Roman Empire, yet their portrayals kept Nicholas attractive through and beyond these historical developments and across hardening confessional divisions. As they wrote, the three authors appealed to their readers for a reform of religion. They did so patriotically. In these respects they were not unlike their contemporaries throughout the empire. While the other chorographically refashioned saints retained or attained new regional significance, Nicholas's extreme asceticism and holy counsel turned him into a saintly celebrity of international significance and attracted visitors to his hermitage from all over Europe. Thanks to the humanists' representations, Nicholas's reputation flourished through and beyond the Reformation. He became in consequence a central figure in the Swiss founding myth, attractive to figures as opposite as Ulrich Zwingli and Peter Canisius.

The enduring attractiveness of Nicholas's cult leads us to the question of continuities between the early humanist and successor projects on the saints. In fact, many German saints who received the attention of early humanists also attracted interest in the late sixteenth and early seventeenth centuries. In addition to Nicholas's cross-confessional appeal, for example, the Wittelsbachs' adoption of Saint Benno into the Bavarian Catholic renewal with the help of the Jesuit order indicates links from one side of the Reformation divide to the other. Likewise, the late sixteenth-century Jesuit reformer, Peter Canisius, reworked numerous older saints' lives, among them those of Ida of Toggenburg and Nicholas of Flue. In fact, such examples only begin to reveal how much later generations of authors relied on the work of the early German humanists. A glance at the early modern scholarly literature in the notes and bibliography of this study provides further indication of a persisting interest in the hagiographical production of the early German humanists, even if these writings did not win a place in the canons of humanist literature. The challenge that emerges then is to determine how systematic or substantive the connection was between the early German humanists and the later participants.

Beyond Confessionalism and Confessionalization: Dürer

In pursuing this line of inquiry it is important to acknowledge that the religious tumult beginning in 1517 had a disruptive effect on creative production related to the cult of the saints in the Empire. Luther's attack on the cult of Saint Benno, both at the elevation in 1524 and upon Henry the Pious's assumption of the Saxon throne in 1539, is a case in point, as we saw in the Introduction. The ambiguous, changing, complex connections between the humanists and the cult of the saints in the same period are also reflected in the works of Albrecht Dürer (1471–1528) and his Nuremberg workshops, several examples of which have illustrated this volume. Woodcuts dating from "Brother Claus in Front of His Hut" (1488; figure 4.1) to the *Austrian Saints* (1515/1517; see figure C.2) show Dürer—the foremost artist of the Northern Renaissance and a member of Nuremberg's humanist Sodalitas Staupitziana—along with the workshops that trained and followed him engaged with the cult of the saints throughout his life.[3]

Many of these artistic pieces reflect the same kinds of aspirations and ambiguities as the written works. The controversies among modern art historians over the significance and authenticity of later, highly "traditional" woodcuts parallel the arguments over early humanists' hagiographical writings that we examined in the Introduction. Sometimes a work's theme and composition are straightforwardly traditional, such as Dürer's woodcut of the Virgin with the Carthusians (1515, figure 3.1).[4] Sometimes the artistic works reflect the same debates that one detects in the humanist narratives: The inclusion of Danish and French royal heraldry in the woodcut of Saint Sebald (ca. 1501, figure 2.2), for example, hearkens back to the royal associations that Meisterlin had tried unsuccessfully to attenuate in the saint's legend.[5]

Some alterations are reminiscent of changes humanists made to their own narratives. Between 1515 and 1517 Dürer (or perhaps a student) added the bishop-saints Poppo of Trier and Otto of Freising to the woodcut of Austrian saints (figure C.2). He placed them next to their father, the margrave saint Leopold the Pious.[6] Later woodcuts suggest that Dürer's engagement with the saints changed in consequence of the new theological and ecclesiological ideas gaining currency in his hometown. After 1520 he and his workshop produced woodcuts such as a Last Supper, a Crucifixion, and a Madonna but no other devotional works. *Nimbi,* which Dürer had always used sparingly, were now carved only around the head of the Christ and the Madonna.[7]

The debate over the degree to which Dürer aligned himself with the Evangelical movement is very much alive today. Although he did not formally

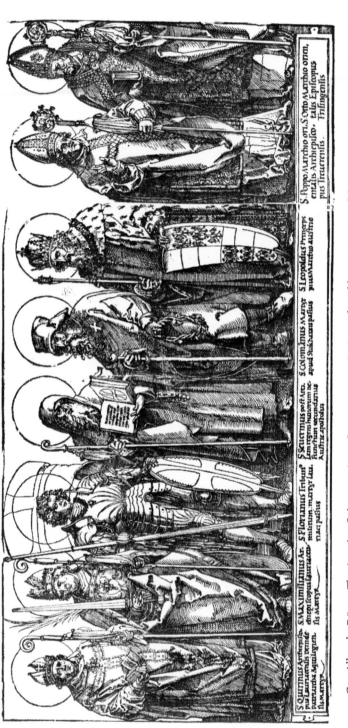

The labels on the figure read:

S. Quirinus Archiepiscopus Laurea censis Deinde Patriarcha Aquilegensis th. martyr.
S. Maximilianus Archiepiscopus Laurea censis fis martyr.
S. Florianus Tribun[us] militum. martyr Lau. th[e]rc[e]baius
S. Seuerinus post Aug. quem regem humaroru[m] ne. kiuetunt secundum Austrie apostolus
S. Colomanus Martyr apud Stokaraw passus
S. Leopoldus Primus pus Marchio austrie
S. Poppo Marchio ori. S. Otto Marchio ori. ertialis Archiepifco. talis Episcopus pus Treurensis. Trifingensis

FIGURE C.2. Albrecht Dürer, *The Austrian Saints,* 1515/1517. Inv. nr. 14 090 D. Reproduced by permission of the Staatliche Graphische Sammlung, Munich.

The original woodcut accompanied verses "to the patron saints of Austria" by Joannes Stabius and appeared in 1515 without the two rightmost bishop saints, the brothers Poppo of Trier and Otto of Freising. In the revised woodcut (1517) the brothers stand to the left of their father, the twelfth-century margrave of Austria, Leopold the Pious, whom Pope Innocent VIII had canonized in 1485 at the behest of Emperor Frederick III. Dürer's disciple and a favorite of Emperor Maximilian I, Hans Springinklee likely added these figures for the opening of Poppo's grave in Trier in anticipation of his canonization. The Habsburgs claimed these saints as ancestors and fostered their cults in the late fifteenth and early sixteenth centuries. Kurth 293; Strauss 174; Schoch 237.

associate himself with Luther's reform, the city of his most active patrons did.[8] And yet, many humanists did not. Of those in this study who lived long enough to have the choice, only Lupulus and Jacobus Montanus (1460–1534), the author of two vitae about Saint Elizabeth of Hungary, adopted the new faiths. But even for the humanist authors who maintained their affiliation with Rome, the religious instability of the 1520s had a distracting effect. The quantity of writing about the saints declined in Germany and across Europe.

Although Luther's critique bears some of the responsibility for this, it should not be too strongly emphasized. In contrast to Calvin and Zwingli's campaigns against the cult of the saints, Luther's opposition to the cult of the saints was derivative of other more contentious theological concerns. His critique of the cult of the saints and its literature was strongest on points that other churchmen had already articulated. Furthermore, there is no evidence that hagiographical production declined because it was fundamentally at odds with long-term and "more perfect" humanist interests. The decline seems rather to have been a matter of priorities: Catholics (analogously to Luther) understood that there were other more fundamental questions that need addressing, critiquing, and defending. It is in this spirit that the Council of Trent rather quietly affirmed the veneration of the saints in principle and condemned certain abuses in practice in its decree "On the invocation, veneration, and relics of saints and on sacred images" (December 3, 1563) [9] The first saint subsequently canonized was the fifteenth-century Andalusian hermit and missionary Didacus in 1588. Shortly after the council, Pope Sixtus V enacted new regulations for canonization, and the church slowly began canonizing a new generation of saints.[10] More than two centuries passed after Benno's canonization before popes again raised any holy figures from German territories to the altar.[11]

Polemical Hagiography: Witzel and Canisius

Canonizations, however, made up only a small part of all activity related to the cult of the saints in these centuries as in all others. Despite the many reformers averse to the traditional cult of the saints, scholarly interest in and popular devotion to the saints sustained itself through the sixteenth century with greater vigor than Roman legislation and theological tracts from the period imply. The tenor of the hagiography produced after the 1520s in Germany and elsewhere tended in two directions. One was, as I describe it here, polemical. It addressed disputed issues of the day and used the lives of the saints to illustrate Catholic responses to Evangelical criticisms. Examples of such hagiography came from the pens of George Witzel (1501–1573) and Peter Canisius (1521–1597). Witzel's

Hagiologium (1541) numbers among the most widely disseminated and least agonistic examples of polemical hagiography. Witzel, a Catholic cleric who had renounced his ordination to follow Luther in the 1520s, returned to the Catholic church in the 1530s. Although many of his exchanges with former Evangelical colleagues following his second conversion were heated, he regularly articulated a hope for reconciliation between Evangelicals and Catholics.

In this spirit he composed the *Hagiologium* while serving as secretary to the abbot of Fulda. The work began with a lengthy introduction arguing the antiquity of veneration of the saints. Along these lines, Witzel sketched a history of the cult's literature beginning with a review of patristic authors and included medieval authors such as Jacobus de Vorgine and humanist authors such as Petrarch, Francisco Pico della Mirandola, Baptista Mantuanus, Bartolomaeo Platina, and Thomas More.[12] In the main part of the work, Witzel reflected new sensibilities about Holy Scripture by incorporating numerous holy men and women from the Old and New Testaments. His post–biblical examples emphasized the earliest martyrs but extended far into the Middle Ages. Witzel avoided any triumphant or denunciatory rhetoric against heresy. He likewise minimized the place of the miracle in the legends by replacing it with an emphasis on inward piety cultivated in, but not confined to, the cloister. These vitae were crafted with a care that bespeaks the author's expressed desire for confessional reconciliation, even as he sought to identify what he saw as the errors of the Reformers. The legends of the saints, Witzel hoped, would inspire readers to adopt Christian virtues and lead to a genuinely Catholic society.[13]

Witzel relied on many of the early German humanists' works in a variety of ways. His life of Saint Afra, a patroness of Augsburg, for example, came entirely from the edited version by Veit Bild, greatly abbreviated and shorn even more extremely of its miracles. His entry for Saint Boniface was a similarly tidied version of the abbreviated life found in *The Golden Legend*. He included an entry for Saint Benno, whom Evangelicals had two years earlier, it will be recalled, exiled from Meissen one last time. Witzel's entry derives from Emser's widely known, published life, not directly, however, but through the canonization documents of 1523. In this instance as throughout his work, Witzel removed the miracles and focused instead on the virtuous manner in which Saint Benno was educated in good morals and piety and led his diocese as its bishop.[14] Moving further than the earlier humanist works, Witzel focused on these saints as exemplars of moral and educational reform and favored presentation of human virtues over miracles as signs of God's power.

Peter Canisius produced more contentious works. Active in the empire slightly after Witzel, Canisius defended the cult of the saints and the Virgin Mary in his catechism and in treatises such as *On Mary, the Peerless Virgin*.[15]

Canisius also revised older vitae sanctorum and used them in his campaign to win back the German lands for the Catholic church. Several of these revised lives had been initially composed less than a century earlier and have been analyzed in earlier chapters, such as the lives of Nicholas of Flue and Ida of Toggenburg.[16] In Canisius's work, the cult of the saints, including life writing, became a tool for the Counter-Reformation just as we saw it turned into a tool for reform by the German humanists before Luther and Calvin.[17]

Critical Hagiography: Surius and the Bollandists

The other direction that late sixteenth-century hagiography took can be desig-nated "critical." The classification reflects in the first instance the philological techniques for determining the oldest and most accurate texts. The most cel-ebrated example from the early modern period is the *Acta sanctorum*, a com-pilation of writings about the saints edited by a group of Jesuit scholars in Antwerp, the Bollandists. Their inspiration came from Jesuit father Heribert Rosweyde (1569–1629), who had judged earlier attempts to edit the texts in-adequate. Antwerp and surrounding Brabant were, at the time, within the Spanish Netherlands part of the Holy Roman Empire; the region also had ecclesiastical ties with Cologne, within which ecclesiastical province Antwerp fell. Cologne, not accidentally, was a place of considerable hagiographical ac-tivity in the fifteenth and sixteenth centuries.

The Carthusian Laurentius Surius (1522–1578) undertook the most in-fluential of these earlier investigations in Cologne. Arriving there to study at the university as an Evangelical, Surius was received into the Catholic church by Peter Canisius. He entered the Cologne charterhouse in 1542.[18] His mon-umental work of hagiography, *The Authenticated Stories of the Saints*, consisted in its first edition of nearly seven hundred lives in six volumes, published between 1570 and 1575.[19] Surius followed medieval practice in organizing his collection according to the liturgical calendar. The core of Surius's work was *The Lives of the Ancient Holy Fathers*,[20] a collection of saints' lives begun by humanist Aloisius Lippomanus (1500–1559), a Catholic cardinal and the scion of a prominent Venetian family.[21]

Surius's volumes were so well received that the duke of Bavaria assigned German translators to begin a vernacular edition in 1574, and a second Latin edition began appearing in 1576.[22] The work distinguished itself from earlier legendary compilations in its stated goal of collecting and editing the impor-tant lives of saints from across Europe. There were, in other words, tendencies toward philological precision and geographical universality such as were un-common up to that point. When there were earlier humanist manuscripts or printed books, Surius used them. At the same time, he sometimes altered older texts with scarcely an explanation, and he did not consistently apply editing criteria.[23] For example, he repeated Emser's *Life of Holy Benno* nearly word for word, among longer sections omitting only the dedicatory letter to Duke George. At the same time, he made no attempt to represent the hagiographical tradition of Saint Bruno the Carthusian and blended the lives written by François Dupuy and Peter Blomevenna haphazardly.[24]

Even if the unfulfilled aspiration for philological precision and documentary thoroughness justifies Surius's place among the earliest "critical hagiographers," his work also serves as an example of how permeable the line between polemical and critical was in this early period of Counter-Reformation. Surius indisputably shaped his writings to address the new Evangelical challenges, and not in the irenic style of a George Witzel. Surius tipped his hand with his expansive use of miracles and revealed his polemical aims. Sometimes he reinserted miracles that earlier humanists had excised; sometimes he added new ones. Miracles occur in *The Authenticated Stories* at a rate of nearly a hundred miracles for every saint, and he authored an entire work on the miraculous.[25] Nevertheless, as a compilation of transcribed manuscripts, the Carthusian's work was remarkable; and later scholars, including the Bollandists, relied heavily on *The Authenticated Stories*. Indeed, there is scarcely a life that Surius edited that does not appear in the *Acta sanctorum*.

The Bollandists' more immediate model for the *Acta sanctorum* was Rosweyde's one-volume *Festival Calendar of the Saints Whose Lives Are in the Manuscripts of Belgian Libraries* (Antwerp, 1607) and *Lives of the Fathers* (Leiden, the Netherlands, 1615). The first volume of the *Acta* was published in Antwerp in 1643 under the supervision of another Flemish Jesuit, Jan van Bolland (1596–1665), whose name these Jesuit scholars later took for their group. Like older legendaries, the *Acta sanctorum* was organized according to the liturgical calendar. More than older legendaries, the *Acta* attempted to encompass saints from across the Christian Mediterranean world, and all historically significant pieces of literature pertinent to a saint's life, including multiple lives of any saint who had them and hagiographical genres other than vitae, such as poetry and miracle accounts. The Bollandists were also committed to providing extensive scholarly commentary and critical notation to each saint's hagiographical dossier.[26]

The Bollandist undertaking bears on this project in two complementary respects: how it relied on the authors who anteceded it and how it compensated for what previous compilations had not included. Bolland acknowledged the reliance in the introduction of the *Acta*'s first volume. In it he named as sources *The Histories of Many Saints*, a collection of some two hundred abbreviated lives, compiled as a supplement to *The Golden Legend* and first printed in Cologne in 1483; the compilations of the Brabantine canon John Gielemans (d. 1487), including the *Sanctilogium*, the *Hagiologium Brabantinorum*, and *Novale sanctorum*, as well as Witzel's *Hagiologium* and Surius's volumes. Individual authors in his acknowledgment included several authors whose writings on the saints we have seen, among them Bonstetten, Celtis, Cincinnius, Emser, and Trithemius, and from outside the German lands Baptista Mantuanus, Lefèvre d'Étaples, Lippomanus, and Mombritius.[27]

Sometimes the Bollandists expressed a lack of interest in (and even disdain for) the writings of the early humanists, as when Suyskens refrained from analyzing Cincinnius's *Life of Blessed Ida*. The Bollandists' overarching goal led them to prefer the oldest materials about saints as being the biographically most significant. Given what we now know about how and why the earlier humanist authors came to their projects, we can safely assume they would take no umbrage at this Bollandist judgment. It is only in answer to the fundamentally different questions of this volume that Cincinnius's life of Saint Ida takes on some historical significance. In contrast, Cincinnius's research on the life of Saint Ludger and his work with Altfrid's medieval life, for example, earned extended comment from and the approval of Bollandist editors.[28] In the case of Saint Benno, who lacked a hagiographical dossier until the fifteenth century, Bollandists Godefroid Henskens and Daniel van Papenbroech reproduced Emser's *Life of Holy Benno* in the *Acta*, carefully noted its philological strengths and weaknesses in their notes, and supplemented it with articles from the canonization acts and accounts of Benno's miracles.[29] In fact, the most enduring negative ramification of the Bollandists' historical ambivalence is found in a practical matter and reveals more about later research and its reliance on the Bollandists than about the Bollandists themselves: Early humanist works were often not reproduced in the *Acta sanctorum* and are usually listed in the *Bibliotheca hagiographica latina*, the Bollandists twentieth century index of Latin sources, without their own index numbers as derivative editions of older works, if at all. Consequently, the works are harder to find even today.

In the final analysis, the very ambivalence of the Bollandists to the earlier humanist work in Germany is the best indicator of its place in the development of the West's literature about saints. The philological priority of *bollandisme* was no less novel to the seventeenth century than, say, humanist chorography was to the fifteenth. The Bollandists were philologically trained and interested in the saints in a way that Jacobus de Voragine, author of *The Golden Legend*, was not and could not possibly have been in the thirteenth century. However, neither could the works of the Bollandists and Jacobus be confused with those of the early German humanists. On the one hand, the reproduction of older hagiography published as such by several humanists (e.g., Wimpfeling's *Life of Saint Adelph* and Harderwyck and Gratius's *Life of Holy Swithbert*) anticipated the kind of research and reproduction developed by the "critical hagiographers" of the seventeenth century. The philological precision for which the humanists (and the German humanists in particular) were renowned manifested itself in the hagiography as a concern for diction and grammar but not as a consistent concern with sources and historiographical precision in the modern sense. These later interests were also tempered by the concerns of patrons, with whom the humanist authors negotiated. Humanists' willingness to adapt to their patrons' tastes also allowed on occasion, as we have also seen, several examples of hagiographical fraud. Furthermore, we have no indication that the early German humanists wanted to do what their Bollandist successors did, that is, to reiterate what the most ancient hagiographers had already written. But then neither did the Bollandists want to reiterate what the earlier humanists had done: These scholars saw another usefulness for their work in their confessionalized and contentious age. Even if each group casts a skeptical eye on the work of its predecessors, an eye was still cast, and what was detected was absorbed. Ambivalence is at the heart of a connection without which later works such as the *Acta sanctorum* would have looked very different indeed.

This study has examined the classicizing Latin, the admixture of pagan and Christian allusion and association, the focus on cultural and historical Germania, the conventional piety, and the ambitious and diverse plans for cultural, political, religious, and ecclesiastical reform in these vitae sanctorum. All of these aspects illustrate defining interests of early humanism in Germany. It has also considered ways that the early German humanists should be understood in the contexts of humanist history in and beyond Germany. As the title of this book suggests, the accomplishment of the early German humanists in their writing of saints' lives was two pronged: The authors searched for saints who could model a reform of both church and society. In the process, the early German humanists reformed saints. The early German humanists would hardly count as the first generation or sort of Western intellectual to turn to the past in the hope of creating new solutions to the problems of their own day. They were certainly also not the last.

Notes

INTRODUCTION

1. For a bibliographical essay on Benno's biography, cult, and canonization, see David Collins, "Bursfelders, Humanists, and the Rhetoric of Sainthood: The Late Medieval *Vitae* of Saint Benno," *Revue Bénédictine* 111 (2001): 546–50. See also Christoph Volkmar, *Die Heiligenerhebung Bennos von Meissen (1523/24): Spätmittelalterliche Frömmigkeit, landesherrliche Kirchenpolitik und reformatorische Kritik im albertinischen Sachsen in der frühen Reformationszeit*, ed. Heribert Smolinsky, vol. 146, *Reformationsgeschichtliche Studien und Texte* (Münster, Germany: Aschendorff, 2002), 30–42.

2. UHM 1: 266 (Aug. 6, 1285); 1: 341 (June 15, 1307); 2: 564 (June 12, 1366). UHM 2: 734 (Feb. 1, 1395). The miracles reported through the fourteenth century can be found in the *Acta sanctorum* (AASS, June 3: 176E–180A). "Miracula s. Bennonis," clm 27044, BHL 1166d.

3. Pierre Delooz, *Sociologie et canonisations*, vol. 30, *Collection scientifique de la Faculté de Droit de l'Université de Liège* (La Haye: Martinus Nijhoff, 1969), 461–62.

4. The popes had canonized Sebald of Denmark (a reputed prince-turned-hermit and Nuremberg's patron saint) in 1425 and Leopold the Pious (a twelfth-century margrave of Austria, the object of the emperor Frederick III Habsburg's veneration) in 1485.

5. VD16 L7433-L7442. "Widder den newen Abgott" (1524), in WA 15: 183–98. Luther had addressed the veneration and canonization of saints briefly in the letter to the emperor appended to his "Open Letter to the Christian Nobility" (1520). Here Luther mentioned and condemned the canonization process of Antoninus of Florence, which was progressing hand

in hand with Benno's. He remained silent on the matter of Benno's canonization, perhaps to avoid exacerbating his poor relations with Duke George.

6. VD16 E1117. Hieronymus Emser, *Divi Bennonis Misnensis quondam episcopi vita miracula et alia quedam non tam Misnensibus quam Germanis omnibus decora.* Emser's vita followed upon an earlier work he composed upon employment at the Dresden court: VD16 ZV4995. Hieronymus Emser, *Epitome ad sanctissimum dominum nostrum papam Julium secundum super vita miraculis et sanctimonia divi patris Bennonis Episcopi quondam insignis et ingenue ecclesie Missnensis.* The vernacular life: VD16 E1118 and ZV4997. Hieronymus Emser, *Das heilig leben und legend des seligen Vatters Bennonis weylund bischoffen tzu Meyssen.* The synopsis was perhaps edited by Emser's colleague Johann Hennig: AASS, June 3: 148A–150C. See Volkmar, *Die Heiligenerhebung,* 99–100.

7. Despite the potential confusion with the modern-day English language usages, I favor the term "evangelical" to "protestant" since in nearly all instances the persons and ideas in question antedate the "protest" at the Diet of Speyer in 1529. "Evangelical" also alludes somewhat less anachronistically to the principle of *sola scriptura* put forth by Luther and other "Protestant" reformers. Cf. David W. Lotz, Siegfried Bräuer, and Hans J. Hillerbrand, "Protestantism," in *The Oxford Encyclopedia of the Reformation,* ed. Hans J. Hillerbrand (New York: Oxford University Press, 1996), Georgetown University, Dec. 21 2006, http://o-www.oxfordreference .com.library.lausys.georgetown.edu:80/views/ENTRY.html?subview=Main&entry =t172.e1144.s0002.

8. VD16 E1083 and E1084. Hieronymus Emser, *Antwurt auff das lesterliche buch wider Bischoff Benno zu Meissen und erhebung der Heiligen iungst außgegangen.* Augustin von Alveldt and Paul Bachmann joined Emser in defending the newly canonized Benno against Luther's assaults in their broadsheet "Wyder das wild geyffernd eber schweyn Luthern, so ynn dem weyngartten des herren der krefften wület, grabet, und sich understehet mit seynem besodelten rüssel umbzustossen die canonizacion divi Bennonis und aller heyligen ehr erbietung zu vertilgen." See Adolf Laube and Ulman Weiss, eds. *Flugschriften gegen die Reformation (1525-1530),* edited by Adolf Laube and Ulman Weiss, 2 vols. (Berlin: Akademie Verlag, 2000). See also Carolus Fridericus Seyffarth, *Ossilegium s. Bennonis episcopi quondam Misnensis seu vita et acta ipsius,* a-3. For an analysis of musical lyrics about Benno composed by Emser and Luther see Rebecca Wagner Oettinger, *Music as Propaganda in the German Reformation (St. Andrews Studies in Reformation History),* 51–53, 81–88; Luther, "Ein newes lied wir heben an" (1523), ibid., 260–63; and Emser, "Ach Benno du vil heilger man" (1524), ibid., 213–14.

9. *Argumentum oder Inhalt der Comedi von S. Benno, zehenden Bischoff der Kirchen zu Meissen in Sachsenlandt, welches heiliger Leib jetzundt allhie in unser lieben Frawen Hauptkirchen herrlich auffbehalten.* See Collins, "Bursfelders," 544–45, and Alois Schmidt, "Der heilige Benno in Bayern," *Monumenta Misnensia: Jahrbuch für Dom und Albrechtsburg zu Meißen* 7 (2005–2006): 30–37.

10. A bibliography and assessment of the historiography can be found in Collins, "Bursfelders," 546–50.

11. WA 15: 183–84.

12. Studies that exploit the distinction between historical persons and their literary and ritual representations in writing about the saints that have influenced me include Peter Brown, *The Cult of the Saints: Its Rise and Function in Latin Christianity* (Chicago: University of Chicago Press, 1981); Caroline Walker Bynum, *Holy Feast and Holy Fast: The Religious Significance of Food to Medieval Women* (Berkeley: University of California Press, 1987); Hippolyte Delehaye, *The Legends of the Saints*, trans. Donald Attwater (Portland, Ore.: Four Courts Press, 1998); and František Graus, *Volk, Herrscher, und Heiliger im Reich der Merowinger: Studien zur Hagiographie der Merowingerzeit* (Prague: Nakladatelstvi Ceskoslovenské akademie věd, 1965).

13. Charles Garfield Nauert Jr., *Humanism and the Culture of Renaissance Europe*, 2d ed., *New Approaches to European History*, vol. 6 (New York: Cambridge University Press, 2006), 102–71. Nauert offers a fine overview. Several points where the present volume attempts to advance the *status quaestionis* have to do with the humanist stances on religious reform and traditional devotions, the place of Erasmus in an evaluation of German humanism, and the relationship of early German humanism to the sixteenth-century Reformations.

14. This is a matter of tendencies, of course, as there are professional expressions by humanists in these latter fields as well.

15. Many authors under consideration in this volume identified themselves with various names, spelled irregularly. In an attempt to make the text readable and the citations pursuable I have followed several general rules: if an author adopted and used widely a Latin surname or cognomen, as many humanists did, I use it in the text with the Latin given name. If the author wrote under his German family name, even if declining it with Latin endings, I use the German surname and anglicize the given name; thus, Joannes Cincinnius and Joannes Trithemius, but John Reuchlin and Albert von Bonstetten. I have allowed exceptions when a certain form is so well known as to be expected; thus Albrecht Dürer rather than Albert. In the citations, I have generally retained the names and spellings found in the libraries and archives where I worked, thus Johannes Cincinnius and Johann Reuchlin (without ever changing a proper name in a book or article's title). Such compromises inevitably cause dissatisfaction at points, even in the author who makes them.

16. Humanist Reuchlin's play *Sergius* criticized devotion to religious relics and the role of monastic orders in promoting that devotion. It is also possible that the student Luther attended Emser's lecture on *Sergius*. Johann Reuchlin, "Sergius," in *Johann Reuchlins Komödien: Ein Beitrag zur Geschichte des lateinischen Schuldramas*, 107–26.

17. "Hagiography," as well as related terms, has changed in meaning over time and today has highly equivocal connotations. Given its pejorative undertones in current English, I generally avoid its use here. When it appears in *Reforming Saints*, the referent is simply writing about holy men and women, recognized as such in medieval Christian society and the early modern Catholic world, in a variety of literary forms, for a range of purposes, including edification, amazement, and instruction. These writings are associated with the cult of the saints and are often parts of canonization processes. Hagiography includes accounts of miracles worked through

the intercession of the saint. Hagiography encompasses a variety of forms (e.g., narrative vitae, poems, liturgical offices, calendars, and legal promulgations) and so is more than a genre. The scholarly literature defining the word is copious; I point here only to one of many helpful essays: Guy Philippart, "Hagiographes et hagiographie, hagiologes et hagiologie: des mots et des concepts," *Hagiographica* 1 (1994): 1–16.

18. VD16 H3482 and ZV7940. Desiderius Erasmus, "Eximii doctoris Hieronymi Stridonensis vita," in *Erasmi Opuscula*, ed. Wallace K. Ferguson, 134–90. The vita served as the introduction to Jerome's collected works as edited by Erasmus and published by Johann Froben in Basel from 1516 to 1520. See David Collins, "A Life Reconstituted: Jacobus de Voragine, Erasmus of Rotterdam, and Their Lives of St. Jerome," *Medievalia et Humanistica* n.s. 25 (1998): 31–51.

19. Early in my research I was much inspired by the introductory theoretical considerations presented in Thomas F. Mayer and D. R. Woolf, eds., "Introduction," in *The Rhetorics of Life-writing in Early Modern Europe: Forms of Biography from Cassandra Fedele to Louis XIV* (Ann Arbor: University of Michigan Press, 1995), 1–38.

20. Monique Goullet has highlighted the importance of taking "mere revisions" more seriously as historical evidence. Monique Goullet, *Écriture et réécriture hagiographiques: Essai sur les réécritures de vies de saints dans l'Occident latin médiéval (VIIIe–XIIIe s.)*, ed. Paul Bertrand, J. Deploige et al., vol. 4, *Hagiologia* (Tournhout, Belgium: Brepols, 2005), 7–27; and Monique Goullet and Martin Heinzelmann, eds., *La réécriture hagiographique dans l'Occident médiéval: Transformations formelles et idéologiques*, vol. 58, *Beihefte der Francia* (Ostfildern, Germany: Jan Thorbecke, 2003).

21. Franz Brendle, Dieter Mertens, Anton Schindling et al., eds., *Deutsche Landesgeschichtsschreibung im Zeichen des Humanismus*, vol. 56, *Contubernium: Tübinger Beiträge zur Universitäts- und Wissenschaftsgeschichte* (Stuttgart: Steiner, 2001); and Johannes Helmrath, Ulrich Muhlack, and Gerrit Walther, eds., *Diffusion des Humanismus: Studien zur nationalen Geschichtsschreibung europäischer Humanisten* (Göttingen: Wallstein, 2002).

22. André Vauchez's seminal work has reinforced the early fifteenth century (1430) as the terminus ad quem for the medievalists; Peter Burke's brief but influential study that begins at the Council of Trent has given the early modernists their conventional terminus a quo. Peter Burke, "How to Be a Counter-Reformation Saint," in *The Historical Anthropology of Early Modern Italy: Essays on Perception and Communication*, ed. idem (New York: Cambridge University Press, 1987), 48–62; and André Vauchez, *Sainthood in the Later Middle Ages*, trans. Jean Birell (New York: Cambridge University Press, 1997). The encyclopedic *Hagiographies* volumes edited by Guy Philippart extend to 1550. The chapters covering the last decades, however, give scant consideration of sixteenth-century literature or humanist contributions. Guy Philippart, ed., *Hagiographies: Histoire internationale de la littérature hagiographique latine et vernaculaire en Occident des origines à 1550*, 4 vols., *Corpus Christianorum* (Turnhout, Belgium: Brepols, 1994–). An excellent exception to this problem is Dörfler-Dierken's study of devotion to Saint Ann, mother of the Virgin Mary. Angelika Dörfler-Dierken, *Die Verehrung der heiligen Anna in Spätmittelalter und früher*

Neuzeit, vol. 50, *Forschungen zur Kirchen- und Dogmengeschichte* (Göttingen: Vanden-hoeck and Ruprecht, 1992).

23. Most recently see Carol Piper Heming, *Protestants and the Cult of the Saints in German-speaking Europe, 1517–1531*, vol. 65, *Sixteenth-century Essays and Studies* (Kirksville, Mo.: Truman State University Press, 2003); and Beth Kreitzer, *Reforming Mary: Changing Images of the Virgin Mary in Lutheran Sermons of the Sixteenth Century*, ed. David Steinmetz, *Oxford Studies in Historical Theology* (New York: Oxford University Press, 2004). See also Brad S. Gregory, *Salvation at Stake: Christian Martyrdom in Early Modern Europe*, vol. 134, *Harvard Historical Studies* (Cambridge, Mass.: Harvard University Press, 1999); Robert Kolb, "Burying the Brethren: Lutheran Funeral Sermons as Life-writing," in *The Rhetorics of Life-writing in Early Modern Europe*, ed. Mayer and Woolf, *Studies in Medieval and Early-modern Civilization* (Ann Arbor: University of Michigan Press, 1995), 97–114; Robert Kolb, *For All the Saints: Changing Perceptions of Martyrdom and Sainthood in the Lutheran Reformation* (Macon, Ga.: Mercer University Press, 1987); Robert Kolb, *Martin Luther as Prophet, Teacher, Hero: Images of the Reformer, 1520–1620* (Grand Rapids: Baker Books, 1999); and James Michael Weiss, "Erasmus at Luther's Funeral: Melanchthon's Commemorations of Luther in 1546," *Sixteenth Century Journal* 16 (1985): 91–114.

24. Simon Ditchfield has called for a more thorough study of this intervening period. As the following chapters show, the complex continuities between early humanists and seventeenth-century authors were anything but a teleological development from medieval superstition to modern philological sophistication. Ditchfield has rightly impugned that hypothesis as "whiggish." Simon Ditchfield, "Sanctity in Early Modern Italy," *Journal of Ecclesiastical History* 47 (1996): 98–112.

25. Monika Rener identifies forty such vitae sanctorum for the thirteenth century and four for the fourteenth century. Hagiogr. 1: 256–58. In Italy, by contrast, vitae sanctorum were produced at a steady rate throughout the fifteenth century. Alison Knowles Frazier's study of Italian humanists and their vitae sanctorum and her hand list of manuscripts cover the period from 1420 to 1521: Alison Knowles Frazier, *Possible Lives: Authors and Saints in Renaissance Italy* (New York: Columbia University Press, 2005), 39–41, 327–494. An argument for a humanist hagiography in anticipation of the reforms of Trent on the basis of a work by a Croatian humanist is made in Brenda Dunn-Lardeau, "*De bene beateque vivendi institutione per exempla Sanctorum* (1498) de Marko Marulic ou l'hagiographie médiévale revue par l'humanisme chrétien pré-tridentin," in *Europa sacra*, ed. Sofia Boesch Gajano and Raimondo Michetti (Rome: Carocci, 2002), 243–57. See Hagiogr. 1: 155–88; 2: 61–72, 95–98; 4: 183–272, 524, 564–70.

26. For an illuminating essay on how monastic reform movements appropriated aspects of humanism and church reform movements, see Kaspar Elm, "Monastische Reformen zwischen Humanismus und Reformation," in *900 Jahre Kloster Bursfelde*, ed. Lothar Perlitt (Göttingen: Vandenhoeck und Ruprecht, 1994), 59–111. Nicholas of Cusa's midcentury reforming visitation through Germany sheds light on the important link between the Councils of Constance and Basel on the one hand and

church reform within the empire on the other; see Wolfgang Seibrich, "Episkopat und Klosterreform im Spätmittelalter," *Römischer Quartalsschrift* 91 (1996): 289–304, 323–32. For an instance of mid-fifteenth-century monastic reformers producing a new *vita sancti* see Collins, "Bursfelders," 536–41. Exemplary lives emanated from the Modern Devotion, as can be found in works of Thomas à Kempis: Thomas à Kempis, *Opera omnia*, ed. Joseph Pohl, 7 vols. (Freiburg: Herder, 1902), vols. 6–7.

27. Heinrich Denzinger and Peter Hünermann, eds., *Enchiridion symbolorum definitionum et declarationum de rebus fidei et morum*, 38th ed. (Freiburg: Herder, 1999), 1821–25.

28. For example, Eric W. Cochrane, *Historians and Historiography in the Italian Renaissance* (Chicago: University of Chicago Press, 1981), 50, 154, 246, 305, 417–20.

29. The limited new scholarship—marked by awareness of and respect for this humanist writing—focuses predominantly on cases and has made only preliminary steps toward developing a synthetic notion of "humanist hagiography." See, for example, Francesco Bausi, "Francesco da Castiglione fra umanesimo e teologia," *Interpres* 11 (1991): 112–81; Francesco Bausi, "Umanesimo e agiographia: Il carme di Ugolino Verino in lode di Antonino Pierozzi," *Memorie domenicane* 29 (1998): 99–158; Sofia Boesch Gajano and Raimondo Michetti, *Europa sacra: Raccolte agiografiche e identità politiche in Europa fra Medioevo ed età moderna* (Rome: Carocci, 2002); Bruno Figliuolo, *La cultura a Napoli nel secondo Quattrocento: Ritratti di protagonisti* (Udine, Italy: Forum, 1997), 149–54; Remo Luigi Guidi, "Questioni di storiografia agiografica nel quattrocento," *Benedictina* 34 (1987): 167–252; Massimo Miglio, *Storiografia pontificia del Quattrocento* (Bologna: Pátron Editore, 1975), 119–54; and Diana Webb, "Sanctity and History: Antonio Agli and Humanist Hagiography," in *Florence and Italy: Renaissance Studies in Honour of Nicolai Rubinstein*, ed. Peter Denley and Caroline Elam, *Westfield Publications in Medieval Studies* (London: Committee for Medieval Studies at Westfield College, 1988), 297–308.

30. Paul Oskar Kristeller called for greater attention to the religious sensibilities of humanists in his *Renaissance Thought: The Classic, Scholastic, and Humanist Strains* (New York: Harper and Row, 1961), 70–91. Ronald Witt's recent assertion that religion remained on the periphery of humanists' interests is the latest major contribution to the conversation animated by Kristeller; see Ronald G. Witt, *In the Footsteps of the Ancients: The Origins of Humanism from Lovato to Bruni*, vol. 74, *Studies in Medieval and Reformation Thought* (Leiden, the Netherlands: Brill, 2000). Objecting to Witt's point, Robert Black, "The Origins of Humanism, Its Educational Context and Its Early Development: A Review Article of Ronald Witt's In the Footsteps of the Ancients," *Vivarium* 40 (2002): 292–95.

31. Erika Rummel, *The Confessionalization of Humanism in Reformation Germany*, ed. David Steinmetz, *Oxford Studies in Historical Theology* (New York: Oxford University Press, 2000), 27.

32. Bernd Moeller, "Die deutschen Humanisten und die Anfänge der Reformation," *Zeitschrift für Kirchengeschichte* 70 (1959): 59.

33. The scholarly tradition suggesting hostility between Christianity—and more specifically Catholicism—and "the Renaissance" includes eminent modern historians of the period: Jacob Burckhardt, *Die Cultur der Renaissance in Italien* (Basel: Schweighauser, 1860); Ludwig Geiger, *Renaissance und Humanismus in Italien und Deutschland* (Berlin: Baumgärtel, 1880); Gerhard Ritter, "Die geschichtliche Bedeutung des deutschen Humanismus," *Historische Zeitschrift* 127 (1923): 393–453; and Georg Voigt, *Die Wiederbelebung des classischen Alterthums, oder das erste Jahrhundert des Humanismus* (Berlin: G. Reimer, 1859).

34. Rummel, *Confessionalization of Humanism in Reformation Germany*, 3–8.

35. Lewis William Spitz, "The Course of German Humanism," in *Itinerarium Italicum*, ed. Heiko A. Oberman and Thomas A. Brady (Leiden, the Netherlands: Brill, 1975), 371–436; Lewis William Spitz, "Humanism and the Protestant Reformation," in *Renaissance Humanism: Foundations, Forms, and Legacy*, vol. 3, ed. Albert Rabil (Philadelphia: University of Pennsylvania Press, 1988), 380–411; Lewis William Spitz, "Luther and German Humanism," in *Luther and Learning*, ed. Marilyn J. Harran (Selinsgrove, Penn.: Susquehanna University Press, 1985), 69–94; Lewis William Spitz, *The Religious Renaissance of the German Humanists* (Cambridge, Mass.: Harvard University Press, 1963); and Lewis William Spitz, "The Third Generation of German Renaissance Humanists," in *Aspects of the Renaissance: A Symposium*, ed. Archibald R. Lewis (Austin: University of Texas Press, 1967), 105–21.

36. Much of the praise for *The Life of Jerome* as a new kind of sacred biography overlooks the implications of its composition not for devotional purposes at all but as the forward to his critical edition of Jerome's writings. Its readership was not preachers or pious devotees but academics. Even once the forward was printed as a freestanding work, Erasmus employed no typical saint's honorific—*sanctus, divus,* or *beatus*—in the title, as he did in his genuinely hagiographical writings. A meticulous synopsis of Erasmus's poetic compositions in honor of the saints can be found in Roland Stieglecker, *Die Renaissance eines Heiligen: Sebastian Brant und Onuphrius eremita*, ed. Dieter Wuttke, vol. 37, *Gratia: Bamberger Schriften zur Renaissanceforschung* (Wiesbaden: Harrassowitz, 2001), 80–94.

37. James Michael Weiss, "Hagiography by German Humanists, 1483–1516," *Journal of Medieval and Renaissance Studies* 16 (1985): 316. Some of Erasmus's writings on the cult of the saints are less skeptical than his *Life of Saint Jerome*, as when he responded to indiscriminate Protestant rejection of the devotion. Hilmar M. Pabel, *Conversing with God: Prayer in Erasmus' Pastoral Writings*, vol. 13, *Erasmus Studies* (Toronto: University of Toronto Press, 1997), 95–108.

38. On the difficulty in identifying Germany in this period, see Thomas A. Brady, "The Holy Roman Empire's Bishops on the Eve of the Reformation," in *Continuity and Change: The Harvest of Late Medieval and Reformation History*, ed. Robert James Bast and Andrew Colin Gow (Leiden, the Netherlands: Brill, 2000), 20–47.

39. Hagiogr. 1: 267–88.

40. Brown, *Cult*, 88.

41. For an enlightening study of poetry about the saints in Renaissance Germany, see Stieglecker, *Renaissance eines Heiligen*.

CHAPTER I

1. For example, Ottonian-era vitae highlight marks of episcopal sanctity that are different from those composed in the Carolingian era. Similarly, humanist authors and bishop-saints dominate the vitae sanctorum of Quattrocento Italy, but in the peninsular writings the monastic origins of bishops, central to the northern vitae, are all but absent.

2. Benjamin Arnold, "Episcopal Authority Authenticated and Fabricated: Form and Function in Medieval German Bishops' Catalogs," in *Warriors and Churchmen*, ed. Timothy Reuter (London: Hambledon Press, 1992), 63–78; František Graus, *Volk, Herrscher und Heiliger im Reich der Merowinger: Studien zur Hagiographie der Merowingerzeit* (Prague: Nakladatelstvi Ceskoslovenské akademie ved, 1965), 114–17; Reinhold Kaiser, "Die *gesta episcoporum* als Genus der Geschichtsschreibung," in *Historiographie im frühen Mittelalter*, ed. Anton Scharer and Georg Scheibelreiter (Munich: Oldenbourg, 1994), 459–80; and Michel Sot, "Arguments hagiographiques et historiographiques dans les 'Gesta episcoporum,'" in *Hagiographie, cultures et sociétés, IVe–XIIe siècles, ed. Centre de recherches sur l'Antiquité tardive et le haut Moyen Age Université de Paris X (Paris: Études Augustiniennes, 1981), 95–104.*

3. Sulpicius Severus's fourth-century *Life of Saint Martin of Tours*, the Venerable Bede's eighth-century *Life of Saint Cuthbert* (bishop of Lindisfarne), and Edward Grim's *Life of Saint Thomas, Archbishop of Canterbury* were episcopal vitae that had great impact on conceptions of sainthood through the Middle Ages. Holy bishops figured prominently in literature about the saints from the sixth-century *Martyrologium Hieronymianum* to the thirteenth-century *Golden Legend* and beyond.

4. GW M32672 and GW M38537, respectively: Petrus de Prussia, *Legenda venerabilis domini Alberti Magni* (Cologne: Johannes Guldenschaiff, 1486–1487); and Rudolphus de Novimagio, *Legenda litteralis Alberti Magni* (Cologne: Johannes Koelhoff de Lübeck, 1490). Although the life writers paid attention to Albertus Magnus's brief tenure as bishop of Regensburg, they were more interested in him as a holy Dominican and natural philosopher. The case highlights a danger of rigid typological approaches to the cult of the saints.

5. "Legenda sancti Bonifatii Thuringica," Jena, ThULB, ms. Sag. q. 5, 80–98. Frequently cited but rarely inspected, a 1940 thesis by Weimar archivist Alfred Keilitz demonstrates the relative independence of the vernacular and Latin legends and dates the Latin legend to ca. 1500. Alfred Keilitz, "Die Thüringische Bonifatiuslegende: Überlieferung und Text" (1940), Weimar, Thüringisches Hauptstaatsarchiv, QE42/10, 40–41. Cf. Wilhelm Levinson's comments on the "Legenda Bonifacii Thuringica" in MGH SRG 37: lxxxiv–lxxxv. Menke's edition of the life is abbreviated, incomplete, and inaccurate in parts. "Legenda patroni Germaniae sancti Bonifacii, libris II," in *Scriptores rerum Germanicarum praecipue Saxonicarum*, ed. Johann Burchard Menke (Leipzig: Joannes Christianus Martinus, 1728), 833–51. This vitae of Boniface is addressed again in chapter three.

6. Johannes Scheckmann, "Vita sancti Basini," Stadtbibliothek Trier, ms. 2002/92, 59r–65v. Also, AASS, March 1: 312–18. In the early twentieth century it was

determined that the "Vita s. Basini" was not of early medieval origin. See Albert Poncelet, "L'auteur de la vie de s. Basin évêque de Trèves," *Analecta bollandiana* 31 (1912): 122–47. Poppo's remains were translated in 1517, indicating an interest in enhancing his cult and perhaps instigating his canonization; AASS, June 1: 105A–106E. The Bollandists report of no other writing about him in either the *Acta sanctorum* or the *Bibliotheca hagiographica latina*; see AASS, Feb. 3: 446A, note c; and Apr. 2: 654B.

7. Trithemius, "Vita beati Maximi, episcopi Moguntini," Rome, Vat. Pal. lat. cod. 850, 110r–121v. As it happens, Trithemius's accounts were not only de novo but also largely fictional, a problem that is considered later in this chapter. On the life of Rhabanus Maurus, see Michele C. Ferrari, "Vitae Hrabani," in *Scripturus vitam*, ed. Dorothea Walz (Heidelberg: Mattes, 2002), 395–98; and Stephanie Haarländer, ed., *Rabanus Maurus zum Kennenlernen: Ein Lesebuch mit einer Einführung in sein Leben und Werk* (Mainz: Bistum Mainz, 2006). Haarländer limits her collection to the medieval sources, thus excluding Trithemius's works.

8. I wish to thank Dr. Markus Müller for bringing this vita to my attention. Nuremberg Staatsarchiv, Rep. 52a, nr. 2. "Handschriftliche Nachrichten über Johannes Schallerman, Bischof zu Gurk." This fragment has recently been analyzed in Franz Fuchs, "Ein Westfale in Kärnten—Eine unbekannte Vita des Bischofs Johann Schallermann von Gurk († 1465)," *Carinthia I: Zeitschrift für geschichtliche Landeskunde von Kärnten* 191 (2001): 143–63. See also BHRR 2: 620.

Additional lives of bishops give no indication that the authors considered their subjects saints. Rudolf von Langen (ca. 1438–1519), vita of Henry (III) of Schwarzburg, bishop of Münster (1440, 1466–1496): StA Münster, ms. VII 1032, II/16. Jh., 17v–18v; Julius Ficker, ed., *Die münsterischen Chroniken des Mittelalters*, vol. 1, *Die Geschichtsquellen des Bisthums Münster* (Münster: Theissing, 1851), 241–43; BHRR 2: 653–64; Arnold Heymerick, "Vita Davidis episcopi Traiectini," in *Schriften des Arnold Heymerick*, ed. Friedrich W. Oediger (Bonn: Gesellschaft für Rheinische Geschichtskunde, 1939), 108–33; BHRR 2: 121–23; Gerardus Noviomagus, "Vita clarissimi principis Philippi a Burgondia," in *Collectanea van Gerardus Geldenhauer Noviomagus, gevolgd door den herdruk van eenige zijner werken* (Amsterdam: Werken Historisch Genootschap, 1901), 223–47; Philip of Burgundy, bishop of Utrecht (1465, 1517–1524), BHRR 2: 532–34; Peter Maier, "Gesta archiepiscopi Johannis II de Baden," LHA Koblenz 701/12; John, margrave of Baden, elector-archbishop of Trier (1430, 1456–1503), BHRR 2: 341–43. Maier also wrote a German-language life of Richard Greiffenklau von Vollrads, archbishop of Trier (1467, 1512–1531), Landeshauptarchiv Koblenz 701/13; BHRR 2: 239–41. See Markus Müller, *Die spätmittelalterliche Bistumsgeschichtsschreibung: Überlieferung und Entwicklung* (Cologne: Böhlau, 1998), 15–250;

9. Veit Bild, *Gloriosorum Christi confessorum Uldarici et Symperti, necnon beatissime martyris Aphre, Augustane sedis patronorum fidelissimorum historie* (1516). In this he followed Berno's *Vita s. Udalrici* (BHL 8362); and Adilbert's *Vita s. Simperti* (BHL 7775).

10. VD16 V1741. Jakob Wimpfeling, *Vita sancti Adelphi patroni Collegii Novillarensis* (1506). There are no extant manuscripts against which to judge Wimpfeling's

edition, and Guy Philippart's source analysis yielded ambiguous results. Still, Wimpfeling clarified some of his aspirations in his dedicatory letter, which is analyzed later in this chapter. Guy Philippart, "La vie anonyme de s. Adelphe de Metz plagiat de la vie de s. Arnoul," *Analecta bollandiana* 104 (1986): 185–86; and Christian Wilsdorf, "Remarques sur la premiere vie connue de saint Adelphe de Metz et le pèlerinage de Neuwiller-les-Saverne (IXᵉ–XIIᵉ)," *Revue d'Alsace* 119 (1993): 31–41.

11. BHL 7941; VD16 M936. Pseudo-Marcellinus, *Vita divi Swiberti Verdensis ecclesie episcopi, Saxonum Frisorumque apostoli,* ed. Gerardus de Harderwyck and Ortwinus Gratius (1508). See Wilhelm Diekamp, "Die Fälschung der *Vita sancti Suidberti,*" *Historisches Jahrbuch* 2 (1881): 272–86; Ursula Rautenberg, *Überlieferung und Druck: Heiligenlegenden aus frühen Kölner Offizinen* (Tübingen: Max Niemeyer, 1996), 225–28; and Knut Schäferdiek, "Suidberht von Kaiserwerth," *Düsseldorfer Jahrbuch: Beiträge zur Geschichte des Niederrheins* 66 (1995): especially 2n9.

12. Veit Bild, *Gloriosorum Christi confessorum Uldarici et Symperti, necnon beatissime martyris Aphre, Augustane sedis patronorum fidelissimorum historie* (1516). Berno's *Vita s. Udalrici* (BHL 8362); the *Conversio et Passio s. Afrae* (BHL 109); Adilbert's *Vita s. Simperti* (BHL 7775). Bild also composed liturgical offices. An additional life of Saint Ulrich dated 1494 appears in an eighteenth-century catalogue of the Augsburg monastery's library: Placidus Braun, *Notitia historico-literaria de codicibus manuscriptis in bibliotheca liberi ac imperialis monasterii ordinis s. Benedicti ad ss. Udalricum et Afram Augustae extantibus,* 6 vols., vol. 3, 93.

13. BHL 7640; GW M38775.

14. The original of the earlier life (BHL 6404–6405)—presumably the one once in Stettin—has since been lost. Older copies can be found in Bamberg manuscripts: Bamberg StB, R.B. mss. 123 and 124; HV ms. 132. The original of the later composition (BHL 6406–6407) is Bamberg StB (1499) R.B. ms. 122. Among later editions, the most commented upon are Andreas Lang, "De vita et operibus beatissimi Ottonis Babenbergensis episcopi, et confessoris Christi ac Pomeranicae gentis apostoli," in *Scriptores rerum episcopatus Bambergensis,* ed. Johann Peter Ludewig, 397–535; Andreas Lang, "De vita s. Ottonis," in *Divi Bambergenses,* ed. Jakob Gretser, 145–368; and Andreas Lang, "De vita s. Ottonis," ed. Valerius Jasche, 1–235. See also Franz Machilek, "Ottogedächtnis und Ottoverehrung auf dem Bamberger Michelsberg," *Historischer Verein Bamberg* 125 (1989): 9–34; Müller, *Die spätmittelalterliche Bistumsgeschichtsschreibung,* 353–57; and Lorenz Weinrich, ed., *Heiligenleben zur deutsch-slawischen Geschichte: Adalbert von Prag und Otto von Bamberg,* vol. 23, *Ausgewählte Quellen zur deutschen Geschichte des Mittelalters* (Darmstadt: Wissenschaftliche Buchgesellschaft, 2005), 17–19.

15. Joannes Cincinnius, "De Historie van deme leven des heiligen gloriosen confessores Cristi sent Ludghers"; VD16 K2477; Johannes Cincinnius von Lippstadt, *Vita divi Ludgeri Mimigardevordensis ecclesie* (1515). See Wilhelm Diekamp, ed., *Die Vitae sancti Liudgeri,* vol. 4, *Die Geschichtsquellen des Bisthums Münster* (1881); and Andreas Freitäger, *Johannes Cincinnius von Lippstadt (ca. 1485–1555): Bibliothek und Geisteswelt eines westfälischen Humanisten,* vol. 18, *Veröffentlichungen der historischen Kommission für Westfalen* (Münster: Aschendorff, 2000), 188–96.

16. Müller, *Die spätmittelalterliche Bistumsgeschichtsschreibung*, 379–87. VD16 F2716.

17. BHL 8990. GW M51767; *Legenda Sancti Wolfgangi* (1475).

VD16 L868 and B8095; *Vita divi Wolfgangi* (1516). The Landshut vita, in both languages, also includes some fifty woodcuts representing episodes in Wolfgang's life. These have justly attracted the attention of art historians, even as the accompanying texts have been overlooked.

See Ulrike Bausewein and Robert Leyh, "Studien zum Wolfgangskult," *Zeitschrift für bayerische Kirchengeschichte* 61 (1992): 9–10; Werner Johann Chrobak, "Literatur über den hl. Wolfgang: Ein Überblick," in *Liturgie zur Zeit des hl. Wolfgang: Der hl. Wolfgang in der Kleinkunst*, ed. Paul Mai (Regensburg: Schnell und Steiner, 1994), 44; Marianne Popp, "Viten und Legenden des hl. Wolfgang in der handschriftlichen Überlieferung," in ibid., 35–43; Karl Schottenloher, *Die Landshuter Buchdrucker des 16. Jahrhunderts* (Nieuwkoop, the Netherlands: B. De Graaf, 1967), 15, 18; Ignaz Zibermayr, *St. Wolfgang am Abersee: Seine Legende und ihr Einfluß auf die österreichische Kunst* (Horn, Austria: Ferdinand Berger, 1961), 39; and Rudolf Zinnhobler, "Das Leben des hl. Wolfgang," in *Der heilige Wolfgang und Oberösterreich*, ed. Rudolf Zinnhobler, *Schriftenreihe des Oberösterreichischen Musealvereins* (Linz, Austria: Oberösterreichischer Musealverein—Gesellschaft für Landeskunde, 1994), 9–13.

18. BHL 227. Jacobus de Gouda, "Legenda metrica Alberti," in *Legenda litteralis Alberti Magni* (Cologne: Johannes Koelhoff de Lübeck, 1490), A'-ii-r–B'-i-r. For an abbreviated edition of the poem see Jacobus de Gouda, "Legenda compendiosa et metrica venerabilis Alberti," in *Beati Alberti magni episcopi quondam Ratisbonensis tractatus de forma orandi eiusdem legenda metrica praemissa*, ed. Albert Wimmer (1902), vii–x.

19. VD16 E1216 and E1217. Philipp "Engentinus" Engelbrecht, *Divi Lamberti Episcopi Traiectensis vita* (1519).

20. See, for example, GW 5067 and 5068. Sebastian Brant, *Carmina in laudem B. Mariae Virginis multorumque sanctorum* (no earlier than 1494); and Sebastian Brant, *Varia Carmina* (1498).

21. The only late medieval Imperial bishop whose canonization was pursued was John of Luxemburg-Ligny, archbishop of Mainz (1342?–1373); BHRR 1: 410–11.

22. AASS, June 5: 498–530. Jakob Obersteiner, "Ein Brief von Johannes Hinderbach an den Gurker Bischof Ulrich III, Sonnenberger," *Carinthia I: Mitteilungen des Geschichtsvereins für Kärten* 175 (1985): 212–13.

23. Thomas Wetzstein, *Heilige vor Gericht: Das Kanonisationsverfahren im europäischen Spätmittelalter*, ed. M. Heckel, P. Landau et al., vol. 28, *Forschungen zur kirchlichen Rechtsgeschichte und zum Kirchenrecht* (Cologne: Böhlau, 2004), 514–45.

24. For an overview see Charles Garfield Nauert, Jr., *Humanism and the Culture of Renaissance Europe*, 2d ed., *New Approaches to European History* (New York: Cambridge University Press, 2006), 1–25, 102–31.

25. Albert was simultaneously the archbishop-elector of Mainz, the archbishop of Magdeburg, and the ecclesiastical administrator of Halberstadt. Albert's 1514 arrangement with the papal curia concerning the sale of indulgences for the building of the new Saint Peter's Basilica in Rome allowed him to keep a generous percentage of the revenues and inspired Martin Luther's protest against indulgences in 1517. BHRR 2: 13–16.

26. VD16 B1184. *Historia horarum canonicarum de s. Hieronymo vario carminum genere contexta* (Augsburg: Ratdolt, 1512). Bild composed a similar work on Saint Dionysius, third-century founding bishop of Augsburg. See Henschenius's "commentarius historicus," AASS, February 3: 631–33. In his only departure from Augsburg after his entrance into the monastery, Bild visited the Austrian abbey at Melk in 1511 to study the monastic reform movement based there, which Bild's monastery had been affiliated with since the mid-fifteenth century. A. Bigelmair, "Der Briefwechsel von Oekolampadius mit Veit Bild," *Reformationsgeschichtliche Studien und Texte* 40 (1922): 117–35; and Alfred Schröder, "Der Humanist Veit Bild, Mönch bei Sankt Ulrich: Sein Leben und sein Briefwechsel," *Zeitschrift des historischen Vereins für Schwaben und Neuburg* 20 (1893): 173–227.

27. The *Vita sancti Basini* [BHL 1028] was originally thought to be an early medieval life by Nithard, abbot of Mettlach. After the discovery in Trier of Scheckmann's epistolary preface in the late nineteenth century, authorship and dating were reevaluated. Poncelet, "L'auteur," 142–47. Trier, Stadtbibliothek, Hs. 2002/92, 59v.; VD16 S2392–S2394. Johannes Scheckmann, *Tractatulus . . . in laudem sancte ecclesie treverensis* (Mainz: Johann Schöffer, ca. 1512); Johannes Scheckmann and Johannes Enen, *Epitome alias medulla Gestorum Trevirorum* (Metz, France: Hochfeder, 1517); Franz-Josef Heyen, ed., *Die Bistümer der Kirchenprovinz Trier: Das Erzbistum Trier*, vol. 6, *Germania Sacra*, n.s. (Berlin: Walter de Gruyter, 1972), 13, 15, 110, 319, 441; J. Marx, *Geschichte des Erzstifts Trier, d.i. der Stadt Trier und des Trier. Landes, als Churfürstenthum und als Erzdiöcese, von den ältesten Zeiten bis zum Jahre 1816*, vol. 2/1 (Trier, Germany: Fr. Linß'schen Buchhandlung, 1860), 126n121; and Müller, *Die spätmittelalterliche Bistumsgeschichtsschreibung*, 429–32, 432n418.

28. BHL 6394; MGH SRG 71.

29. BHL 6395; Jan Wikarjak, ed., *Ebonis vita S. Ottonis episcopi Babenbergensis*, vol. 7/2, *Monumenta Poloniae historica, s. n.* (Warsaw: Panstwowe wydawnictwo naukowe, 1969), 45–146; BHL 6397; Jan Wikarjak, ed., *Herbordi dialogus de vita s. Ottonis episcopi Babenbergensis*, vol. 7/3, *Monumenta Poloniae historica, s. n.* (Warsaw: Panstwowe wydawnictwo naukowe, 1974), 3–212. See also Weinrich, ed., *Heiligenleben*.

30. Gerd Zimmermann, "Lang, Andreas" in VL 5 (1985): 572–78. See also Kurt Eisenmann, "Studien über Voraussetzungen und Rezeption des Humanismus in den fränkischen Territorien Würzburg, Bamberg und der Markgrafschaft Ansbach-Bayreuth" (PhD diss., Julius-Maximilians-Universität, 1953), 104–107; Markus Müller, "Die humanistische Bistumsgeschichtsschreibung," in *Deutsche Landesgeschichtsschreibung*, ed. Franz Brendle, Dieter Mertens et al. (Stuttgart: Steiner, 2001), 182–83; Müller, *Die spätmittelalterliche Bistumsgeschichtsschreibung*, 353–59, 377–78; and Jürgen Petersohn, "Otto von Bamberg und seine Biographen: Grundformen und Entwicklung des Ottobildes im hohen und späten Mittelalter," *Zeitschrift für bayerische Kirchengeschichte* 43 (1980): 23.

31. "Libros illos sanctissimorum auctorum multis seculis ignoratos diligentissime inquisitos et inventos accepit: a mendis quibus undique scatebant castigationis luna eripuit et ut impressorio opere tunc in lucem prodierent constituit."

Ortwinus Gratius, introduction, in Pseudo-Marcellinus, *Vita divi Swiberti*, A-1-r. The *libri* also include a report of Ludger's canonization.

32. Erich Meuthen has used this term to describe the appropriation of a humanist esteem for linguistic and literary education at the university hostels in Cologne. Under humanist influence these hostels began designating themselves *gymnasia* in the sixteenth century. Erich Meuthen, *Kölner Universitätsgeschichte* (Cologne: Böhlau, 1988), 203–62. Ulrich Muhlack has used the term to apply to scholastically trained theologians who appropriated a humanist esteem for classical Latin and ancient literature. Muhlack designates Wimpfeling, for example, a scholastic humanist. Ulrich Muhlack, *Geschichtswissenschaft im Humanismus und in der Aufklärung: Die Vorgeschichte des Historismus* (Munich: C. H. Beck, 1991), 91. Richard Southern's use of the term is unrelated.

33. Jacobus Montanus, author of *The Life of Holy Elizabeth, Daughter of the King of Hungary* [*Vita illustre ac dive Helisabet Hungarorum regis filie*], was also one of Hegius's students.

34. His work *Fasciculus rerum expetendarum ac fugiendarum* (Cologne: Peter Quentel, 1535) was a compilation of treatises on church reform and councils (VD16 G2924). Diekamp, "Die Fälschung der *Vita sancti Suidberti*," 272–87; and Rautenberg, *Überlieferung*, 225–29. Regarding Gerhard's and Ortwinus's relations to the university, see James V. Mehl, "Humanism in the Home Town of the 'Obscure Men,'" in *Humanismus in Köln*, ed. idem (Cologne: Böhlau, 1991), 1–38; Meuthen, *Kölner Universitätsgeschichte*, 64, 93, 180, 184, 190, 219–26, 229–30, 268–71, 295; and Götz-Rüdiger Tewes, *Die Bursen der Kölner Artisten-Fakultät: Bis zur Mitte des 16. Jahrhunderts, Studien zur Geschichte der Universität zu Köln* (Cologne: Böhlau, 1993), 62–63, 378–85, 417–27, 447–49, 720–22, 725–30, 734–36, 748–68.

35. Diekamp, "Die Fälschung der *Vita sancti Suidberti*," 272–87.

36. Alison Knowles Frazier. *Possible Lives: Authors and Saints in Renaissance Italy* (New York: Columbia University Press, 2005), 11.

37. MGH SRG 38: 290–95.

38. Richard Doebner, "Aktenstücke zur Geschichte der *Vita Bennonis Misnensis*," *Neues Archiv für Sächsische Geschichte und Alterthumskunde* 7 (1886): 135–39.

39. Hieronymus Emser, *Divi Bennonis Misnensis quondam episcopi vita miracula et alia quedam non tam Misnensibus quam Germanis omnibus decora* (1512), C-i-v.

40. For an edition and analysis of the Hildesheim vita, see David Collins, "Bursfelders, Humanists, and the Rhetoric of Sainthood: The Late Medieval Vitae of Saint Benno," *Revue Bénédictine* 111 (2001): 508–56. An alternative hypothesis judges this earlier vita to be a sixteenth-century counterfeit composed by a monk of Saint Michael in Hildesheim, Henning Rose, in league with Emser and the other canonization advocates in Meissen. For an analysis of the historiographical problem see ibid., 546–50. The counterfeit thesis has recently resurfaced in Christoph Volkmar's *Die Heiligenerhebung Bennos* (2002). Volkmar has expressed a concern that there is no (other) evidence of a cult in Hildesheim before 1510. Advocates of the counterfeit hypothesis, however, have not yet addressed several problems: (1) that the content of the Hildesheim vita does not correspond well to the canonization interests of

petitioners who visited Hildesheim in 1510, (2) that the purported counterfeiter made fraudulent claims elsewhere about Benno that were not reiterated in the Hildesheim vita, and (3) that the paleographical and codicological analysis concludes that neither the paper of the manuscript nor the handwriting of the text corresponds to a date as late as 1510 (the earliest point at which the vita could have been counterfeited, according to Volkmar) or as early as the twelfth century (to make the vita adequately "ancient"). The alleged counterfeiter Rose was, to be sure, a creative manipulator of historical texts, and he had indeed passed falsified texts to the canonization advocates. But conspiracy theorists continue to reheat nineteenth-century speculations without examination of the Hildesheim manuscript or its text. For example, in 1911 Johannes Kirsch proposed that certain passages in the Hildesheim vita were dependent on passages in the vita of Hildesheim's most famous medieval bishop, Bernward, by Thangmar. More recently it was discovered that Rose had even made a manuscript copy of Thangmar's *Vita Bernwardi*. The conspiracy theorists take his transcription as yet another piece of evidence that Rose counterfeited the Hildesheim vita. In point of fact, however, the parallel passages are not so similar as to suggest plagiarism from the one to the other. See, for example, note k in the edition of the vita prima. It is no more than an accidental similarity, but for Kirsch it was decisive, and subsequent conspiracy theorists have left the parallels untested. In any event, if echoing or even outright imitation of older texts is evidence of counterfeit, then hardly a single vita from this period could be counted "authentic." The burden of proof belongs to those who would exclude the authenticity of a work; in this instance the judgment must be rendered "unproved." "Vita prima Bennonis," *Revue Bénédictine* III (2001): 555. Cf. Christoph Volkmar, *Die Heiligenerhebung Bennos von Meissen (1523/24): Spätmittelalterliche Frömmigkeit, landesherrliche Kirchenpolitik und reformatorische Kritik im albertinischen Sachsen in der frühen Reformationszeit*, ed. Heribert Smolinsky, vol. 146, *Reformationsgeschichtliche Studien und Texte* (2002), 125–31. See my review of Volkmar's otherwise laudable book in the *Catholic Historical Review* 72 (2003): 553–55.

41. Hieronymus Emser, *Das heilig leben und legend des seligen Vatters Bennonis weylund bischoffen tzu Meyssen* (1517). See Hagiogr. 1: 267–70.

42. BHL 4955–59.

43. Poncelet, "L'auteur," 142–47.

44. "Sed in contrarium ut ego sententiam Megenfridi solidissime auctoritatis viri me compellit adamissim exquisita digentia, qui temporibus Ottonis secundi ac tertii imperatorum, monachus fulde vivens in humanis, libros quatuor et viginti historiarum de temporibus gratie composuit in quibus aliter multo sensit et scripsit, quam auctores incerti omnes memorati," Trithemius, *Vita s. Maximi presulis Moguntini*, Vatican, Palat. lat. 850ff., 110v–11.

Many have attempted to explain Trithemius's dissimulation. To my mind the most persuasive is Nikolaus Staubach, "Auf der Suche nach der verlorenen Zeit: Die historiographischen Fiktionen des Johannes Trithemius im Lichte seines wissenschaftlichen Selbstverständnisses," in *Fälschungen im Mittelalter* (Hannover: Hahnsche Buchhandlung, 1988), 1: 279–80.

45. Philippart, "La vie anonyme," 185–86.

46. "Nomine suo Liudgerus appellatus est levante illum beatae ac nobili Ida ex ducum sanguine in Francie partibus orta." Joannes Cincinnius von Lippstadt, *Vita divi Ludgeri Mimigardevordensis ecclesie* (Cologne: Quentel, 1515), 5v.

47. Klaus Schreiner, " 'Discrimen veri ac falsi': Ansätze und Formen der Kritik in der Heiligen- und Reliquienverehrung des Mittelalters," *Archiv für Kulturgeschichte* 48 (1966): 1–53; Klaus Schreiner, "Zum Wahrheitsverständnis im Heiligen- und Reliquienwesen des Mittelalters," *Saeculum* 17 (1966): 131–69.

48. Examples are his use of *contraversia* for *controversia* and *confirmavit* for *conformavit*. His use of *poeticando* was an unusual medievalism, whereas the classically ringing reference to Benno's death as *astra peciit* fit clumsily into the surrounding passages.

49. James Michael Weiss, "Hagiography by German Humanists, 1483–1516," *Journal of Medieval and Renaissance Studies* 16 (1985): 310. *Divus* was a favored honorific by the humanists. It suggested an analogy, irresistible to humanists, between ancient Roman and contemporaneous Christian exultations of the person.

50. Collins, "Bursfelders," 533–34.

51. These sources include Helmold's *Chronica Slavorum*, the *Chronica episcoporum Hildesheimensis*, the *Chronica Hildesheimensis*, *Annales Hildesheimensis*, *Chronica Goslariensis*, and the *Chronicon Episcoporum et Abbatarum*. See the apparatus for "Vita prima Bennonis," 551–56.

52. Emser, *Divi Bennonis vita*, B-v-r.

53. Collins, "Bursfelders," 520n536.

54. Emser, *Divi Bennonis vita*, A-vi-v.

55. Ibid. Reference to the school ("Parisiensi olim Gymnasio")—a prestigious educational institution in the early sixteenth century yet undistinguished in the eleventh—surely conjured up associations, ugly to some humanists, of scholastic learning.

56. Ibid.

57. Ibid., B-i-r.

58. "Vita prima Bennonis," 553.

59. Emser, *Divi Bennonis vita*, B-i-r.

60. "Nobilissimo stemate progenitus," Johannes Scheckmann, "Vita sancti Basini" (Trier, Stadtbibliothek, ms. 2002/92: 59–65v), 60v.

61. "Hec cordis in alveolo ubi frequenter revolveret, demum votis morem gessit, sciens absque facto vanas esse cogitationes hominum. In ipso itaque etatis flore gloriam, voluptates, opes, parentes, tellurem hereditatariam, mundum denique et seipsum talem fugiens, ut se alium inveniret, totum ad cenobialis vite studium se contulit. At ille quidem e seculo exeunti, divis bonarum litterarum disciplinis comitantibus, haud procul a Trevericis menibus ad S. Joannis Evangelistae monasterium, quod in preurbio fate civitatis ad Aquilonarem plagam in Campo-Martio situm, et B. Maximini nomine pretitulatum est, saltus fuit." Ibid., 60v–61r.

62. "Beatus Maximus testante Megenfrido honestis et christianis parentibus ortus, in urbe Moguntina, more gentis adhuc puer studio deputatus est litterarum. In quo cum tempore adeo proferit, quod sibi coetaneos pene omnes superavit." Johannes

Trithemius, "Vita beati Maximi, episcopi Moguntini," Rome, Vat. Pal. lat. cod. 850, f. 115.

63. "Consuetudo fuit illo in tempore valde necessaria clericis ac sacerdotibus soli deo vacare, sacro ministerio verbi et orationis insistere; . . . mundi honores, divinitias quoque et omnes voluptates moriture carnis vilipendere." Ibid., 115v.

64. "Vita prima Bennonis," 554.

65. Emser, *Divi Bennonis vita*, B-iii-r.

66. Ibid.

67. Ibid. B-iii.

68. Ibid. B-iii-r.

69. Ibid. C-i-r.

70. Ibid. C-iii-r.

71. Ibid.

72. Lampert of Hersfeld, "Annales," MGH SRG 38: 149, 231, 268–69. See also Benjamin Arnold, *Medieval Germany, 500–1300: A Political Interpretation* (Toronto: University of Toronto Press, 1997), 92–107; Lutz Fenske, *Adelsopposition und kirchliche Reformbewegung im östlichen Sachsen: Entstehung und Wirkung des sächsischen Widerstandes gegen des salischen Königtums während des Investiturstreits* (Göttingen: Vanderhoeck und Ruprecht, 1977), 71n244, 275n275, 110; and Hanna Vollrath, "The Western Empire under the Salians," in *The New Cambridge Medieval History*, ed. David Luscombe and Jonathan Riley-Smith (New York: Cambridge University Press, 2004), 4/2: 50–61.

73. "Eo vasaniae Imperatorem induxerat caeca Sacerdotum (qui tunc frequentes apud eum erant) libido." Emser, *Divi Bennonis vita*, A-v-r.

74. Ibid., B-iiii-r.

75. "Vita prima Bennonis," 554; and Emser, *Divi Bennonis vita*, A-v-r. See Stephanie Haarländer, *Vitae episcoporum: Eine Quellengattung zwischen Hagiographie und Historiographie, untersucht an Lebensbeschreibungen von Bischöfen des Regnum Teutonicum im Zeitalter der Ottonen und Salier*, ed. Friedrich Prinz, vol. 47, *Monographien zur Geschichte des Mittelalters* (Stuttgart: Anton Hiersemann, 2000), 467–68.

76. "Vita prima Bennonis," 555–56.

77. Emser, *Divi Bennonis vita*, C-ii-v.

78. Haarländer, *Vitae episcoporum*, 377–78, 413–14.

79. "Sub his turbationibus ecclesie multa christianorum milia propter catholice fidei confessionem ab infidelibus et hereticis apud Moguntiam et in omnibus terminis eius crudeliter fuerunt occisa. . . . Quapropter pontifices et ministri domini sacerdotes in quos furor persequentium crudelius seriebat in urbibus et vicis publice non audentes comparere quotiens persecutio imminebat cum suis ad nemora secesserunt in speluncis et cavernis montium latitantes inedia fame ac siti ultra quam credi potest afflicti longum pro fide Christi martyrium sustinebant." Trithemius, "Vita b. Maximi," 112.

80. Johannes Scheckmann, "Vita s. Basini," 62–63.

81. Joannes Trithemius, letter to Pope Julius II (June 21, 1506) ("Sanctissimo in Christo Patri, Iulio Papae Secundo Iohan. Trithemius abbas Spanheimensis hu-

millima pedum oscula beatorum"), in *Opera Historica*, letter 64, ed. Marquard Freherr, 2:491–92. Trithemius repeated the contents of this first letter in another letter of the same year, dated Oct. 31 (*Opera* 2:514–17), and in a brief entry in the *Annales Hirsaugienses* 1:199.

82. Emser, *Divi Bennonis vita*, A-iii-r.

83. Ibid., B-iiii-r.

84. Joachim Herrmann, "Materielle und geistige Kultur," in *Die Slawen in Deutschland*, ed. Joachim Hermann (Berlin: Akademie, 1972), 250–52; Christian Lübke, *Das östliche Europa, die Deutschen und das europäische Mittelalter* (München: Siedler, 2004), 276–89; and Helmut Schröcke, *Germanen—Slawen: Vor- und Frühgeschichte des ostgermanischen Raumes* (Viöl, Germany: Verlag für ganzheitliche Forschung, 2000), 245–64.

85. Emser, *Divi Bennonis vita*, B-iiii-r and C-i-r.

86. For consideration of the military metaphors used in hagiography to describe missionary activity see Thomas Scharff, *Die Kämpfe der Herrscher und Heiligen: Krieg und historische Erinnerung in der Karolingerzeit* (Darmstadt: Wissenschaftliche Buchgesellschaft, 2002), 32–52.

87. "His igitur acceptis literis a Papa, profectus est inde ad Longobardorum Regem Luitbrandum, a quo honorifice susceptus, aliquandiu cum eo est hospitatus. Profectus vero exinde, incognitos Baijoariorum et Germaniae terminos perlustrans, in Thuringiam devenit, et inibi aliquot dies commorans, omnes principes illius provinciae verbis spiritualibus alloquens, ad sacrae fidei agnitionem incitavit. Sed et sacerdotes, quos variis deditos erroribus comperit, sermonibus Evangelicis admonens, ad institutionis Canonicae normam correxit." Jena, ThULB, ms. Sag. q. 5, 80v–81r.

88. "His igitur acceptis literis a Papa, profectus est inde ad Longobardorum Regem Luitbrandum, a quo honorifice susceptus, aliquandiu cum eo est hospitatus. Profectus vero exinde, incognitos Baijoariorum et Germaniae terminos perlustrans, in Thuringiam devenit, et inibi aliquot dies commorans, omnes principes illius provinciae verbis spiritualibus alloquens, ad sacrae fidei agnitionem incitavit. Sed et sacerdotes, quos variis deditos erroribus comperit, sermonibus Evangelicis admonens, ad institutionis Canonicae normam correxit." Jena, ThULB, ms. Sag. Q. 5, 80v–81r. Indeed, a key theme of the entire work is showing Boniface as the apostle to the Thuringians. As for example, "Eo tempore, quo sanctus Bonifacius se cum omnibus suis Karolo primo subiecit, ut supra memoravimus, cum suis Thuringiae fines adijt, intendens, huiusmodi populum deo acquirere." Ibid., f. 89r. And "S. Bonifacius, repletus gaudio attamen cum magno tremore expectans judicium Dei, Thuringos ad se vocavit, eos a decimis absolvit, necnon et in timore et fide Christi instruxit atque baptizavit, exhortansque, ut susceptam fidem verbo et opere servarent, quousque judicii Dei, quod in foribus existeret, viderent finem, intimans, se ab eis non recessurum, nisi prius viderent virtutem altissimi." Ibid., f. 91r-v.

89. Pseudo-Marcellinus, *Vita divi Swiberti*, A-5-v–A-6-v, C-6-v–D-2-v.

90. For example, "De prefato autem rege Ratbodo plura alia iniqua legimus. Ut videlicet ipse crudelis tyrannus impius ac perfidus strennuissimusque idolatra quodam, tempore proprie salutis contemptu, pedes suos de sacro baptismatis fonte

retraxerit, malens cum pluribus reprobris ad inferos descendere, quam cum paucis salvandorum celos intrare." Cincinnius, *Vita divi Ludgeri*, 4v.

91. Lang, "De vita b. Ottonis," 460–89; Petersohn, "Otto," 23.

92. See Philip M. Soergel, *Wondrous in His Saints: Counter-Reformation Propaganda in Bavaria*, vol. 17, *Studies on the History of Society and Culture* (Berkeley: University of California Press, 1993), 187–88. See also Brad S. Gregory, *Salvation at Stake: Christian Martyrdom in Early Modern Europe*, vol. 134, *Harvard Historical Studies* (Cambridge, Mass.: Harvard University Press, 1999), 31–50. Gregory argues against strong continuities between late medieval and sixteenth-century interests in martyrs.

93. Sulpicius Severus, *Life of Saint Martin of Tours*, ch. 10.

94. Graus, *Volk, Herrscher und Heiliger im Reich der Merowinger*, 115; and Thomas Wünsch, "Der heilige Bischof: Zur politischen Dimension von Heiligkeit im Mittelalter und ihrem Wandel," *Archiv für Kulturgeschichte* 82 (2000): 262–64, 271–72. For general consideration of the participation of saints in wars, see Scharff, *Die Kämpfe*, 45–50.

95. Hagiogr. 4: 273–520; Wilhelm Janssen, "Biographien mittelalterlicher Bischöfe und mittelalterliche Bischofsviten: Über Befunde und Probleme am Kölner Beispiel," *Römischer Quartalsschrift* 91 (1996): 131–47; Wilhelm Janssen, "Der Bischof, Reichsfürst und Landesherr (14. und 15. Jahrhundert)," in *Der Bischof in seiner Zeit: Bischofstypus und Bischofsideal im Spiegel der Kölner Kirche*, ed. Peter Berglar and Odilo Engels (Cologne: J. P. Bachem, 1986), 208–209; Oskar Köhler, *Das Bild des geistlichen Fürsten in den Viten des 10., 11., 12. Jahrhunderts* (Berlin: Verlag für Staatswissenschaften und Geschichte, 1935), 45, 54, 138; and Wünsch, "Der heilige Bischof," 266–77.

96. Haarländer, *Vitae episcoporum*, especially 89–229, 312–47, 463–72. These generalities do not hold true in Italy, where, for example, canons frequently authored episcopal vitae.

97. Wünsch, "Der heilige Bischof," 268–78, 288–97.

98. Rainald Becker, "Der Breslauer Bischof Johannes Roth (1426–1506) als *instaurator veterum* und *benefactor ecclesiae suae*: Eine Variation zum Thema des Humanistenbischofs," *Römischer Quartalsschrift* 96 (2001): 100–23; Thomas A. Brady, "The Holy Roman Empire's Bishops on the Eve of the Reformation," in *Continuity and Change: The Harvest of Late Medieval and Reformation History*, ed. Robert James Bast and Andrew Colin Gow (Leiden, the Netherlands: Brill, 2000), 20–47; Daniela Rando, *Dai margini la memoria: Johannes Hinderbach (1418–1486)* (Bologna: Società editrice il Mulino, 2003); and Alois Schmid, "Humanistenbischöfe: Untersuchungen zum vortridentinischen Episkopat in Deutschland," *Römischer Quartalsschrift* 87 (1992): 159–92.

99. Müller, "Die humanistische Bistumsgeschichtsschreibung," 167–87.

100. Trithemius, "Vita b. Maximi," 110–21v. See Weiss, "Hagiography," 307–308.

101. Müller, "Die humanistische Bistumsgeschichtsschreibung," 171; Müller, *Die spätmittelalterliche Bistumsgeschichtsschreibung*, 412.

102. For example, "Beatissimi patris Bennonis Bennopolitani, insignis ecclesiae Misnensis decimi quondam Episcopi, vitam descripturus: opere praecium duxi: ante omnia, urbis ipsius Misnae, situm, originem, ac veteris ecclesiasticae disciplinae, in haec usque tempora, servata vestigia, litteris demandare, tum quia id a nemine prius attentatum: tum quia indignum sit eam urbem apud exteros esse incognitam, quae caput et mater est, populi Misnensis, Germanorum omnium (quod cum pace tamen aliorum dixerim) facile principis: ne dum soli ubertate et bonorum omnium abundantia: verum etiam urbanitate ac moribus nitidissimis. Est enim idem populus Misnensis peculiariter in superos pius: in hospites liberalis: domi splendidus: foris compositus, ager vero non solum Cerere et Baccho, sed et auro et argento luxuriat. Ex gemmis adamanta, berillum, iaspida, amethisthum, topasion ac uniones parturit. Stanno, ferro, et universo fere metalli genere scaturit. Marmor praeterea gignit: et omnium novissime repertum electrum ac succinum. Flumina colligit ratibus ac navibus pervia, Albim germaniae olim terminum, Muldam, Tschoppen, Ellestram, et alia quamplurima, torrentes vero ac rivulos pene innumeros, nec desunt illi sylvae caeduae, et nemora stabula alta ferarum, nec laeta pecoribus pascua, et florida prata. Aeris quoque tanta fruitur temperiae, ut et crocum, et nonnullos alios peregrinos frutices non invite etiam nutriat. Huc ego tam mites ac placidos Misnensis populi mores, tamque formosa corpora referenda censeo: siquidem Aristotele etiam teste, haud parum refert, hac vel illa caeli facie, homines procreari. Domos hic aedificat, vel sectili lapide excisas, vel coctili compactas." Emser, *Divi Bennonis vita*, A-ii-v.

103. For example, the author of "The Thuringian Life of Boniface" addresses the "privilegia Thuringorum"; Jena, ThULB, ms. Sag. q. 5, f. 93v.

104. "Lotharingiam provinciam primum Austrasiam vel Austeriam sive Austriam superiorem Brabantiam vero Austrasiam vel Austeriam sive Austriam inferiorem nuncupatam tradunt cosmographi et economiste Austrasie vocabulum derivatum astruunt ab Austrasio principe magnificentissimo nepote Caroli pulchri ex Landone filio." Scheckmann, "Vita s. Basini," 60v.

105. Müller, "Die humanistische Bistumsgeschichtsschreibung," 170–83.

106. Markus Müller, "Fürstenspiegel und Bischofsspiegel: Der Beitrag Jakob Wimpfelings," in *Humanisten am Oberrhein*, ed. Sven Lembke and Markus Müller (Leinfelden-Echterdingen, Germany: DRW-Verlag, 2004), 9–61.

107. Dieter Mertens, "Der Humanismus und die Reform des Weltklerus im deutschen Südwesten," *Rottenburger Jahrbuch für Kirchengeschichte* 11 (1992): 13–23.

108. BHRR 2: 776–77.

109. Ibid., 719–20; Volkmar, *Die Heiligenerhebung*, 133–35.

110. Jacob Wimpfeling, "Catalogus archiepiscoporum Moguntinorum (1514)," HofB Aschaffenburg, ms. 22, J. 1515. He also composed the "Argentinensium episcoporum catalogus cum eorundem vita atque certis historiis rebusque gestis et illustratione totius fere episcopatus Argentinensis." This was printed in Strassburg by John Grüninger in 1508 (VD16 W3344).

111. Lewis William Spitz, *The Religious Renaissance of the German Humanists* (Cambridge, Mass.: Harvard University Press, 1963), 41.

112. Jakob Wimpfeling, *Opera selecta: Epistolae (187–358)*, ed. Otto Herding and Dieter Mertens, vol. 3/2 (Munich: Wilhelm Fink, 1990), 553. Frederick I "the Victorious," duke of Bavaria and palatine count (1425–1476), foreswore marriage and adopted his deceased elder brother's minor son (with the nobility's approval) so that he could combine full rulership in his person over his own territory and that of his brother. Emperor Frederick III opposed the plan but in the end could not prevent it. Frederick of Bavaria participated actively in monastic reforms and in Imperial reform movements as well. Such passages support other research into Wimpfeling's ideal prince, such as Bruno Singer, *Die Fürstenspiegel in Deutschland im Zeitalter des Humanismus und der Reformation*, ed. Ernesto Grassi, vol. 34, *Humanistische Bibliothek (Abhandlungen)* (Munich: Wilhelm Fink, 1981), 173–249.

113. Volkmar, *Die Heiligenerhebung*, 1–7, 140–56.

114. Duke George supported several sites of popular devotion within Saxony. See Angelika Dörfler-Dierken, *Die Verehrung der heiligen Anna in Spätmittelalter und früher Neuzeit*, vol. 50, *Forschungen zur Kirchen- und Dogmengeschichte* (Göttingen: Vandenhoeck and Ruprecht, 1992); Virginia Nixon, *Mary's Mother: Saint Anne in Late Medieval Europe* (University Park: Pennsylvania State University Press, 2004), 92–98; and Volkmar, *Die Heiligenerhebung*, 7–12.

CHAPTER 2

1. In 1996 Patrick Geary made a thoughtful plaidoyer for the consideration of revisions in medieval writings about saints. Patrick J. Geary, "Saints, Scholars, and Society: The Elusive Goal," in *Saints: Studies in Hagiography*, ed. Sandro Sticca (Binghamton, N.Y.: Medieval and Renaissance Texts and Studies, 1996), 13–20. More recently, Monique Goullet has developed a conceptual framework (along with Martin Heinzelmann) and provided a helpful range of case studies taken from several chronological periods and cultural regions. Monique Goullet, *Écriture et réécriture hagiographiques: Essai sur les réécritures de vies de saints dans l'Occident latin médiéval (VIIIᵉ–XIIIᵉ s.)*, ed. Paul Bertrand, J. Deploige et al., vol. 4, *Hagiologia* (Turnhout, Belgium: Brepols, 2005); and Monique Goullet and Martin Heinzelmann, "Avant-propos," in *La réécriture hagiographique dans l'Occident médiéval*, ed. eidem (Ostfildern, Germany: Jan Thorbecke, 2003), 7–14.

2. VD16 M5078. Daniel Agricola, *Almi confessoris et anachorete Beati, Helveciorum primi Evangeliste et Apostoli a sancto Petro missi vita iam pridem exarata*. German humanist Beatus Rhenanus took issue with Agricola's contrivance of Beat's ancient past; Beatus Rhenanus, *Libri tres rerum germanicarum nov-antiquarum, historico-geographicarum*, 602–603. More recent historians have argued over whether this particular Beat existed at all. Cf. Beat of Vendôme, from which Agricola likely derived his life: BHL 1064, AASS, May 2: 363–64; and BHL 1066: Charles Métais, *Saint Bienheuré de Vendôme: Vie et office inédits, XI–XIIIᵉ siècles* (Vendôme, France: Lemercier, 1888), 27–34. See M. Bihl, "Agricola (Daniel), franciscain observant (†1540)," DHGE 1 (1912): 1022; Henri Moretus, "La légende de saint Béat, apôtre de Suisse," *Analecta bollandiana* 26 (1907): 423–49; Lutz Röhrich, *Erzählungen des späten Mittelalters und*

ihr Weiterleben in Literatur und Volksdichtung bis zur Gegenwart, 2 vols. (Bern: Francke, 1962, 1967), vol. 1, 116–19; Otmar Scheiwiller, "Zur Beatusfrage," *Zeitschrift für schweizerische Kirchengeschichte* 5 (1911): 21–52; and A. Wrede, "Beatus, hl. Bekenner," in *Handwörterbuch des deutschen Aberglaubens* (Berlin: Walter de Gruyter, 1927), vol. 1, 964–65. The printed work includes an artistically significant set of Renaissance illustrations by Swiss artist Urs Graf. Hans Koegler, "Die illustrierten Erbauungsbücher, Heiligenlegenden und geistlichen Auslegungen im Basler Buchdruck der ersten Hälfte des XVI. Jahrhunderts," *Basler Zeitschrift für Geschichte und Altertumskunde* 39 (1940): 132–34.

3. The interest that Nicholas of Flue inspired not just among humanists but also across fifteenth-century Europe is the subject of chapter four.

4. BHL 5878, "Passio s. Meginradi." In Latin: Paris, Bibliothèque Nationale de France, ms. 5656, ff. 32r–42r. In German: "Dis ist die legende von unser frawen cappelle zu den einsidlen wie sie gewicht ward und von sant Meinratsz leben," Nuremberg, Staatsarchiv Nürnberg, Reichstadt Nürnberg, Ratskanzlei, A-Laden, 142, nr. 16 (Rep. 15a) (film S3484). Also, including a poem by Sebastian Brant, GW M29714, *Passio sancti Meinradi*, ed. Albrecht von Bonstetten (Basel: Michael Furter, 1496).

5. Albrecht von Bonstetten, "Legenda beati Geroldi, heremite olim quoque Saxonie ducis," (Weimar, Thüringisches Hauptstaatsarchiv HS Reg. O 157; HS Reg. O 29a; HS Reg. O 29b); and Albrecht von Bonstetten, "Legenda beati Geroldi, heremite olim quoque Saxonie ducis," in *Der Gute Gerhart Rudolfs von Ems in einer anonymen Prosaauflösung und die lateinische und deutsche Fassung der Gerold-Legende Albrechts von Bonstetten nach den Handschriften Reg. O 157 und Reg. O 29A und B im thüringischen Hauptstaatsarchiv Weimar*, vol. 81, *Deutsche Texte des Mittelalters*, ed. Rudolf Bentzinger, Christina Meckelnborg, Franzjosef Pensel, and Anne-Beate Riecke (Berlin: Akademie Verlag, 2002), 124–38. Bentzinger argues that the German version is a translation of the original Latin; ibid., 106–16.

6. The vita of Ida of Herzfeld is analyzed in chapter three.

7. A metrical vita about Empress Saint Adelheid was composed and printed in 1516: VD16 V1739. Patrick Corbet, Monique Goullet, and Dominique Iogna-Prat, eds., *Adélaïde de Bourgogne: Genèse et représentations d'une sainteté impériale* (Paris: Comité des Travaux Historiques et Scientifiques, 2002); Robert Folz, *Les saintes reines du Moyen Age en Occident: VIe–XIIIe siècles*, vol. 76, *Subsidia hagiographica* (Brussels: Société des Bollandistes, 1992), 67–80; Herbert Paulhart, "Die 'Vita sancte Adelhaydis': Ein Druck des 16. Jahrhunderts aus Durlach," *Mitteilungen des Instituts für österreichische Geschichte* 69 (1961): 100–104; and Klaus Schreiner, "Hildegard, Adelheid, Kunigunde: Leben und Verehrung heiliger Herrscherinnen im Spiegel ihrer deutschsprachigen Lebensbeschreibungen aus der Zeit des späten Mittelalters," in *Spannungen und Widersprüche*, ed. Susanna Burghartz, Hans-Jörg Gilomen et al. (Sigmaringen, Germany: Thorbecke, 1992), 37–50.

8. The monks in Kempten venerated Hildegard as a saint, and the abbot of Kempten directed the composition of the hagiographical vita in 1471. See Robert Folz, "Tradition et culte de Hildegarde," in *Actes du Colloque "Autour d'Hildegarde,"* ed.

Pierre Riché, Carol Heitz, and François Héber-Suffrin (Paris: Centre de Recherches sur l'antiquité tardive et le haut moyen age, 1987), 19–26; Norbert Hoerberg, "Geistige Entwicklung in Stift und Stadt," in *Geschichte der Stadt Kempten*, ed. Volker Dotterweich, Karl Filser et al. (Kempten, Germany: Tobias Dannheimer, 1989), 143–45; Georg Kreuzer, "Gründung und Frühgeschichte des Klosters," in *Geschichte der Stadt Kempten*, ed. Dotterweich et al., 71; Wolfgang Maaz, "Hildegardis," *Enzyklopädie des Märchens* 6 (1990): 1017–21; Riché et al., eds., *Actes du Colloque "Autour d'Hildegarde"*; Klaus Schreiner, "Hildegard, Schwabens heilige Königin," *Schwäbische Heimat: Zeitschrift zur Pflege von Landschaft, Volkstum, Kultur* 23 (1972): 111–23; Schreiner, "Hildegard, Adelheid, Kunigunde," 37–50; and Klaus Schreiner, "'Hildegardis regina': Wirklichkeit und Legenda einer karolingischen Herrscherin," *Archiv für Kulturgeschichte* 57 (1975): 24n93.

9. As part of a canonization petition in the early 1480s Italian canonist Pavini composed a vita of Austrian margrave Leopold the Pious, and Thomas Stretzinger, a member of the faculty of the arts in Vienna delivered a panegyric there to the saint in 1512 that has been preserved. One aspect of Leopold's holiness was his sponsorship, with his wife, of several monasteries. *Bulla canonizationis sancti Leopoldi marchionis* (1485); Johannes Franciscus de Pavinis, *Oratio in laudem Leopoldi Marchionis Austriae* (1484); Johannes Franciscus de Pavinis, *Rede auf den Heiligen Leopold*, ed. Ludwig Bieler (1936); and Thomas Stretzinger, *Oratio de divo Leopoldo III Austriae marchione in Universitate Vindobonensi habita*, ed. Hermann Maschek, *Bibliotheca scriptorum Medii Recentisque Aevorum . . . Saec. XVI* (1934). GW M27563, M27564, M27567, M27572, M30412, M30431, and M30434.

A similar foundress saint is Saint Irmina of Trier, who was a prominent patroness of Saint Willibrord and about whom Trithemius composed a life, since lost, probably dependent on an older vita. BSS 7 (1966): 905–906. Klaus Arnold, *Johannes Trithemius (1462–1516)*, ed. Klaus Wittstadt, 2d ed., vol. 23, *Quellen und Forschungen zur Geschichte des Bistums und Hochstifts Würzburg* (Würzburg: Kommissionsverlag Ferdinand Schöningh, 1991), 20, 52, 258.

Jacobus Montanus's writings on Elizabeth of Thuringia represent divergences from these tendencies. Saint Elizabeth, once widowed, became a Franciscan tertiary (*"Confestim igitur ut Elisabeth precandi studium remisit, remisso pariter calore, juvenis est velocissime refrigeratus, adsumturum sese maturius Francisci Assisiatis institutum pollicitur, quod et non multo post tempore adsumsit, adsumtum coluit, cultum viriliter consummavit,"* c. 24) and used her resources to support the sick and poor. The earliest edition of Montanus's work, titled *Vita illustris ac dive Helisabeth Hungarorum regis filie*, was published in 1511 in Marburg. The vita was printed a second time in Cologne: *Divae Helisabet Hungarorum regis filiae vita* (1521). The second edition has been edited in Jacobus Montanus, *Vita illustris ac divae Elisabeth Hungarorum regis filiae*, ed. Herrman Müller (1878). See its introduction, pp. v–viii.

10. Hippolyte Delehaye, *Les origines du culte des martyrs*, vol. 20, *Subsidia hagiographica* (Brussels: Société des Bollandistes, 1912); and Paul-Albert Février, "Martyre et sainteté," in *Les fonctions des saints dans le monde occidental (IIIe–XIIIe siècle)*, Collection de l'École française de Rome (Rome: École française de Rome, 1991), 51–80.

11. Monika Rener, "Lateinische Hagiographie im deutschsprachigen Raum von 1200–1450," in *Hagiographies*, ed. Guy Philippart, *Corpus Christianorum* (Turnhout, Belgium: Brepols, 1994), vol. 1, 201–204; André Vauchez, *Sainthood in the Later Middle Ages*, trans. Jean Birell (New York: Cambridge University Press, 1997), 207–12, 336–54; and Donald Weinstein and Rudolph M. Bell, *Saints and Society: The Two Worlds of Western Christendom, 1000–1700* (Chicago: University of Chicago Press, 1982), 168–70, 197–99, 224–26.

12. See Rener, "Lateinische Hagiographie," Hagiogr. 1, 207–21.

13. For an overview of the earlier trends, now ended, see ibid., 219–33. Many of the bishop saints had in fact begun their careers as coenobites; as chapter one demonstrates, however, they were not venerated or written about as coenobites per se.

14. Petrus de Prussia, *Legenda venerabilis domini Alberti Magni;* and Rudolphus de Novimagio, *Legenda litteralis Alberti Magni.*

15. Trithemius wrote a "Life of Saint Macharius the Abbot." It has since been lost. Arnold, *Trithemius,* 149, 258. Trithemius's *On Illustrious Benedictines* consisted of chapters on individual coenobites drawn from the past, but veneration and canonization were not his goal. Johannes Trithemius, "De viris illustribus ordinis sancti Benedicti (1492)," in *Joannis Trithemii opera pia et spiritualia,* ed. Johannes Busaeus (1604–1605), 16–149. See Arnold, *Trithemius,* 22–55, 233.

16. An excellent overview of humanist poetry in honor of the saints can be found in the introduction of Roland Stieglecker, *Die Renaissance eines Heiligen: Sebastian Brant und Onuphrius eremita,* ed. Dieter Wuttke, vol. 37, *Gratia: Bamberger Schriften zur Renaissanceforschung* (Wiesbaden: Harrassowitz, 2001), 47–108.

17. Many of the fifteenth- and sixteenth-century sources can be found in the *Bruder Klaus* anthology edited by Durrer and Amschwand and abbreviate here BK. See chapter four.

18. Noel L. Brann, *The Abbot Trithemius (1462–1516): The Renaissance of Monastic Humanism,* vol. 24, *Studies in the History of Christian Thought* (Leiden, the Netherlands: Brill, 1981); Jacques Chomarat, "Erasme et le monachisme," in *Acta conventus neo-Latini Hafniensis,* ed. Ann Moss, Philip Dust et al. (Binghamton, N.Y.: Medieval and Renaissance Texts and Studies, 1994), 5–20; Kaspar Elm, "Monastische Reformen zwischen Humanismus und Reformation," in *900 Jahre Kloster Bursfelde,* ed. Lothar Perlitt (Göttingen: Vandenhoeck und Ruprecht, 1994), 59–111; Andreas Freitäger, "Klosterhumanismus," in *Das Jahrtausend der Mönche,* ed. Jan Gerchow and Reinhild Stephan-Maaser (Cologne: Wienand, 1999), 248–54; and Franz Machilek, "Klosterhumanismus in Nürnberg um 1500," *Mitteilungen des Vereins für Geschichte der Stadt Nürnberg* 64 (1977): 10–45.

19. Berndt Hamm, "Hieronymus-Begeisterung und Augustinismus vor der Reformation: Beobachtungen zur Beziehung zwischen Augustinismus und Frömmigkeitstheologie (am Beispiel Nürnbergs)," in *Augustine, the Harvest and Theology (1300–1650): Essays Dedicated to Heiko Augustinus Oberman in Honor of His Sixtieth Birthday,* ed. Kenneth Hagen (Leiden, the Netherlands: Brill, 1990), 127–236; Eugene F. Rice, *Saint Jerome in the Renaissance* (Baltimore: Johns Hopkins University Press,

1984), 84–136; and B. Vogler, "Erasmus and Saint Augustine or Influence of Saint Augustine on Humanism of Erasmus," *Annales* 31 (1976): 535–36.

20. *Secretum de contemptu mundi* (GW M31627, M31628, M31630), *De vita solitaria* (GW M3175210, M31754, M31765, M31766), and *De otio religioso*. See also K. A. E. Enenkel, "Die humanistische *vita activa/vita contemplativa* Diskussion: Francesco Petrarcas *De vita solitaria*," in *Acta conventus neo-Latini Hafniensis*, ed. Moss et al., 249–57; and Jürgen Geiß, *Zentren der Petrarca-Rezeption in Deutschland (um 1470–1525): Rezeptionsgeschichtliche Studien und Katalog der lateinischen Drucküberlieferung* (Wiesbaden: Ludwig Reichert, 2002), 407–13.

21. Geiß, *Zentren der Petrarca-Rezeption*, 83–84, 283–98.

22. Beat Matthias von Scarpatetti, "Heynlin, Johannes, de Lapide (von Stein)," *VL* 3 (1981): 1213–15.

23. Sigismund Meisterlin, "Apologia," Munich, Bayerische Staatsbibliothek, clm. 901, ff. 118–19.

24. "Non propria temeritate, optimi viri, illud negotium attempto: sed rogatu plurimorum maxime tamen quia sepius Babenberge ac ubique audivi irrisiones fieri de illa moderna simplici et notabiliter sibi contraria legenda rusticitatem quam sancto quam etiam nobis omnibus improperando." Ibid., clm. 901, f. 118r.

25. "Ne noter et plus errata faciam manifesta sed tacite declaro vel circumlocutionibus utor." Ibid.

26. "Modus autem publicandi saluo meliori iudicio is videtur, ut secreto modo imprimatur hec in numero certo proponantur post venales tam in latino quam in vulgari. Et una ponatur ad bibliothecam S. Sebaldi et S. Laurencij etc., una tacite in ecclesiam. Alie divulgentur non facta mencione de novitate vel auctore quia si per dominos doctores et aliquos peritos probata fuerit non de facili notari potest." Ibid., f. 118v.

27. "Translationem eius facerem ita quod unus in cancellaria emendaret ydioma meum. Noveritis etiam quod nec emendavi incongruitatem nec correxi eo quod prius iudicium dominorum expecto. Ergo rogo instantissime, ut nulli communicetur sed ut non perdatur labor meus ut corrigatur quo ad dicta et mihi remittatur. Eciam sciant quod certa mente teneo: de ista materia, que melius est silere quam prodere." Ibid., ff. 118v–19r.

28. "Me queso commendatum habete et facite nec istam appoleticam epistolam ad legendam scribite vel addite: sed Vulcano tradite." Ibid., 119r. Fortunately for posterity, neither the apologia nor the accompanying vita was handed over to Vulcan; they, along with the revision version datable to circa 1488, can be found in the Bavarian State Library in Munich.

29. Compare Meisterlin's "Loquatur materia historiam, non loquatur auctorem," with Sulpicius's "loquatur materiam, non loquatur auctorem."

30. The most significant writings about Saint Sebald circulating in the late fifteenth century were the following: (1) the thirteenth-century rhyming office *Nuremberg extolleris*, Nuremberg, Stadtbibliothek Nürnberg, cod. cent. VII, 43, ff. 246v–48r; and Munich, Bayerische Staatsbiliothek, clm. 692, 76r; clm. 27372, 155r–68r; (2) the late fourteenth-century vernacular legend *Es was ein kunek*, Nuremberg, Stadtbibliothek

Nürnberg, cod. Solger 37, 271v–77v; and Munich, Bayerische Staatsbibliothek, cgm. 409, 199r–206r; (3) its revision and translation into Latin for the canonization of 1425 *Si dominum* (BHL 7535), AASS, Aug. 3: 769–75; Nuremburg, Stadtbibliothek Nürnberg, cod. cent. III, 69, 62r–66v; Munich, Bayerische Staatsbibliothek, clm. 27372, 147r–54v; and (4) most importantly, since it was chained in the Sebalduskirche and thus accessible to the venerating public, a mid-fifteenth-century popularization by Henry Leubing, a priest of the Sebalduskirche, *Czu den zeiten*, Nuremberg, Landeskirchliches Archiv Nürnberg, Rep. 14, St. Sebald, nr. 465. For additional manuscripts and printed editions see Arno Borst, "Die Sebaldslegenden in der mittelalterlichen Geschichte Nürnbergs," *Jahrbuch für fränkische Landesforschung* 26 (1966): 36n65, 60n160, 171n205, and 191n255. See also Werner Williams-Krapp, "Deutschsprachige Hagiographie von ca. 1350 bis ca. 1550," in *Hagiographies*, ed. Guy Philippart, *Corpus Christianorum* (Turnhout, Belgium: Brepols, 1994), vol. 1, 277–82.

31. Borst, "Die Sebaldslegenden," 120–22.

32. Concerning the strong humanist sensibilities of Nuremberg's political and social elites, see Berndt Hamm, "Humanistische Ethik und Reichsstädtische Ehrbarkeit in Nürnberg," *Mitteilungen des Vereins für Geschichte der Stadt Nürnberg* 76 (1989): 66–68, 73–106; and Nine Miedema, "Die Nürnberger Humanisten und die *Germania Illustrata*: Tradition und Innovation im Bereich der Geographie um 1500," in *Tradition and Innovation in an Era of Change*, ed. Rudolf Suntrup and Jan R. Veenstra (Frankfurt: Peter Lang, 2001), 51–72.

33. Paul Fritz Joachimsen, *Die humanistische Geschichtschreibung in Deutschland: Die Anfänge, Sigismund Meisterlin* (Bonn: P. Hanstein, 1895).

34. Augsburg, Bischöfliche Ordinariatsbibliothek, cod. 50. See also Placidus Braun, *Notitia historico-literaria de codicibus manuscriptis in bibliotheca liberi ac imperialis monasterii ordinis s. Benedicti ad ss. Udalricum et Afram Augustae extantibus*, vol. 3 (1793), 54–70; and Joachimsen, *Die humanistische Geschichtschreibung*, 281–84. The *Liber miraculorum s. Simpert*, AASS, Oct. 6: 251–56. See also Katherina Colberg, "Meisterlin, Sigismund," VL 6 (1987): 356–66; RFHMA 7 (1997): 554–56; Nonnosus Bühler, *Die Schriftsteller und Schreiber des Benediktinerstiftes St. Ulrich und Afra in Augsburg während des Mittelalters* (Borna-Leipzig: Robert Noske, 1916), 44–64; Joachimsen, *Die humanistische Geschichtschreibung*, 23–26; and Dieter Weber, *Geschichtsschreibung in Augsburg: Hektor Mülich und die reichsstädtische Chronistik des Spätmittelalters*, ed. Wolfram Baer, vol. 30, *Abhandlungen zur Geschichte der Stadt Augsburg* (Augsburg: Hieronymus Mühlberger, 1984), 10–11, 16–45, 59–64, 85, 121, 154, 179, 220, 253.

35. Meisterlin, "Vita sancti Sebaldi alterior," Munich, Bayerische Staatsbibliothek, clm. 23877, ff. 182r–92r.

36. Another significant indicator of humanist participation in Saint Sebald's cult is the broadsheet bearing an image by Albrecht Dürer and a poem by Conrad Celtis (BHL 7536d).

37. "Cuius corpus mox ut pauperes potuerunt indomitis bobus grabato iunctis divino implorato favore absteactis frenis ad oppidum Neronperg ductum: quod sub castro imperiali dudum per romanos cesares ex electis fidelibusque colonis hinc inde

aggregatis constructum erat, cuiusque cives in subsidium ac auxilium officiali comiti prefati castri ac circumiacenti[s] provincie gubernatori ab imperatore associati fuere ut cum eorum consilio imperii negocia ibidem disponeret. Ita tamen ut merum dominium in cives et castrum romano pro tempore imperatori reservaretur. Ibidem boves in loco ubi eclesiola [sic] in honore principis apostolorum constructa erat fixerunt vestigia nec inde moveri potuerunt. Intellexerunt sagaces incole celitus eis destinatum futuus temporibus profuturum pateonum, qui suis tam meritis quam precibus vallaret tam melitum oppidum ipsius prope tutamine recepturus incrementum." Meisterlin, "Vita s. Sebaldi prior," clm. 901, ff. 131v–32r.

38. Borst, "Die Sebaldslegenden," 122–25.

39. "Sebaldus seriosus seu gravis valde vel pocius serens waldum quod est silvam nomen suum quod iuxta accidencia habuit decorans gravitate morum." Meisterlin, "Vita Sebaldi prior," clm. 901, f. 123r.

40. For example, drawing from his research on the history of Augsburg and the cult of Bishop Saint Simpert, Meisterlin wrote, "In quibus deo militabant ut Simpertus primo abbas deinde episcopus Augustensis nepos ex sorore Karoli filia Pipini monasterium Morbacense, neptis vero monasterium in Kitzingen et alia que longum et extra propositum est enarrare." Ibid., f. 124v. Or, revealing a typical humanist concern for the Roman origins of German society, he wrote, "Tiberius Cesar prenomine Claudius agnomine Nero quia de familia Neronorum civitatem condiderat ad ripas Danuby Vindelicia ubi terminatur et Baioariorum provincia ubi habitant attingit Noricorum fines ubi olim regnum contra cuius regem dimicavit et hybernias cum exercitu habuit donec eundem victum in provinciam redigeret. Ea civitas nunc Ratispona quasi in modum ratis dicitur vel a fluvio Regensburg. Ad hanc veniens post reditum ex Ytalia sanctus Sebaldus relictis iam suis sociis, quibus incumbebat officium predicandi ac dispensandi sacramenta dei." Ibid., ff. 128v–29r; Borst, "Die Sebaldslegenden," 122–25; and Joachimsen, Die humanistische Geschichtschreibung, 143–52. We have already seen geographical and historical elaborations within the saints' lives in the previous chapter. This kind of alteration is the primary focus of the next chapter.

41. Borst, "Die Sebaldslegenden," 122–25; Joachimsen, Die humanistische Geschichtschreibung, 143–52; and James Michael Weiss, "Hagiography by German Humanists, 1483–1516," Journal of Medieval and Renaissance Studies 15 (1985): 301–304.

42. On the debate over hermits in fifteenth-century Germany, particularly the case of Johannes Frankfurter, see Wilhelm Baum, "Johannes Frankenfurter, ein Tiroler 'Aussteiger' im 15. Jahrhundert: Die Eremiten im Halltal zwischen Meister Eckhart und Nikolaus Cusanus," Tiroler Heimatblätter 62 (1987): 11–15; Karl Bosl, "Eremus: Begriffsgeschichtliche Bemerkungen zum historischen Problem der Entfremdung und Vereinsamung des Menschen," in Polychordia, ed. Peter Wirth (Amsterdam: Adolf M. Hakkert, 1967), 73; Otmar Doerr, Das Institut der Inclusen in Süddeutschland, ed. Ildefons Herwegen, vol. 18, Beiträge zur Geschichte des alten Mönchtums und des Benediktinerordens (Münster: Aschendorffsche Verlagsbuchhandlung, 1934), 11–21; Eugen Gruber, "Beginen und Eremiten der Innerschweiz," in Festschrift Oskar Vasella (Freiburg, Switzerland: Universitätsverlag, 1964), 79–106;

Hermann Grundmann, "Deutsche Eremiten, Einsiedler und Klausner im Hochmittelalter," *Archiv für Kulturgeschichte* 45 (1963): 60–73; Hermann Hallauer, "Johannes Frankfurter und die Waldbrüderstatuten des Nikolaus von Kues," in *Cusanus Gedächtnisschrift*, ed. Nikolaus Grass (Innsbruck: Universitätsverlag Wagner, 1970), 375–79; Philipp Hofmeister, "Eremiten in Deutschland," in *Wahrheit und Verkündigung: Michael Schmaus zum 70. Geburtstag*, ed. Leo Scheffczyk, Werner Dettloff et al. (Paderborn, Germany: Ferdinand Schöningh, 1967), 1191–1214; Edgar Mills, *Die Geschichte der Einsiedlergestalt vom mittelalterlichen Epos über Barock und Empfindsamkeit bis zum Roman der Romantik* (Vienna: Europäischer Verlag, 1968), 17–29; Ralph Weinbrenner, *Klosterreform im 15. Jahrhundert zwischen Ideal und Praxis: Der Augustinereremit Andreas Proles (1429–1503) und die privilegierte Observanz*, ed. Heiko A. Oberman, vol. 7, *Spätmittelalter und Reformation* (Tübingen: J. C. B. Mohr [Paul Siebeck], 1996); and Hellmut Zschoch, *Klosterreform und monastische Spiritualität im 15. Jahrhundert: Conrad von Zenn, OESA († 1460) u. sein Liber de vita monastica*, ed. Johannes Wallmann, vol. 75, *Beiträge zur historischen Theologie* (Tübingen: J. C. B. Mohr [Paul Siebeck], 1988).

43. Borst, "Die Sebaldslegenden," 122–25.

44. Meisterlin, "Vita s. Sebaldi alt.," clm. 23877, ff. 182r–192r.

45. "Denique apostolus Germanie Bonifacius archiepiscopatum Wangionensem, que modo Wormacia, in Moguntiam transferens, quatuor archiepiscopales sedes fecit in Germania, inter quos et primatem constituit, videlicet in Moguntia primam, secundam in Agripina, que modo Colonia, terciam in Treveris, quartam in Iuvaro que modo ut diximus Salzburg. Primatem vero voluit esse Mogontiacensem. Hijs prefecit peregrinos in terra, ut nos facet cives celi et domesticos dei. Inclusum fuit tunc in limitibus et in finibus Wirczeburgensis diocesis Neronbergense oppidum, tunc quoque ob imperialis promunctorii fidumque asilum Romanis apice famosum. Ut fundamentum ponamus cum sanctus noster Sebaldus parentum natalisque soli spreverit dulcedinem ut sequentia declarabunt." Ibid., f. 183r.

46. "Que Belgica est pars Gallie unde mater eius de stemate regali.... Sewaldus regalis proles Dacorum regis qui olim Dani dicti matre vero stirpe regum Francie sub temporibus Pipini regis natus extitit.... Quo factum est ut multo studio quesita sibi regalis desponsaretur alto Francorum de regibus virgo sanguine exorta, duplicique ex linea paterno ac materno stemate inclitus adolescens nupcys proleque beandus estimaretur, non quod ea laudanda sint in habentibus sed quod earum contemptus rerum in renunciantibus predicandus." Ibid., f. 188v.

47. Albert Büchi, *Albrecht von Bonstetten: Ein Beitrag zur Geschichte des Humanismus in der Schweiz* (Frauenfeld, Switzerland: J. Huber, 1889); Albert Büchi, "Vorwort," in *Albrecht von Bonstetten: Briefe und ausgewählte Schriften*, ed. Albert Büchi (1893), i–xi; Richard Feller and Edgar Bonjour, *Geschichtsschreibung der Schweiz vom Spätmittelalter zur Neuzeit*, 2d ed., 2 vols. (Basel: Helbing und Lichtenhahn, 1979), vol. 1, 81–83; Gall Morel, "Albert von Bonstetten," *Der Geschichtsfreund* 3 (1846): 3–39; Rudolf Pfister, *Kirchengeschichte der Schweiz* (Zurich: Zwingli, 1964), 404; Joachim Salzgeber, "Albrecht von Bonstetten, ein bedeutender Humanist, Geograph und Genealog," in *775–1975: Neue Beiträge zur Geschichte von Uster* (Uster, Switzerland:

Eugen Weilenmann, 1976), 33–38; and Paulus Volk, "Bonstetten (Albert de), doyen d'Einsiedeln," DHGE 9 (1937): 1111–12.

48. Albrecht von Bonstetten, "Germanica praelia Karoli quondam Burgundiae ducis et finis ejus," *Archiv für Schweizerische Geschichte* 13 (1862): 283–98; Albrecht von Bonstetten, "Historia domus Austrie," in *Geschichte der ganzen österreichischen, weltlichen, und klösterlichen Klerisey,* ed. M. Fidler (Vienna, 1782), 90–180 (partial edition); and Albrecht von Bonstetten, "Superioris Germanie confederacionis descriptio," *Mittheilungen der antiquarischen Gesellschaft Zürich* 3 (1846–1847): 93–105.

49. Albrecht von Bonstetten, "Provisio vacantis ducatus Burgundie," *Archiv für Schweizerische Geschichte* 13 (1862): 319–24.

50. St. Gallen, Stiftsbibliothek, cod. lat. 719, ff. 173–280, and cod. lat. 1428. Editions of many letters can be found in Albrecht von Bonstetten, *Briefe und ausgewählte Schriften,* ed. Albert Büchi (Basel: Adolf Geering, 1893); Morel, "Albert von Bonstetten," 15, 40; and Jean-François-Nicolas Richard, *Histoire des diocèses de Besançon et de St. Claude,* 2 vols. (Besançon, France: Cornu, 1847–1851), vol. 2, 166.

51. "Passio s. Meginradi," BHL 5878. In Latin: Paris, Bibliothèque Nationale de France, ms. 5656, ff. 32r–42r. In German: "Dis ist die legende von unser frawen cappelle zu den einsidlen wie sie gewicht ward und von sant Meinratsz leben," Nuremberg, Staatsarchiv Nürnberg, Reichstadt Nürnberg, Ratskanzlei, A-Laden 142, nr. 16 (Rep. 15a) (Film S3484). Also, including a poem by Sebastian Brant, *Passio sancti Meinradi.* See GW M29712 and M29714.

52. BHL 1204. "Oratio b. Bernhardi," Odilo Ringholz, *Der selige Markgraf Bernhard von Baden in seinem Leben und seiner Verehrung* (Freiburg im Breisgau, Germany: Herder'sche, 1892), 156–84.

53. GW 4920. Albrecht von Bonstetten, *Septem horae canonicae virgineae matris Mariae* (Freiburg: Friedrich Riederer, 1493).

54. "Varia de origine, indulgentiis, rebus et gestis insignis monasterii dive Marie loci heremitarum," Paris, Bibliothèque Nationale de France, ms. lat. 5656. Albrecht von Bonstetten, *Chronik von der Stiftung des Gotteshauses Unserer Lieben Frau zu Einsiedeln* (Ulm: Johann Reger, 1494). See also GW 4919.

55. BHL 4148 and 4149. Regarding the relationships between texts and manuscripts, see Leo M. Kern, "Die Ida von Toggenburg-Legende," *Thurgauische Beiträge zur vaterländischen Geschichte* 64/65 (1928): 1–136; Bruno Meyer, "Die heilige Ita von Fischingen," *Thurgauische Beiträge zur vaterländischen Geschichte* 112 (1976): 23–29, 77–89; Pius Rimensberger, "Hl. Idda (von Toggenburg) in Fischingen vor einem erweiterten Horizont: Ein essayistischer und historiographischer Beitrag," in *Barockes Fischingen,* ed. Hans Peter Mathis (Fischingen, Switzerland: Verein St. Iddazell, 1991), 129–94; and Werner Williams-Krapp, "Die deutsche Ida-Legende des schweizerischen Humanisten Albrecht von Bonstetten," *Zeitschrift für die Geschichte des Oberrheins* 130 (1982): 71–80.

56. "Nuper a me valde expetisti, venerabilis pater, ut vitam divae Iddae, illustris quondam comitissae Togkenburgensis, tui monasterii beatissimae incolae, ex obsoleta lingua Germanica Latine redderem." Einsiedeln A.n.D.85, cist. 7 (1580) (lost between 1928 [Kern] and 1976 [Meyer]); and Frauenfeld Kantonsbibliothek Y 68 (1701), Y 68a

(1704); Albrecht von Bonstetten, "Vita divae Iddae ex antiquis codicibus descripta (1481)," *Thurgauische Beiträge zur vaterländischen Geschichte* 64/65 (1928). In the later edition this line is altered slightly: "Oratum me apprime nuper fecisti, abba pater, super legendam beate Ite, inclite olim comitisse Toggenburgensis, cenobii tui felicis incole atque matrone, ut eam ex materna nostra lingua in Latinam converterem." Frauenfeld, StATh, Schachtelsignatur 7' 41' 102; Fulda, Hessische Landesbibliothek, cod. Aa96 (pre-1496); AASS, Nov. 3: 120–25; Albrecht von Bonstetten, "Legenda beate Ite comitisse in Toggenburg (1485)," *Thurgauische Beiträge zur vaterländischen Geschichte* 112 (1976). The German life in question is "Von der wirdigen frowen sanct Yta leben," St. Gallen, Stiftsbibliothek 603: "Von der wirdigen frowen sanct Yta leben (1470)," *Thurgauische Beiträge zur vaterländischen Geschichte* 64/65 (1928): 62–83. See Williams-Krapp, "Die deutsche Ida-Legende," 71–80.

57. "Translationem haut de verbo ad verbum, sed e sensu ad sententiam, ut absque macrologio et longa ambigine fieri debet." Albrecht von Bonstetten, "Legenda beate Ite (1485)," *Thurgauische Beiträge zur vaterländischen Geschichte* 64/65 (1928): 61. "Currente quidem calamo, non reddens verbum verbo, sed sensum, ne prolixior fieret sermo." Bonstetten, "Vita Iddae (1481)," 61.

58. "Verum tamen nolui tibi, pater, adversari, sed potius voluntati tuae gerere morem. Nec rem Hebraica, Graeca et Latina lingua dignam diu differendam esse duxi. Verti igitur in Latinum pro viribus, quantum potui." Ibid. "Nolui tamen tibi, pater, adversari, sed morem gerere voluntatitue, nec rem ipsam tum Hebraicis, Grecis, tum Latinis dignam in amplum differe. Bonstetten, "Legenda Ite (1485)," 61. It is unlikely that Bonstetten knew Hebrew at all. Büchi, *Albrecht von Bonstetten*, 29.

59. "Faxit deus, ut opera mea aliquid supernae suavitatis inspirem legentibus atque ex hoc pyrite eliciam aliquem devotionis ignem accendamque! Jam tibi mitto hanc vitam, ac rem tibi pergratam dono offero, ut acceptum habeas meum obsequium rogans." Bonstetten, "Vita Iddae (1481)," 61. "Propter gloriam divi nominis eius et tua in me merita exuberantissima, quoad potui, quam prepropere effeci. Utinam lectituris cum ea dulcedinem mellifluam instillare possem ex illoque ignili nostro excutere aliquam devotionis scintillam! Hanc ad te nunc mitto atque dono do tamquam materiam tibi conducibilem; tuum sit placite eam capessere." Bonstetten, "Legenda Ite (1485)," 61.

60. Karl Kuhn, *Thurgovia Sacra*, 3 vols. (Frauenfeld, Switzerland: Gromann, 1876), vol. 2. 15–23; Bruno Meyer, "Fischingen," in *Helvetia Sacra: Die Orden mit Beneditinerregel*, ed. Elsanne Gilomen-Schenkel (Bern: Francke, 1986), 693–95; Meyer, "Die heilige Ita von Fischingen," 77–89; and Rimensberger, "Hl. Idda," 158–67.

61. Wilhelm Ehrenzeller, *Kloster und Stadt St. Gallen im Spätmittelalter* (St. Gallen, Switzerland, 1931), 369–436; Kuhn, *Thurgovia Sacra*, 3–16, 24–48; Meyer, "Fischingen," 672–78, 693–95; and Rimensberger, "Hl. Idda," 149–50.

62. Meyer, "Die heilige Ita von Fischingen," 77–89. See also Kern, "Die Ida von Toggenburg-Legende," 1–23; Kuhn, *Thurgovia Sacra*, 15–23; and Rimensberger, "Hl. Idda," 139–46.

63. Genevieve has fascinated authors into modern times: Robert Schumann and Jacques Offenbach both composed operas in the mid-nineteenth century out of her legend. Readers are likely familiar with the melody of at least one aria from Offenbach's *opéra bouffe*: The melody of the Marines' Hymn, "From the Halls of Montezuma," originally accompanied a duet of two gendarmes in his *Genevieve de Brabant* (1859).

64. BHL 5394. G. Kentenich, *Die Genovefalegende: Ihre Entstehung und ihr ältester datierter Text* (Trier, Germany: Jacob Lintz, 1926), 27–51. See René de Cériziers, *L'innocence reconnue ou la Vie de Ste Geneviève de Brabant* (Paris, 1634). See also BSS 6: 156–57; R. Aubert, "Geneviève de Brabant, héroïne légendaire qui fut l'objet d'un culte populaire en Rhénanie," DHGE 20 (1984): 454–55; Felix Brüll, "Die Legende von der Pfalzgräfin Genovefa nach dem noch ungedruckten, bisher verschollenen Texte des Johannes Seinius," in *Jahresbericht des Gymnasiums zu Prüm für 1898/1899* (Prüm, Germany: M. J. Goergen, 1899), 1–21; Maurice Coens, "Geneviève de Brabant, une sainte?: Le terroir de sa légende," in *Recueil d'Études bollandiennes, Subsidia hagiographica* (Brussels: Société des Bollandistes, 1963), 101–18; Franz Görres, "Neue Forschungen zur Genovefa-Sage: Beiträge zur Kirchen- und Kulturgeschichte des Rheinlandes," *Annalen des Historischen Vereins für den Niederrhein* 66 (1898): 1–39; G. Kentenich, "Die Genovefalegende," *Trier'scher Volksfreund*, Jan. 31, 1927, 1; and Heinrich Sauerborn, *Geschichte der Pfalzgräfin Genovefa und der Kapelle Frauenkirchen* (Regensburg: G. Joseph Manz, 1856).

65. Hippolyte Delehaye, "La légende de la bienheureuse Ida de Toggenburg," *Nova et Vetera* 4 (1929): 359–65.

66. "Wir lesent von der hailgen frowen sancta Yta, daz sy waz ain gräffin von Kirchberg in Schwaben und ward gemächlet ainem graffen, der was gesessen uff der alten Toggenburg. Der mächlet ir ainen ring, der was guldin, als es gewonlich ist under grossen heren." "Von Yta leben (1470)," 62.

"Beata igitur Idda e stirpe nobili comitum Kirchbergensium prognata, quorum dicio, genus et nomen maximis adhuc apud Suevos claret honoribus. Quae matrimonio erat coniuncta comiti nomine Henrico ex Toggenburg, qui admodum celsam beneque munitam habitabat arcem silvis monasterii Vischingensis circumseptam sitamque in apicibus montium, qui fluvium ex Turthal provenientem in duas dividunt partes. Acceperat autem ab Heinrico annulum pronubum ex auro Arabico constantem, ut illi pro lege coniugali vellet esse fidelis." Bonstetten, "Vita Iddae (1481)," 62.

67. "Von Yta leben (1470)," 72; Bonstetten, "Vita Iddae (1481)," 72.

68. "Von Yta leben (1470)," 74; Bonstetten, "Vita Iddae (1481)," 74.

69. For example, "Von Yta leben (1470)," 82; and Bonstetten, "Vita Iddae (1481)," 82.

70. Williams-Krapp, "Die deutsche Ida-Legende," 71–80.

71. Bonstetten, "Legenda beate Ite (1485)," 66; Bonstetten, "Vita Iddae (1481)," 70.

72. Agricola, *Almi Beati vita*.

73. "She asked that her hut be built at the foot of the mountain called Hürnli next to the chapel dedicated to the Blessed Virgin Mary" (1481). "I choose a place next to the basilica whose patron is the Virgin Mother in the meadows of the Augia, through which the mountain commonly called Hürenli is climbed. There I wish to live in the

house of the Lord" (1485). Bonstetten, "Legenda beate Ite (1485)," 68; Bonstetten, "Vita Iddae (1481)," 74. See also Meyer, "Die heilige Ita von Fischingen," 26.

74. These dates were given by Bonstetten only in their liturgical form in the earlier vita *(ad diem omnium animarum ferias consequentem)*, but in the later vita the classical form is added (III nonas Novembres, hoc est die proxima post animarum omnium commemorationem), a notable combination of his various revisory interests; Bonstetten, "Legenda beate Ite (1485)," 70; Bonstetten, "Vita Iddae (1481)," 80.

75. Bonstetten, "Legenda beate Ite (1485)," 70.

76. Meyer, "Die heilige Ita von Fischingen," 26–27, 34–35.

77. VD16 C757. Petrus Canisius, *Kurtze beschreibung der Gottseligen Frauwen Sanct Yta Gräfin von Kirchberg* (Fribourg, Switzerland: Abraham Gemperlin, 1590). Petrus Canisius, *I fioretti di santa Ida di Fischingen*, ed. Roberto Busa, trans. Ilsemarie Brandmair Dallera (1996).

78. Peter Brown, *The Cult of the Saints: Its Rise and Function in Latin Christianity* (Chicago: University of Chicago Press, 1981), 1–22.

79. A work that neatly summarizes the elements that created these "humanist circles" in the German territories is "From Outsiders to Insiders: Some Reflections on the Development of a Group Identity of the German Humanists between 1450 and 1530," by Eckhard Bernstein, in *In laudem Caroli*, ed. James V. Mehl (Kirksville, Mo.: Thomas Jefferson Press, 1998), 45–64.

CHAPTER 3

1. GW M33835. Pius II [Aeneas Silvius Piccolomini], *De ritu, situ, moribus et conditione Teutoniae descriptio* (Cologne: Wolfgang Stöckel, 1496). Evaluation of Aeneas Silvius's influence in the appropriation of humanism into German learned culture and his inspiration to patriotic humanism continues to be a much researched topic. Johannes Helmrath, "*Vestigia Aeneae imitari:* Enea Silvio Piccolomini als 'Apostel' des Humanismus—Formen und Wege seiner Diffusion," in *Diffusion des Humanismus*, ed. Johannes Helmrath, Ulrich Muhlack et al. (Göttingen: Wallstein, 2002), 99–141; Ludwig Krapf, *Germanenmythos und Reichsideologie: Frühhumanistische Rezeptionsweisen der taciteischen 'Germania'* (Tübingen: Max Niemeyer, 1979), 50–53; Jacques Ridé, *L'image du Germain dans la pensée et la littérature allemandes de la redécouverte de Tacite à la fin du XVIème siècle: Contribution à l'étude de la genèse d'un mythe* (Paris: H. Champion, 1977), 115–29; Adolf Schmidt, ed., *Aeneas Silvius, "Germania" und Jakob Wimpfeling, "Responsa et replicae ad Eneam Silvium"* (Cologne: Böhlau, 1962), 3–7; and Klaus Voigt, *Italienische Berichte aus dem spätmittelalterlichen Deutschland von Francesco Petrarca zu Andrea de' Franceschi (1333–1492)*, ed. Horst Braunert, Karl Dietrich Erdmann et al., vol. 17, *Kieler Historische Studien* (Stuttgart: Ernst Klett, 1973), 2–23.

2. "*Amplior est vestra natio quam umquam!*" Pius II [Aeneas Silvius Piccolomini], *Germania*, ed. Schmidt, 6.

3. Donald R. Kelley, "'*Tacitus noster*': The *Germania* in the Renaissance and Reformation," in *Tacitus and the Tacitean Tradition*, ed. T. J. Luce and A. J. Woodman

(Princeton, N.J.: Princeton University Press, 1993), 152–67; Ulrich Muhlack, "Die *Germania* im deutschen Nationalbewußtsein vor dem 19. Jahrhundert," in *Beiträge zum Verständniss der Germania des Tacitus*, ed. Herbert Jankuhn and Donald Timpe (Göttingen: Vandenhoeck und Ruprecht, 1989), 128–30; L. D. Reynolds, ed., *Texts and Transmission: A Survey of the Latin Classics* (Oxford: Clarendon, 1983), 410–11; and Ridé, *L'image du Germain*, 165–91.

4. Ulrich Muhlack, "Das Projekt der *Germania Illustrata:* Ein Paradigma der Diffusion des Humanismus?," in *Diffusion des Humanismus*, ed. Helmrath et al., 141.

5. In particular, see Jeffrey White's introduction in the newest critical edition and translation of the *Italia Illustrata*, issued by the I Tatti Renaissance Library: Flavio Biondo, *Italy Illuminated*, ed. and trans. Jeffrey A. White (Cambridge, Mass.: Harvard University Press, 2005). See also Ottavio Clavuot, "Flavio Biondos *Italia Illustrata:* Porträt und historisch-geographische Legitimation der humanistischen Elite Italiens," in *Diffusion des Humanismus*, ed. Helmrath et al., 56–57, 75–76.

6. Conrad Celtis, *Oratio in Gymnasio in Ingelstadio publice recitata, cum carminibus ad Orationem pertinentibus*, ed. Hans Rupprich, *Bibliotheca scriptorum medii recentisque aevorum saec. XV–XVI* (Leipzig: Teubner,1932). See GW 6466.

7. Eckhard Bernstein, *German Humanism* (Boston: Twayne, 1983), 65–66; Clavuot, "Flavio Biondos *Italia Illustrata*," 55–76; Nine Miedema, "Die Nürnberger Humanisten und die *Germania Illustrata:* Tradition und Innovation im Bereich der Geographie um 1500," in *Tradition and Innovation in an Era of Change*, ed. Rudolf Suntrup and Jan R. Veenstra (Frankfurt: Peter Lang, 2001), 51–72; and Ridé, *L'image du Germain*, 215–23.

8. VD16 H5278. Conrad Celtis, ed., *Opera Hrosvite, illustris virginis et monialis Germane, gente Saxonico orte* (Nuremberg: Sodalitas Celtica, 1501).

9. Bernstein, *German Humanism*, 65–66; Paul Fritz Joachimsen, *Die humanistische Geschichtschreibung in Deutschland: Die Anfänge, Sigismund Meisterlin* (Bonn: P. Hanstein's Verlag, 1895), 279–300; Peter Johanek, "Weltchronistik und regionale Geschichtsschreibung im Spätmittelalter," in *Geschichtsschreibung und Geschichtsbewußtsein im späten Mittelalter*, ed. Hans Patze, *Vorträge und Forschungen* (Sigmaringen, Germany: Thorbecke, 1987), 287–330; Dieter Mertens, "Schlußbemerkungen," in *Deutsche Landesgeschichtsschreibung*, ed. Franz Brendle, Dieter Mertens et al. (Stuttgart: Steiner, 2001), 279–81; Ulrich Muhlack, "Die humanistische Historiographie: Umfang, Bedeutung, Probleme," in ibid., 3–18; Muhlack, "Das Projekt," 142–58; Ridé, *L'image du Germain*, 223–229; Jacques Ridé, "Un grand projet patriotique: 'Germania Illustrata,'" in *L'humanisme allemand, 1480–1540* (Paris: J. Vrin, 1979), 99–113; Reinhard Stauber, "Hartmann Schedel, der Nürnberger Humanistenkreis und die 'Erweiterung der deutschen Nation,'" in *Diffusion des Humanismus*, ed. Helmrath et al., 159–87; and Gerald Strauss, *Sixteenth-century Germany: Its Topography and Topographers* (Madison: University of Wisconsin Press, 1959), 8.

10. In modern scholarship the term "historical topography" has been more commonly employed. "Chorography," however, was the term familiar to medieval and early modern writers and is favored here. Patrick Gautier Dalché, "Limite, frontière et organisation de l'espace dans la géographie et la cartographie de la fin du Moyen

Age," in *Grenzen und Raumvorstellungen (11.–20. Jh.)/Frontières et conceptions de l'espace (11ᵉ–20ᵉ siècles)*, ed. Guy P. Marchal (Zurich: Chronos, 1996), 93–122; Christian Halm and Jan Hirschbiegel, "Reiseberichte, ethnographische und geographische Schriften," in *Aufriß der Historischen Wissenschaften*, ed. Michael Maurer (Stuttgart: Philipp Reclam jun., 2002), 215–38; Frank Lestringant, "Chorographie et paysage à la Renaissance," in *Le Paysage à la Renaissance*, ed. Yves Giraud (Fribourg: Eds. Universitaires, 1988), 9–26; and Strauss, *Sixteenth-century Germany*, 6–18, 49.

11. In Greek the word χωρογραφία can, for example, be found in Polybius (203–120 B.C.), *Histories*, 34.1.5, and in Strabo (63 B.C.–A.D. 24), *Geography*, 8.3.17. In Latin, Publius Terrentius Varro (82–36 B.C.) authored a poem with the title "Chorographia," and Cicero (106–43 B.C.) wrote a work titled "De Chorographia," now lost.

12. Tamsyn Barton, *Ancient Astrology*, *Sciences of Antiquity* (London: Routledge, 1994), 179–85.

13. Ptolemy, *Geographia nova*, 1.1. See also J. A. May, "The Geographical Interpretation of Ptolemy in the Renaissance," *Tijdschrift voor Economische en Sociale Geografie* 73 (1982): 350–52; Dieter Mertens, "Landeschronistik im Zeitalter des Humanismus und ihre spätmittelalterlichen Wurzeln," in *Deutsche Landesgeschichtsschreibung*, ed. Brendle et al., 19; Mertens, "Schlußbemerkungen," 280–81; and Strauss, *Sixteenth-century Germany*, 49, 55.

14. Farmer offers a splendid example in Saint Martin's cult in medieval Tours. Sharon A. Farmer, *Communities of Saint Martin: Legend and Ritual in Medieval Tours* (Ithaca, N.Y.: Cornell University Press, 1991).

15. VD16 B5746. Petrus Blomevenna, *Vita sancti Brunonis* (Cologne: St. Barbara Charterhouse, 1516). The Bollandists relied for their edition on Surius, whose version diverges at points from the text printed in 1516; the AASS also does not include the prologue. AASS, Oct. 2: 724–36. See Gérald Chaix, "La gloire de Dieu, l'honneur de Bruno et la sainteté de Cologne: Les tâches de la Chartreuse Sainte Barbe," in *Die Kölner Kartause um 1500: Aufsatzband*, ed. Werner Schäfke (Cologne: Kölnisches Stadtmuseum, 1991), 273; Gérald Chaix, *Reforme et Contre-reforme catholiques: Recherches sur la Chartreuse de Cologne au XVIᵉ siècle*, ed. James Hogg, vol. 80, *Analecta Cartusiana* (Salzburg: Institut für Anglistik und Amerikanistik, 1981), 149; and James Hogg, "Petrus Blomevenna: *Vita sancti Brunonis* and *Sermo de sancto Brunone*," *Analecta Cartusiana* 130 (1995): 1–2.

16. GW V, 573. Franciscus Puteus, *Vita beati Brunonis primi institutoris ordinis Carthusiensium* (Basel: Johann Froben, 1515). Jodocus Badius included the vita in the *Opera et Vita sancti Brunonis*, published in Paris in 1524. AASS, Oct. 2: 707–24.

17. BHL 1467. "Vita Antiquior auct. Primorum quinque Cartusiae Priorum chronologo anonymo," AASS, Oct. 3: 703–707.

18. BSS 3: 561–77. The contribution of Heinrich Scheve (also known as Scheveus, Scaevius, Scheeve, and Schaefe) to this resurgent interest in Bruno has been overlooked in all recent bibliographic and source studies of the cult: Henricus Scheveus, *In divi Brunonis primi Carthusianae religionis fundatoris ac patroni, montisque Carthusiae praeconium* (Cologne, 1519).

19. Alain Girard, "Les premières images de saint Bruno," *Analecta Cartusiana* 192 (2004): 47–62; and Ulrike Mader, "Heiligenverehrung als Ordenspropaganda: Zur Interpretation eines Bilderzyklus aus der Kölner Kartause," in *Die Kölner Kartause: Aufsatzband,* 275–76.

20. Mary Alvarita Rajewski, "Sebastian Brant: Studies in Religious Aspects of His Life and Works with Special Reference to the 'Varia Carmina' " (PhD diss., Catholic University of America, 1944), 238–240; and Roland Stieglecker, *Die Renaissance eines Heiligen: Sebastian Brant und Onuphrius eremita,* ed. Dieter Wuttke, vol. 37, *Gratia: Bamberger Schriften zur Renaissanceforschung* (Wiesbaden: Harrassowitz, 2001), 417–39.

21. Chaix, "La gloire de Dieu," 272–73; Chaix, *Reforme,* 147–51; Hogg, "Petrus Blomevenna," 1–2; Gerardo Posado, ed., *Der heilige Bruno, Vater der Kartäuser: Ein Sohn der Stadt Köln* (Cologne: Wienand, 1987); Rita Wagner, "Eine kleine Geschichte der Kölner Kartause St. Barbara," in *Die Kölner Kartause um 1500: Eine Reise in unsere Vergangenheit,* ed. Rita Wagner and Ulrich Bock (Cologne: Kölnisches Stadtmuseum, 1991), 12; and Adam Wienand, "Der heilige Bruno und seine Vaterstadt," in *Der heilige Bruno, Vater der Kartäuser,* ed. Posado, 15–18.

22. Jodocus Badius Ascencius (Josse Bade, 1462–1535) is likewise a humanist who cannot be neatly categorized if the best humanism indeed drew humanists ineluctably toward Protestantism. His failure to adopt religious reforms that rejected Roman primacy has led recent studies torturously to label him "conservative" and "medieval." E.g. Mark L. Crane, "A Conservative Voice in the French Renaissance: Josse Bade (1462–1535)" (PhD diss., University of Toronto, 2005); and Isaac Meir Gewirtz, "The Prefaces of Badius Ascensius: The Humanist Printer as Arbiter of French Humanism and the Medieval Tradition in France (Jocodus Badius Ascensius)" (PhD diss., Columbia University, 2003).

23. James Hogg has edited much relevant primary material and incorporated it into an article. See James Hogg, "The Memory of Saint Bruno and the Recovery of the Charterhouse of Serra San Bruno," in *San Bruno di Colonia,* ed. Pietro de Leo (Soveria Mannelli, Italy: Rubbettino, 2004), 71–106. See also Gérald Chaix, "L'hagiographie de Bruno à travers les vies composées dans les chartreuses allemandes au tournant du XVIe siècle," *Analecta Cartusiana* 189 (2003): 189–95; and Pierrette Pavary, "Dom François Du Puy, biographe de saint Bruno à l'aube du XVIe siècle," *Analecta Cartusiana* 192 (2004): 19–30.

24. Franciscus Puteus, "Vita b. Brunonis." AASS, Oct. 2: 708–709.

25. "Beatus Bruno sacri carthusiensis ordinis initiator, natione teutonicus ex insigni civitate Colonia (que antiquitus Agrippina a Marco Agrippa genero Octaviani dicebatur) de parentibus tam genere, quoque virtute claris duxit originem." Blomevenna, *Vita sancti Brunonis,* A-iii-r.

26. "De his ortus est beatus Bruno ex parte patris ex parte vero matris sanguinem traxit de tribu nobili romanorum de parva cogitatione nuncupata, ex familia que postmodum de rubro stessen dicta est. Huius a cunabulis mater sapientia lactabat infantiam, et semper in profectu etatis proficere ad meliora edocuit, hic est, dum puer esset nihil puerile gessit in opere, sed quasi future religionis speciem ostentans

plurium monachorum institutor a domino parabat. Sortitus est autem a domino animam bonam, laudabilem indolem, ingenium docilem, memoriam tenacem." Ibid., A-iii-r–A-iii-v.

27. "Quia vero sanctus Bruno natione coloniensis fuit prefatus dominus Matheus restituaverat portionem parvam de eodem capite pro priore domus Colonie eique in presentia reverendi patris maioris Carthusie donavit plurimum gaudenti et devotione magna suscipienti anno 1516. . . .

"Montibus siquidem artum satis, et cinctum nemoribus eiusdem vallis extrema claudentibus de viis et solitariis, nec ultra aditum humano usui prebentibus. Supra isto antrum edificatum est haud grande sacullum cum altari sub titulo sancti Brunonis coloniensis, magistri eremi sancte marie de turris ordinis carthusiensis institutoris primi cuius ibi imago depicta cernitur." Ibid., I-iii-r–I-iii-v.

28. "Ex insigni civitate Colonia (que antiquitus agrippina a Marco Agrippa genero Octaviani dicebatur) de parentibus tam genere quoque virtute claris duxit originem. Imperator quippe Traianus et senatus romanorum nobiles illuc olim romanos pro incolatu civitatis terreque custodia direxerant, quibus matrimonialiter vicini nobiles coniungebantur. Ex quibus una tribus dicta fuit de sapientibus, ex romanis vero una appellabatur de duro pungno." Ibid., A-iii-r.

29. VD16 B5756. Petrus Blomevenna, *Sermo de sancto Brunone* (Cologne: St. Barbara Charterhouse, 1516).

30. For example, "Religio enim virtus moralis, utitur omnibus virtutibus ad cultum divinum tanque actibus imperatis testatur sanctus Thomas." Blomevenna, *Sermo de sancto Brunone*, c-ii-r.

31. The chapter numeration in these notes are taken from my critical edition of the two extant manuscripts (Lippetal-Herzfeld, Pfarrgemiende–St.-Ida, Pfarrarchiv and Münster, Nordrhein-Westfälisches Staatsarchiv, Altertumsverein Münster [Dep.], ms. 356, pp. 14–25): David Collins, "Renaissance Revisions: A Brief Analysis and Critical Edition of Cincinnius's *Vita s. Ida*, a Revision of BHL 4143," *Analecta bollandiana* 124 (2006): 343-358.

32. *Annales regni Francorum*, MGH SRG 6, years 775, 776, 779, 780, 783.

33. Wilhelm Diekamp, ed., *Die Vitae sancti Liudgeri*, vol. 4, *Die Geschichtsquellen des Bisthums Münster* (Münster: Theissing'schen Buchhandlung, 1881); and Eberhard Kaus, "Zu den Liudger-Viten des 9. Jahrhunderts," *Westfälische Zeitschrift* 142 (1992): 9–55.

34. Wilhelm Stüwer, "Kloster Werden," in *Die Benediktinerklöster in Nordrhein-Westfalen*, ed. Rhabanus Maurus Haacke, *Germania Benedictina* (St. Ottilien, Germany: Eos, 1980), 580–81.

35. BHL 4143: *Vita et miracula sanctae Idae Herzfeldensis auct. Uffingo mon. Werthinensi*. AASS, Sept. 2: 260–69. See Uffing, "Ex Vita s. Idae," MGH SS (folio) 2 (1829): 569–76; Uffing, "Das Leben und die Wunder der heiligen Ida von Herzfeld (um 980)," in *Heilige Ida von Herzfeld, 980–1980*, ed. Géza Jászai (Münster, 1980), 9–25; and Uffing, "Vita sanctae Idae," in *Die Kaiserurkunden der Provinz Westfalen, 777–1313*, ed. Roger Wilmans (1867), vol. 1, 470-88. See also Andreas Freitäger, *Johannes Cincinnius von Lippstadt (ca. 1485–1555): Bibliothek und Geisteswelt eines westfälischen*

Humanisten, vol. 18, *Veröffentlichungen der historischen Kommission für Westfalen* (Münster: Aschendorff, 2000), 187; and Nicolaus Gussone, "Die Erhebung Idas zur Heiligen," in *Heilige Ida von Herzfeld, 980–1980,* 65–72.

36. Stüwer, "Kloster Werden," 584–85. Bursfeld monks authored saints' lives, most prominently Trithemius, suggesting that enhancing the cult of the saints was a specific element in the congregation's plan for religious reform.

37. AASS, Sept. 2: 257.

38. Wilmans, ed., *Die Kaiserurkunden der Provinz Westfalen,* vol. 1, 469-70.

39. Augustin Hüsing, *Die heilige Ida, Gräfin zu Herzfeld in Westfalen* (Münster [in Westfalen]: 1880), 3.

40. Freitäger, *Johannes Cincinnius,* 56–112.

41. Ibid., 144–75. The relationship between Werden and Cincinnius was similar to that between Kempten and Johannes Birk, a possible author of *The Life of the Queen Saint Hildegard.*

42. Ibid., 347–79. The register of these acquisitions is an appendix in Freitäger's monograph and are henceforth cited CB (Cincinnius-Bibliothek).

43. CB 129, 142.

44. P. Anastase de Saint-Paul, "Baptiste de Mantoue (Bienheureux), général des carmes, philosophe, théologien et poète célèbre de la Renaissance," DHGE 6 (1932): 525–27.

45. CB 14, 17, 27.

46. Cincinnius acquired Erasmus of Rotterdam's *Hieronymi Stridonensis vita* in 1519 (ibid., 59; VD16 E2968). In this vita of Saint Jerome, Erasmus sharply criticized the practices of medieval authors. In this regard, Cincinnius did not conform to Erasmus's model. Freitäger's observation that "Cincinnius's reworking of saints' legends are marked by critical analysis of the sources" does not lend itself to confirmation in the *Vita b. Idae;* cf. Freitäger, *Johannes Cincinnius,* 173.

47. CB 1, 148.

48. VD16 ZV9238. Johannes Cincinnius von Lippstadt, *Frageboich van CCCC fragen gotlicher und naturlicher dingen* (Cologne: Melchior von Neuß, 1527). See also Freitäger, *Johannes Cincinnius,* 247–72.

49. Johannes Cincinnius von Lippstadt, "Von der Niederlage des Varus," in *200 Jahre Landes- und Stadtbibliothek Düsseldorf,* ed. Gerhard Rudolph, 109-20 (Düsseldorf: Landes- und Stadtbibliothek, 1970); VD16 K2476. See also Freitäger, *Johannes Cincinnius,* 273–92.

50. Frank L. Borchardt, *German Antiquity in Renaissance Myth* (Baltimore: Johns Hopkins Press, 1971), passim; Freitäger, *Johannes Cincinnius,* 273–92; and Ridé, *L'image du Germain,* 471–625.

51. Cincinnius, *De historie van deme leven des heligen gloriosen Confessoers cristi sent Ludghers,* and Cincinnius, *Vita divi Ludgeri Mimigardevordensis ecclesie,* Münster, Nordrhein-Westfalen Staatsarchiv, Altertumskundeverein Münster (Dep.), ms. 136. (Printed, VD16 K2477.) See also Diekamp, ed., *Die Vitae sancti Liudgeri,* lxxxvii, ci–cii, civ–cv; and Freitäger, *Johannes Cincinnius,* 188–97.

52. Cincinnius, "Divorum septem fratrum Maccabaeorum Hebraeorum martyrum et matris eorum Solomonae agones stupendi," Paris, Bibliothèque nationale, ms. lat. 10161, 59r–91r; and Cologne, Dombibliothek, cod. 271, 79r–119r.

53. Freitäger, *Johannes Cincinnius*, 212–17; and Daniel E. Joslyn-Siemiatkoski, "The Maccabean Martyrs in Medieval Christianity and Judaism" (PhD diss., Boston College, 2005).

54. Diekamp, ed., *Die Vitae sancti Liudgeri*, 260–61.

55. A history of the manuscripts can be partially reconstructed from the following: Aloys Bömer, "Eine volkstümliche deutsche Enzyklopädie eines Werdener Bibliothekars aus dem Jahre 1527," in *Festschrift Georg Leyh: Aufsätze zum Bibliothekswesen und zur Forschungsgeschichte*, ed. Ernst Leipprand (Leipzig: O. Harrassowitz, 1937), 38–53; P. Jacobs, *Geschichte der Pfarreien im Gebiete des ehemaligen Stiftes Werden an der Ruhr, Beiträge zur Geschichte des Stiftes Werden* (Düsseldorf: L. Schwann, 1893), 4, 17, 177, 178, 194, 228; Gerhard Karpp, "Die Bibliothek der Benediktinerabtei Werden im Mittelalter," in *Das Jahrtausend der Mönche*, ed. Jan Gerchow and Reinhild Stephan-Maaser (Cologne: Wienand, 1999), 244–46; Adolf Schmid, "Handschriften der Reichsabtei Werden," *Beiträge zur Geschichte des Stiftes Werden* 11 (1905): 116–17, 124; and Wilhelm Stüwer, *Die Reichsabtei Werden an der Ruhr*, vol. 12, *Germania Sacra, n.s.* (Berlin: Walter de Gruyter, 1980), 72–73.

56. Cincinnius, "Vita b. Idae," ep. nunc. The letter is dated 1517, thus the year beyond which Cincinnius could not have undertaken his work. Despite earlier speculation, there is no reason to assume that Cincinnius prepared his work much earlier than 1517. Circumstantial evidence supports a composition date in the later 1510s. David Collins, "Chorography and Hagiography: Johannes Cincinnius's Revision of Uffing's 'Vita sanctae Idea,'" in *Heiliges Westfalen: Heilige, Reliquien, Wallfahrt und Wunder im Mittelalter*, ed. Gabriela Signori (Bielefeld, Germany: Verlag für Regionalgeschichte, 2003), 214–16; and David Collins, "Renaissance Revisions: A Brief Analysis and Critical Edition of Cincinnius's *Vita s. Ida*, a Revision of BHL 4143," *Analecta bollandiana* 124 (2006): 337–38.

57. Cincinnius, *Vita b. Idae*, ep. nunc.

58. This led Freitäger to conclude cautiously that Cincinnius wrote both the *Vita b. Idae* and the *Vita d. Ludgeri* around the same time, namely, in or around December 1512.

59. Peter Ilisch, "Die volkstümliche Verehrung der heiligen Ida in Westfalen vor 1800," in *Heilige Ida von Herzfeld, 980–1980*, 147; Bernhard Lübbers, "Ida von Herzfeld—Notizen zum Ida-Jubiläum 1980," in ibid., 168; and Siegfried Schmieder, "Herzfeld—Liesborn—Werden," in ibid., 143.

60. Du Cange defined "liber sermocinalis" as a book with sermons or homilies read in Christian liturgies and dated the term to the thirteenth century. Charles (du Cange) du Fresne, *Glossarium mediae et infimae latinitatis*, 10 vols. (Paris: Librairie des sciences et des arts, 1937–1938), vol. 7, 438.

61. Freitäger, *Johannes Cincinnius*, 184.

62. Ibid., 187–88, 190.

63. For example, Cincinnius's replacement of Uffing's *quae angelico relatu didicerat* (I.3) with *que ab angelo audierat* (c. 3), of *marmoreum sarcophagum* (I.6) with *lapideum monumentum* (c. 4), and of *homo quidam cephalargiae concussione nimis vexabatur* (I.15) with *homo quidam cephalargie in capitis dolore unius torquibatur* (c. 13). Chapter references of the Cincinnius text follow the manuscripts as edited in Collins, "Renaissance Revisions," 343-58. Those of the Uffing text follow Wilmans, ed., *Kaiserurkunden*, 470–87.

64. "Patrati sacrilegii poenas luit." Uffing, *Vita s. Idae*, I.11; Cincinnius, *Vita b. Idae*, c. 9.

65. Uffing, *Vita s. Idae*, I.11.

66. Guy Philippart, "Legendare," *VL* 5 (1984): 644–647; and Guy Philippart, *Les légendiers latins*, vols. 24–25, *Typologie des sources du moyen âge occidental* (Turnholt, Belgium: Brepols, 1977).

67. Uffing, *Vita s. Idae*, proemium.

68. Cincinnius, *Vita b. Idae*, c.1. Regarding the baptism as it is described in related texts see "Vita Ludgeri II," in *Die Vitae sancti Liudgeri*, ed. Wilhelm Diekamp (1881), 55; and Altfridus, "Vita sancti Ludgeri," in ibid., 6–9. Cincinnius, it should be noted, left unanswered the questions of who Ida's parents were and whether she had remained childless in marriage, issues that remain contested to this day. Augustin Hüsing, "Genealogie der heiligen Ida," *Zeitschrift für vaterländische Geschichte und Alterthumskunde* 38 (1880): 1–21; Franz-Josef Jakobi, "Zur Frage der Nachkommen der heiligen Ida und der Neuorientierung des sächsischen Adels in der Karolingerzeit," in *Heilige Ida von Herzfeld, 980–1980*, 53–63; Jürgen Kemper, "Das Leben der heiligen Ida von Herzfeld im Spannungsfeld von Christianisierung und fränkischer Politik in Sachsen," in ibid., 43–50; Lübbers, "Ida von Herzfeld: Notizen zum Ida-Jubiläum 1980," in ibid., 163–68; Reinhard Wenskus, "Die deutschen Stämme im Reiche Karls des Großen," in *Karl der Grosse, Lebenswerk und Nachleben*, ed. Wolfgang Braunfels and Helmut Beumann (Düsseldorf: L. Schwann, 1965); and Reinhard Wenskus, *Sächsischer Stammesadel und fränkischer Reichsadel*, vol. 93, *Abhandlungen der Akademie der Wissenschaften in Göttingen, Philologisch-historische Klasse 3. Folge* (Göttingen: Vandenhoeck and Ruprecht, 1976).

69. "Odilia enim (ut legimus) in Francia patre Adelardo nata fuit: qui sub Childerico francorum rege, totius Burgundie Principatum gerebat." Cincinnius, *Vita b. Idae*, c. 1.

70. "Usque ad tempora Pippinii regis et Caroli magni filii eius, Westphalia et omnes regiones inter Rhenum et Albiam et inter Phrisiam et Hassiam tota Saxonia dicte fuere." Ibid.

71. Regarding the late medieval hagiographical concern with popular married saints in late-medieval Germany such as Ann, the mother of the Virgin Mary, and Leopold the Pious, margrave of Austria, see Amelia Carr, " 'Because He Was a Prince': St. Leopold, Habsburg Ritual Strategies, and the Practice of Sincere Religion at Klosterneuburg," in *Ceremony and Text in the Renaissance*, ed. Doug Rutledge (Newark: University of Delaware Press, 1996), 35; Heide Dienst, *Agnes, Herzogin, Markgräfin, Ehefrau und Mutter* (Vienna: Österreichischer Bundesverlag, 1985); Angelika

Dörfler-Dierken, "Annenkult und humanistische Hagiographie," in *Humanismus und Theologie in der frühen Neuzeit*, ed. Hanns Kerner, *Pirckheimer-Jahrbuch* (Verlag Hans Carl, 1993), 57–90; Floridus Röhrig, *Leopold III. der Heilige, Markgraf von Österreich* (Vienna: Herold, 1985); and Floridus Röhrig and Gottfrie Stangler, eds., *Der Heilige Leopold: Landesfürst und Staats-Symbol: Ausstellung Stift Klosterneuberg, 30. März–3. November 1985*, vol. 155, *Katalog des Niederösterreichischen Landesmuseums* (Vienna: Amt der Niederösterreichischen Landesregierung Abt. III/2 Kulturabt., 1985).

72. Uffing, *Vita s. Idae*, I.4.

73. Cincinnius, *Vita b. Idae*, c. 1.

74. Edith Mary Whitman, *Gallia Belgica* (London: B. T. Batsford, 1985), 45–61.

75. I am grateful to Dr. Natalia Lozovsky for her assistance in determining that Cincinnius's division of Gaul most likely has no precedent.

76. Jacopo d'Angelo prepared the first Latin translation of Ptolemy's work in 1406, and by the time of its first printing in 1475 it was serving as the key reference work for European geographers.

77. VD 16 P5211.

78. VD 16 P5207; CB 129.

79. Written reference to Westphalia as a political, cultural, and territorial region with priority over a people occupying a certain area and distinguished from Saxony first appeared in a mid-eleventh-century document that located a village in "Westvalen." This document, dated 1054, places the *villa* Holthausen "in Westvalen"; the latinization, Westfalia, is first found in 1067. "Westfalia, quae autem versus Rhenum occidentem intendit," MGH SS 12: 229. Caesarius von Heisterbach in the early thirteenth century wrote of the three duchies of Saxony, Bavaria, and Westphalia. *Catalogus aepiscoporum Coloniensium* in Böhmer, *Fontes rerum Germanicarum*, 2 (1845): 278. Furthermore, the *Annales Pegavienses* describe both a *ducatus Saxoniae* and a *ducatus in Westfalia*, separated by the River Weser. MGH SS 16: 263; Chronica Slavorum, MGH SRG 32: 59ff. See also Harm Klueting, *Geschichte Westfalens: Das Land zwischen Rhein und Weser vom 8. bis zum 20. Jahrhundert*, ed. Klueting Harm (Paderborn, Germany: Bonifatius, 1998), 10.

80. Hermann Aubin and Christian Schulte, *Der Raum Westfalen: Untersuchungen zu seiner Geschichte und Kultur* (Berlin: R. Hobbing, 1934), 3–4.

81. Pius II (Aeneas Silvius Piccolomineus), "Europa in qua sui temporis varias historias complectitur," in *Opera quae extant omnia* (1551), 431.

82. He cited the work thus: "Uti considerare licet ex historiis diversis et praesertim ex libello de antiquitate Westphalie," Cincinnius, *Vita b. Idae*, c. 3.

83. Hermann Bücker, *Werner Rolevinck, 1425–1502: Leben und Persönlichkeit im Spiegel des Westfalenbuches*, ed. Alois Schöer, vol. 4, *Geschichte und Kultur: Schriften aus dem Bischöflichen Diözesanarchiv Münster* (Münster: Regensbergsche Verlagsbuchhandlung, 1953); and Ellen Widder, "Westfalen und die Welt: Anmerkungen zu Werner Rolevinck," *Westfälische Zeitschrift* 141 (1991): 93–122.

84. His writings most frequently reproduced in the late fifteenth and sixteenth centuries include the *Chronicon Westphaliae*, printed first in Cologne by Arnold Ther Hoernen in ca. 1472 as *De laude antiquae Saxoniae, nunc Westphaliae dictae* (GW

M38774), and the *Fasciculus tempororum*, an overview of world history composed, revised, and printed frequently in the fifteenth and sixteenth centuries (GW M38692; Cologne: Arnold Ther Hoernen, 1472).

85. Bücker, *Werner Rolevinck*, 41–52; Widder, "Westfalen," 93–122.

86. Cincinnius, *Vita b. Idae*, c. 1. Cf. Werner Rolevinck, *De laude antiquae Saxoniae nunc Westphaliae dictae*, ed. Hermann Bücker (Münster: Aschendorff, 1953), 12–13, 114–15.

87. Margret Lugge, *"Gallia" und "Francia" im Mittelalter: Untersuchungen über den Zusammenhang zwischen geographisch-historischer Terminologie und politischem Denken vom 6.–15. Jahrhundert*, ed. Max Braubach, vol. 15, *Bonner Historische Forschungen* (Bonn: Ludwig Röhrscheid, 1960), 208–15.

88. Cincinnius, *Vita b. Idae*, c. 3.

89. Rolevinck, *De laude Saxoniae*, 58–59. Valla's ridicule of the term *satrap* in his *Declamatio* of 1439 might well explain why Cincinnius steered clear of the name in 1517.

90. Cincinnius, *Vita b. Idae*, c. 3. Cf. BHL 4937 and 4939: "Vita Ludgeri II," 67; and Altfridus, "Vita sancti Ludgeri," 27–29, 39.

91. "Vita Lebuini presbiteri et confessoris," MGH SS 30.2 (1934): 793. The *Vita sancti Lebuini* (BHL 4812) antedates Altfrid's *Vita s. Ludgeri* by a century. The reference to "satraps" in Saxony appears, however, only in the *Vita s. Lebuini*, whose author most likely used Bede as his source. Bede, *Ecclesiastical History*, 5.10.

92. Discovery of these elements in late fifteenth- and early sixteenth-century hagiographical writings—pointed to here and throughout this chapter—call to mind Simon Ditchfield's arguments regarding hagiography's substantive contribution to the development of national historiographies in the post-Tridentine, early modern period. Such resonances suggest yet more cultural, political continuity between the "late medieval" and the "early modern." Simon Ditchfield, *"Tota regio nil nisi religio:* Nations, Nationalisms, and 'historia sacra,' Some Preliminary Reflections," *Annali di storia moderna e contemporanea* 10 (2004): 593–605.

CHAPTER 4

1. Flue is also indicated in Swiss German as Flüeli.

2. Most of these have been collected in the three volumes, abbreviated BK throughout: Rupert Amschwand, ed., *Bruder Klaus: Ergänzungsband zum Quellenwerk von Robert Durrer* (Sarnen, Switzerland: Regierungsrat des Kantons Obwalden, 1987); and Robert Durrer, ed., *Bruder Klaus: Die ältesten Quellen über den seligen Nikolaus von Flüe, sein Leben und seinen Einfluss*, 2 vols. (Sarnen, Switzerland: Louis Ehrli, 1917). Although Nicholas of Flue is virtually unstudied outside of Switzerland, the modern scholarship has a distinguished pedigree. The first critical historical investigation into the life of Nicholas was undertaken by Guido Görres, son of Johann Joseph Görres: Guido Görres, *Der selige Nikolaus von der Flüe und die Eidgenossen auf dem Tage zu Stanz: Ein Bild aus dem Ende des fünfzehnten Jahrhunderts* (Munich: Rösl, 1831).

3. BHL 6228. Only one manuscript of this important account has survived, an autograph of the Latin original and the German translation that Bonstetten sent to the Nuremberg city council at its request in May 1485. Bonstetten, "Prologus et Hystoria sancti Nicolai de Rupe, heremite Underwaldensis et conmilitonis sui" and "Vorred und Leben Bruder Niclausen," Staatsarchiv Nürnberg, Reichstadt Nürnberg, Losungsamtliche Reverse (Repertorium 2), nr. 19. Also printed in BK 1, 81–90. See Albrecht von Bonstetten, *Deux visites à Nicolas de Flue*, ed. Johann von Waldheim, trans. Eduard Fick (Geneva: J.-G. Fick, 1864). See also Oskar Vasella, "Bruder Klaus und die Stadt Nördlingen," *Zeitschrift für schweizerische Kirchengeschichte* 43 (1949): 68–71.

As for Bonstetten's relation to foreign ambassadors, see the following: letter from Albert of Aucha to Albert von Bonstetten, Lucerne, Feb. 20, 1479, letter 63; letter from Johannes Hux to Albert von Bonstetten, St. Gallen, 1479, letter 76; letter by Albert von Bonstetten dedicating his *Descriptio Helvetiae* to King Louis XI of France, Einsiedeln, July 13, 1481 (unnumbered, p. 175n1); letter by Albert von Bonstetten dedicating his history of Austria to King Charles VIII of France, Einsiedeln, Apr. 22, 1491, letter A5. Letters numbered as in Albrecht von Bonstetten, *Briefe und ausgewählte Schriften*, ed. Albert Büchi (Basel: Adolf Geering, 1893).

4. For example, a report of Bernardino Imperiali, a legate of the duke of Milan, 1483, BK 1, 223–31.

5. BK 3, 108. See also Wilhelm Baum, "Niklaus von Flüe und Sigmund des Münzreiche von Österreich," *Zeitschrift für schweizerische Kirchengeschichte* (1987): 5–29.

6. BK 1, 41–44, 50–52, 98–101; BK 3, 3–6, 182–85.

7. "Zcu deme lebenden heyligin," in Hans von Waldheim journal, BK 1, 58.

8. Gundelfingen, *Hystoria Nicolai*, BK 3, 108.

9. BK 1, 350–53.

10. Ibid., 353–55, 582–88. See also Rupert Amschwand, "Bonstetten und Trithemius: Über den heiligen Nikolaus von Flüe, genannt Bruder Klaus," *Studien und Mitteilungen zur Geschichte des Benediktiner-Ordens und seiner Zweige* 95 (1984): 165–68; and Klaus Arnold, *Johannes Trithemius (1462–1516)*, ed. Klaus Wittstadt, 2d ed., vol. 23, *Quellen und Forschungen zur Geschichte des Bistums und Hochstifts Würzburg* (Würzburg: Kommissionsverlag Ferdinand Schöningh, 1991), 243–45.

11. GW M40784. Hartmann Schedel, *Liber chronicarum* (Nuremberg: Anton Koberger, 1493).

12. GW 7075. *Bruder Claus* (Nuremberg: Marx Ayrer, 1488).

13. BK 1, 400–401.

14. Ibid., 47–49.

15. Ibid. 3, 201. (Charles de Bouelles) Bovillus's visit to the Ranft seems to have inspired eremitical tendencies, and his study of Nicholas's life may have influenced his biography of Raimundus Lull. See Curt Wittlin, "Charles de Bovelles davant dos models de vida santa i solitària: Nicolau de Flüe (1503) i Ramon Llull (1511)," *Randa* 50 (2003): 61–76, which includes editions of Bovillus's letters on Nicholas. See also BK 1, 559–72; 3, 201–202.

16. BK 2, 635–37; 3, 203.

17. Canisius, *Zwey und neunzig Betrachtung und Gebett*, BK 2, 817–34. See also Joseph Bütler, "Die Jesuiten als Förderer der Bruder Klaus Verehrung," *Mitteilungen aus der Deutschen Provinzen* 12, no. 99 (1932): 406–409; E. Wymann, "Kardinal Friedrich Borromeo erhält 1625 ein Biographie des seligen Nikolaus von Flüe," *Zeitschrift für schweizerische Kirchengeschichte* 29 (1935): 61–65; and E. Wymann, "Karl Borromeo und Peter Canisius über den seligen Nikolaus von Flüe," *Zeitschrift für schweizerische Kirchengeschichte* 11 (1917): 55–60.

18. The Holy See sanctioned the cult in 1669 but limited it to the region of Obwalden (one of two larger jurisdictions within Unterwalden). In 1761 this permission was extended to all of Switzerland and the diocese of Constance. Pope Pius XII canonized Nicholas in 1947. Carolus (Cardinalus) Salottus, "Canonizationis beati Nicolai de Flüe confessoris eremitae Helvetici: Positio super Validitate Processus" (Rome: Sacred Congregation of Rites, 1941); Carolus (Cardinalus) Salottus, "Canonizationis beati Nicolai de Flüe confessoris heremitae Helvetici: Positio super tuto" (Rome: Sacred Congregation of Rites, 1944). See also Ferdinand Rüegg, "Ein bio-bibliographisches Dokument über Bruder Klaus im Riten-Archiv zu Rom," *Zeitschrift für schweizerische Kirchengeschichte* 41 (1947): 89–100.

19. The three German-language lives were all derived from the second of the Latin lives, Heinrich "Lupulus" Wölflin's *Divi Nicolai de Saxo vita*. Sebastian Rhaetius, a pastor in the Ranft, revised and translated the *Divi Nicolai vita* in 1521 (BK 3, 157–70). Hans Salat, a history writer who had enjoyed previous careers as a sailmaker, surgeon, and battlefield courier, composed the next—the *Rechte ware History, legend und leben des frommen andächtigen lieben säligen Niclausen von der Flüe*—which was also the first to appear in print (Augsburg: Heinrich Steiner, 1537, VD16 S1326; BK 2, 668–91). Third, Ulrich Witwyler, a conventual monk with pastoral duties in Einsiedeln and a prolific vernacular writer about the saints, composed the *Wahrhaftige wunderbarliche Historie und leben des recht frommen, andächtigen, gottseligen, weitberümpten Nicolausen von der Flüe*. The work draws heavily on Salat's *Rechte ware History*, and Witwyler credited Salat on the title page when Sebald Meyer first printed the work in Dillingen in 1571. BK 2, 769–89 (VD16 S1327).

20. BHL 6227z. Gundelfingen, *Hystoria Nicolai*, BK 3, 105–16.

21. Heinrich "Lupulus" Wölflin, *Divi Nicolai de Saxo vita*, BK 3, 126–50.

22. Bonstetten, "Hystoria fratris Nicolai," BK 1, 81–90.

23. The other significant case involving the contemporaneity of saint and author is that of blood-libel saint Simon Unferdorben of Trent. Simon was a two-year-old who was found murdered under the house of a prominent Jewish moneylender on Easter 1475. Several Jewish residents of Trent confessed to the crime. Fourteen executions followed, as did indiscriminate penalties against the city's Jewish population. The reputed facts of the case were in print within a year as a passion with miracles and poetic decorations. The author, Johannes Mathias Tuberinus, dedicated his work to the prominent humanist bishop of Trent, John Hinderbach (1418–1486). See also chapter one, notes 22 and 98.

24. Guy P. Marchal, "Staat und Nation in der schweizerischen Geschichtskultur," in *Historiographie in Polen und in der Schweiz*, ed. Krzysztof Baczkowski and

Christian Simon, *Studia Polono-Helvetica* (Kraków: Uniwersytet Jagiellonski, 1994), 112–18.

25. Although less is known today outside of Switzerland than the other Swiss national symbols, William Tell and Helvetia, Nicholas is still an important national symbol to the Swiss themselves. A visit to Ranft is one way of experiencing the devotion the Swiss have for Brother Claus and the current significance of his persona. An Internet search for "Bruder Klaus" on the Swiss Google site (www.google.ch) in the summer of 2007 resulted in 130,000 hits (more than quadruple the hits from two years before). See, for example, the Stiftung Bruder Klaus at www.stiftung-bruderklaus.ch and the pilgrimage office in Sachseln at www.bruderklaus.ch.

26. For example, from Bonstetten's "Hystoria": "In Germanos se erigit quidam preruptus alius et scopolosus qui Mons Fractus dicitur, caput inter nubila condens et volgariori nomine Pilati petra, nam eius in apice ad paludem quandam infelix Pontius perjuratus esse ruminatur. Erga Gallorum latus Brunick mons situs est, ingentis eminencie verticem erigens sidera versus. Is tamen (ut liquet) conterraneis graditur. Propterea autem Underwalden nominatum arbitror, nam ex utraque parte Penninorum moncium radicibus atre silve affixe, quibus postea remissius terra adiacet (absque cerere et bacho) satis frugifera, graminosa longe, lacus habens torrentes soniferos, magna in amenitate et copia." BK 1, 82.

"Situs heremi talis est: Dum veniebamus lucum ultra ad villam que Kerns vulgo dicitur, iterando versus montem Brunick prescriptum, paululum ante ville limites a directa via sinistrorsum secesseramus erga alpes glaciatas pervinatasque, et quom eos montes collesque pene ad medium miliare scandebamus, ad verticem valliculi (quod torrentum rapidissimi cursus cum fragore et ingenti sonitu ducit) e superioribus minantibus ruinam petris manentem venimus, quo statim de vili et precipiti descensu ad imum gradiebamur et de hink reascendendo fluviolum versus ortum suum, ad quingentos (credo) passus non longum sed quantum lapidis iactus est a ripa dextrorsum in pede gemminati montis habitacio est heremite." Ibid., 85–86.

And "interea circumflexi lumina prospiciens singula et personam et cellulam haud summotene considerando. Est bone stature, totus macer et fuscus et rugosus, capillos disiectos, minus pectine deductos, nigros mixta canicie, non perdensos, sic quoque barba longitudinem pollice habens, oculos mediocres bona in albedine, eburneos dentes optime serie et nasum faciei pulchre dispositum. Non loquax necque in cognitis corrigibilis. Credo eum in etate sexaginta annos habere. Dum tangitur manus tota gelida notatur; discopertus capite et pedibus, grisea toga tantum super nudo indutus." Ibid., 87.

From the other two hagiographers, for example: "Qui eciam ubi res domesticas ordinavit, omnes facultates suas, nil sibi reservans, liberis uxorique reliquit sicque nudus penitus et Christi fide armatus statim haud procul a suis edibus et Saxelon et Kerns superioris silve vicis ad vallem quandam altam se contulit, quam torrens celerrimi sevientissimique fluxus adeo alluit, ut semper albam lacteamque ex sese gignat aquam." Gundelfingen, *Hystoria Nicholai*, BK 3, 107; and "Qui primo statim mane abscendens, iter unde venerat repetit, ita tamen, ut contemptis, quibus iam abiens renuncitiarat, familiaribus impedimentis, in fundum suum ad vallem Melchae concito gradu pergeret, atque ibi inter densas veprium spinas octo continuos dies absque cybi et potus alimento, nulli hominum conscius latitabat." Wölflin, *Divi Nicholai vita,* ibid., 135.

For an insightful article on the notion of a "desert" in the Alps suitable for the hermit's life, see Catherine Santschi, "Errance et stabilité chez les ermites des Alpes occidentales," *Zeitschrift für schweizerische Kirchengeschichte* 82 (1988): especially 75; and Catherine Santschi, "La solitude des ermites: Enquête en milieu alpin," *Médiévales* 28 (1995): especially 26–29. See also Guy P. Marchal, "Das 'Schweizeralpenland': Eine imagologische Bastelei," in *Erfundene Schweiz: Konstruktionen nationaler Identität/La Suisse imaginée: Bricolages d'une identité nationale,* ed. Guy P. Marchal and Aram Mattioli (Zurich: Chronos, 1992), 37–49.

I henceforth translate *Orte* as "states."

27. The term "canton" has its origins with reforms of the 1790s, as does the term "Switzerland," which I avoid in favor of "the Swiss Confederation." For a history of terms used, see Wilhelm Oechsli, "Die Benennungen der alten Eidgenossenschaft und ihrer Glieder (T. 2)," *Jahrbuch für schweizerische Geschichte* 42 (1917): 89–155.

28. Richard Feller and Edgar Bonjour, *Geschichtsschreibung der Schweiz vom Spätmittelalter zur Neuzeit,* 2d ed., 2 vols. (Basel: Helbing and Lichtenhahn, 1979), 76–78, 80; and Joseph Ferdinand Rüegg, *Heinrich Gundelfingen: Ein Beitrag zur Geschichte des deutschen Frühhumanismus und zur Lösung der Frage über die ursprüngliche Königsfelderchronik,* ed. Albert Büchi, Joseph Peter Kirsch et al., vol. 6, *Freiburger historische Studien* (Fribourg, Switzerland: Universitäts-Buchhandlung Otto Gschwend, 1910).

29. Gundelfingen's visit to the Ranft is disputed by some. See Amschwand's summary, BK 3, 103–104.

30. Heinrich Gundelfingen, *L'office chante de Nicolas de Flue 1488–1650–1950, das Offizium von Gundelfingen 1488, édition critique,* ed. Jean-Marie Curti (Geneva: Opéra-Studio de Genève, 1991).

31. Durrer, ed., *Bruder Klaus,* 418; and Robert Ludwig Suter, *Die Verehrung des hl. Bruder Klaus im Michelsamt, Heimatkunde des Michelsamtes* (Beromünster, Switzerland: Geschichtsverein, 1987), 5–6.

The liturgical office was, in fact, used at Nicholas's tomb in Sachseln, the hermit's hometown, until 1603, when the local bishop on visitation prohibited its use on the grounds that Nicholas had not yet been beatified or canonized. Demonstrating the success of humanist composition no less than the spreading impact of the Council of Trent, witness Johann Zimmermann testified in the canonization process of 1652 and described both how active public devotion to Nicholas was at the shrine and how abruptly its suppression came. BK 1, 422n426.

Canonization documents (1941–1944, see note 18) contradict the claim in the *Allgemeine Deutsche Biographie* that the deceased Nicholas lay in Ranft until 1518 before being translated to Sachseln. It is more likely that he was buried in 1487 in Sachseln. See Ludwig Schmugge, "Der Streit um die Grablege des heiligen Nikolaus von Flüe," in *Studia in honorem eminentissimi cardinalis Alphonsi M. Stickler,* ed. Rosalius Iosephus Castillus Lara, *Studia et Textus Historiae Iuris Canonici* (Rome: LAS, 1992), 530–31.

32. Gundelfingen, *Hystoria Nicolai,* BK 3, 106.

33. Gundelfingen's grandfather, Heinrich von Gundelfingen, had been abbot of the monastery of St. Gall and in that capacity hosted Poggio Bracciolini, Bartolomeo de Montepulciano, and Cincio Romano in 1416 as they distracted themselves during the Council of Constance by searching nearby libraries for interesting texts. Cincio wrote, "There were in the monastery an abbot and monks divorced from any knowledge of letters." Nonetheless, Poggio discovered there a complete copy of Quintilian's *Institutio oratoria*, overlooked for nearly six centuries. The importance of this rediscovery in the history of humanist learning cannot be overestimated. Poggio wrote, "Erant enim non in Bibliotheca libri illi, ut eorum dignitas postulabat, sed in teterrimo quodam, et obscuro carcere, fundo scilicet unius turris, quo ne capitalis quidem rei damnati retruderentur." Tommaso de Tonelli, ed., *Poggii epistolae*, 3 vols. (Florence: Typis L. Marchini, 1832–1861), 1, 25–29. Reported by James J. Murphy, *Rhetoric in the Middle Ages: A History of Rhetorical Theory from Saint Augustine to the Renaissance* (Berkeley: University of California Press, 1974), 357–58. See also Remigio Sabbadini, *Storia e Critica di Testi Latini* (Catania, 1914), 379–407; and L. D. Reynolds, ed., *Texts and Transmission: A Survey of the Latin Classics* (Oxford: Clarendon, 1983), 333.

34. Rüegg, *Heinrich Gundelfingen*, 14–28, 29–65.

35. Universitätsbibliothek, Freiburg im Br., cod. 159, 3r, 4v, 7v–8v, 76r–133r, 136r–139r, and cod. 260, 5v–12v.

36. Titles, in order: *Austriae principum chronici epitome triplex, Herkommen der Schwyzer und Oberhasler, De thermis Badensibus, Militaria monumenta, Amoenitates urbis Lucernensis,* and *Topographia urbis Bernensis.* See also Dieter Mertens, "Gundelfingen, Heinrich," in VL 3 (1981): 306–10; RFHMA 5 (1984): 353–54; and Rüegg, *Heinrich Gundelfingen*, 10–13.

37. For example, accounts of the city council seeking political and commercial advice in BK 1, 75–76, 102–104, 190–91; and accounts of the city council giving financial support to Brother Claus in BK 1, 108–10.

38. For example, the account of counsel privately received by residents of Lucerne in BK 1, 53–55; and accounts of other pilgrims who used Lucerne as the Ranft's closest major city (e.g., Hans von Waldheim in BK 1, 56–67; Paulus Walther von Güglingen in BK 2, 1015; and Heimo am Grund in Amschwand, BK 1, 193).

39. For example, *Lucerne Chronicle* in BK 1, 157–64; and Diebold Schilling's description in BK 1, 596–97.

40. BK 1, 418–58, 3, 103–105. See also Gundelfingen, *L'office chante.*

41. Gundelfingen, *Hystoria Nicolai*, BK 3, 105–106.

42. Ibid., 106. Durrer speculated that it was sickness that drove Gundelfingen to the vita solitaria, BK 1, 420.

43. Beat Matthias v. Scarpatetti, "Heynlin, Johannes, de Lapide (von Stein)," in VF 3 (1981), 1213–19.

44. Johannes Jetzer (ca. 1483 to after 1520) was a Dominican lay brother in Bern and reputed stigmatic who began in 1507 to claim visions in which the saints and the Blessed Virgin visited him. During one of these, the Blessed Virgin admitted her maculate conception, affirming the Dominican position on the disputed question of whether she had been conceived without sin. Jetzer attracted considerable public

attention until he admitted that his claims were fraudulent. As a result of the subsequent trial, four Dominican masters in Bern were executed. Jetzer escaped, however, before his sentence could be carried out. For humanists, the Jetzer affair became
emblematic of how badly the church settled theological controversies.

45. Feller and Bonjour, *Geschichtsschreibung*, 164–65; Hans von Greyerz, *Nation
und Geschichte im bernischen Denken* (Bern: Herbert Lang, 1953), 43; and Hans von
Greyerz, *Studien zur Kulturgeschichte der Stadt Bern am Ende des Mittelalters* (Bern:
Gustav Grunau, 1940), 433–55.

46. "Missus est itaque Bernam ad Heinrichum Lupulum virum doctissimum, et
poetico spiritu clarum, nec non primum qui ludum bonarum literarum in Helvetiis
aperuit." Oswald Mykonius, *Vom Leben und Sterben Huldrych Zwinglis: Das älteste
Lebensbild Zwinglis*, ed. Ernst Gerhard Rüsch, vol. 50, *Mitteilungen zur vaterländischen
Geschichte* (1979), 36–38. See also Anna Rapp-Buri and Monica Stucky-Schurer, "Der
Berner Chorherr Heinrich Wolfli," *Zwingliana* 25 (1998): 65–105.

47. For example, Obwalden's recommendation to the duke of Milan on behalf of
Nicholas's son in BK 1, 505–508; the city of Neuenburg's contribution for the canonization process in BK 2, 1020; and contributions for Masses and candles from
individuals in BK 1, 511, 556–57.

48. Named bishop of Sitten in 1499 and created cardinal in 1511, Schiner was
the most powerful nonmonastic prelate in the region. He was renowned and
somewhat feared for the vigor of his ecclesiastical visitations and his enforcement
of clerical discipline even though he himself had had a mistress and by her fathered at
least two daughters and a son. He was an advisor to emperors Maximilian I and
Charles V. At the Diet of Worms in 1521 he opposed Luther, and later the same year he
was a leading candidate for the papacy at the conclave that elected Hadrian Florent
van Trusen (Pope Hadrian VI). Peter Arnold, "Kurzbiographie von Matthäus Schiner," *Blätter aus der Walliser Geschichte* 14 (1967/1968): 5–60; Albert Büchi, *Kardinal Schiner als Staatsmann und Kirchenfürst: Ein Beitrag zur allgemeinen und
schweizerischen Geschichte von der Wende des XV./XVI. Jahrhunderts*, 2 vols. (Zurich,
1923, 1937); Albert Carlen, "Kardinal Matthäus Schiner in Spiegel der Dichtung,"
Blätter aus der Walliser Geschichte 14 (1967/1968): 61–98; L. Carlen, "Kardinal Schiner
in Rom," *Walliser Jahrbuch* 56 (1987): 19–26; Hellmut Gutzwiller, "Die Beziehungen
zwischen Matthäus Schiner und Solothurn," *Blätter aus der Walliser Geschichte* 14
(1967/1968): 133–60; and Rudolf Pfister, *Kirchengeschichte der Schweiz* (Zurich:
Zwingli Verlag, 1964), 453–55.

49. See the documentation of the chapel's consecration in July 1504 in BK 1, 573–74.

50. Feller and Bonjour, *Geschichtsschreibung*, 28, 81, 164, 323; and Walter Rup-
pen, "Kunst um Schiner," *Blätter aus der Walliser Geschichte* 14 (1967/1968): 115–32.

51. Matthäus Schiner, *Korrespondenzen und Akten zur Geschichte des Kardinals
Matthäus Schiner*, ed. Albert Büchi (1920, 1925).

52. Lupulus, dedicatory letter to Matthaeus Schiner, "Sedunensis ecclesiae antistiti ac Vallesiae praefecto," BK 3, 121–122; the "Ad eundem pontificem et prae-
fectum Matthaeum eiusdem Henrici Lupuli carmen," BK 3, 122–24; and the
"Praefatiuncula," BK 3, 126–27.

53. Lupulus, dedicatory letter to Matthaeus Schiner, "Sedunensis ecclesiae antistiti ac Vallesiae praefecto: "Benivolentia et mansuetudine," "ut et adversantium incursus benignitate conciliet," "te inquam celeberrime antistes... qui cum utriusque gladii gubernacula magnificentissime geras." BK 3, 122.

54. For example, "Est itaque mihi novus et ut ita dicam, implumis quidam libellus, quem superioribus diebus de Undervaldensis Nicolai (cuius iamdiu ad exteras nationes fama evolavit) vita conscripsi. Is ubi diutius a me criticis manibus revolveretur, non est visus tutorem adipisci fideliorem, quam si tuis alis sus tentatus in lucem prodire coeperit." BK 3, 122.

Also, the "Ad Matthaeum carmen": "Haec tibi, iam nuper tenui descripta libello, / Offero censuris excrucianda novis // Limatusque tuo cunctum volitabit in orbem / Munere; notus per te Nicolaus erit." Ibid., 124.

Finally, the *praefatiuncula*: "Qua in re longius etiam sumendum erat exordium, quo ipsa vestra laudatissima civitas, inter Helvetii foederis partes non minima, quibusdam tamen exteris adhuc ignota regionibus, divi huius Nicolai fama eminus illustrata, nostris quoque scriptis, dum locum ipsum ac gentem pandimus, fidem augmentaret." Ibid., 127.

55. Matthias von Kemnat, *Pfälzische Chronik*, BK 2, 1013.

56. Hartmann Schedel, *Liber Chronicarum* (1493), BK 1, 499.

57. Peter Numagen in his "theological investigation" in the summer of 1483 recounted the visit of the bishop, who wanted to ensure against fraud and, more importantly, heterodoxy (BK 1, 260). Carolus Bovillus, French humanist and biographer of Raymond Lull, wrote between 1508 and 1510 that the story was still circulating in Ranft during his visit there in 1503 (BK 2, 568), and Trithemius included it in his chronicles (ibid., 583–84). Gundelfingen made no reference to the bishop's visit; Lupulus did: "Quibus permaxima difficultate comestis, vini quoque pauxillum vix absque nausea exorpsit"; Wölflin, *Divi Nicolai vita*, BK 3, 137.

58. "Qui quamvis in etate florida cum uxore remanens competentibus habundasset diviciis, in bellis vexillifer, manipulariusque ac primipularius, in pace minister nonnunquam Underwaldensium extitisset spectatissimus." Gundelfingen, *Hystoria Nicolai*, BK 3, 107.

59. The oldest *Churchbook* testimonials are dated September 1488, eighteen months after Nicholas's death. Gundelfingen did not have this book at his disposal when writing the *Hystoria Nicolai*. The statements were neither signed nor witnessed, and the book did not name the interrogators or indicate who directed the collection of evidence. It is likely that local officials—probably ecclesiastical, with the encouragement of the civil—organized the composition of *The Churchbook*, the original manuscript of which lies in the parish archives in Sachseln, as a testimonial both for the sake of local veneration and an anticipated canonization. All of the witnesses came from in or around Unterwalden. They claim a variety of relationships with Nicholas: family members, local church officials, spiritual advisors, lifelong friends, neighbors, and so on. The content of the testimonials in *The Churchbook* tends in three directions: descriptions of Nicholas's virtues; accounts of his spiritual life, mainly with the recounting of visions; and attestations of miracles ascribed to his intercession both while

he was alive and since his death. Lupulus drew from all three kinds of testimony. He copied the posthumous miracles—of which the Gundelfingen vita has none—almost word for word. Lupulus's descriptions of Nicholas's youth were developments on testimony in *The Churchbook.* He diligently took the accounts of Nicholas's visions into his vita. His trueness to this written source was then the justification for including materials like miracles and visions, about which he appears ambivalent. *Kirchenbuch von Sachseln,* BK 1, 461–79.

60. Wölflin, *Divi Nicolai de Saxo vita,* BK 3, 134.

61. Such as the report of Peter Numagen of Trier, BK 1, 234–331.

62. See Werner T. Huber, *Dorothea: Die Ehefrau des heiligen Niklaus von Flüe: Auszüge aus dem Quellenmaterial über Bruder Klaus aus dem 15. Jahrhundert bis heute* (Fribourg, Switzerland: Universitätsverlag, 1994).

63. Gundelfingen, *Hystoria Nicolai,* BK 3, 107.

64. Wölflin, *Divi Nicolai vita,* BK 3, 134.

65. Ibid.

66. Ibid., 142.

67. Gundelfingen, *Hystoria Nicolai,* BK 3, 108.

68. Ibid.

69. Ibid.

70. Lupulus even noted that this skepticism was often stronger among Nicholas's relatives than among outsiders; ibid., 136.

71. For example, Wölflin, *Divi Nicolai vita,* ibid., 126.

72. Ibid., 140.

73. BHL 5096. "Non sumpsit panem, non aquam, non genu flexit, non sedit, non accubuit, nihil aliud gustauit praeter pauca cruda crambes folia, quae sumebat die Dominico, vt videretur comedere." AASS, Jan. 1: 87.

74. Peter Dinzelbacher, "Mirakel oder Mirabilien? Heilige und unheilige Anorexie im ausgehenden Mittelalter," in *Das Wunderbare in der mittelalterlichen Literatur,* ed. Dietrich Schmidtke (Göppingen, Germany: Kümmerle, 1994), 204–205. See also Rudolph M. Bell, *Holy Anorexia* (Chicago: University of Chicago Press, 1985), ix–xi; and Caroline Walker Bynum, *Holy Feast and Holy Fast: The Religious Significance of Food to Medieval Women* (Berkeley: University of California Press, 1987).

75. BHL 4922–27; BHL 4926: Johannes Brugman, *Vita alme virginis Lijdwine* (BHL 4926), vol. 2, *Teksten en Documenten* (Groningen, the Netherlands: Rijksuniversiteit te Utrecht, 1963), 1–173; RFHMA 2 (1967): 588; F. A. H. Hombergh, "Brugman, Johannes," in VF 1 (1977): 1048–52. This first printing of Brugman's *Vita alme virginis Lijdwine de Schiedam* corresponds to GW 5579.

76. "Quod qum divino intersit sacrificio videatque illic presbyterum corpori et sanguini Christi communicare, sentire se ac percipere miram ex ea sumptione confortationem." Wölflin, *Divi Nicolai vita,* BK 3, 140.

77. Bell, *Holy Anorexia;* Dinzelbacher, "Mirakel oder Mirabilien?," 187–93; Peter Dinzelbacher, "Religiöses Erleben von bildender Kunst in autobiographischen und biographischen Zeugnissen des Hoch- und Spätmittelalters," in *Frömmigkeit im Mittelalter: Politisch-soziale Kontexte, visuelle Praxis, körperliche Ausdrucksformen,* ed.

Klaus Schreiner (Munich: Fink, 2002), 330; and Peter Dinzelbacher and Dieter R. Bauer, *Religiöse Frauenbewegung und mystische Frömmigkeit im Mittelalter*, vol. 28, *Beihefte zum Archiv für Kulturgeschichte* (Cologne: Böhlau, 1988), 395–404. See also Bynum, *Holy Feast and Holy Fast*; and Richard Kieckhefer, "Holiness and the Culture of Devotion: Remarks on Some Late Medieval Male Saints," in *Images of Sainthood in Medieval Europe*, ed. Renate Blumenfeld-Kosinski and Timea Klara Szell (Ithaca, N.Y.: Cornell University Press, 1991), 296–99.

78. Peter Biller, "Multum ieiunantes et se castigantes: Medieval Waldensian Asceticism," in *Monks, Hermits, and the Ascetic Tradition* (Cambridge: Basil Blackwell, 1985), 215–29; Henry Chadwick, "The Ascetic Ideal in the History of the Church," in ibid., 3–4, 7, 14–15; Virginia Davis, "The Rule of St. Paul, the First Hermit, in Late Medieval England," in ibid., 203; and Kieckhefer, "Holiness and the Culture of Devotion," 297.

79. Ulla Williams and Werner J. Hoffmann, " 'Vitaspatrum,' " in VL 10 (1999): 449–66; and Karl Langosch, "Caesarius von Heisterbach," in VL 1 (1977): 1156–61.

80. Edward Cuthbert Butler, *Benedictine Monachism: Studies in Benedictine Life and Rule*, 2d ed. (Cambridge, UK: Speculum Historiale, 1961), 35–45.

81. David Collins, "A Life Reconstituted: Jacobus de Voragine, Erasmus of Rotterdam, and Their Lives of St. Jerome," *Medievalia et Humanistica*, n.s. 25 (1998): 31–51; Berndt Hamm, "Hieronymus-Begeisterung und Augustinismus vor der Reformation: Beobachtungen zur Beziehung zwischen Augustinismus und Frömmigkeitstheologie (am Beispiel Nürnbergs)," in *Augustine, the Harvest and Theology (1300–1650): Essays Dedicated to Heiko Augustinus Oberman in Honor of His Sixtieth Birthday*, ed. Kenneth Hagen (Leiden, the Netherlands: E. J. Brill, 1990), 127–263; Eugene F. Rice, *Saint Jerome in the Renaissance* (Baltimore: Johns Hopkins University Press, 1984), 49, 75, 81, 84–136; Lewis William Spitz, *The Religious Renaissance of the German Humanists* (Cambridge, Mass.: Harvard University Press, 1963), 43, 49, 200; Rudolf Velhagen, "Eremiten und Ermitagen in der Kunst vom 15. bis zum 20. Jahrhundert," in *Eremiten und Ermitagen in der Kunst vom 15. bis zum 20. Jahrhundert*, ed. Rudolf Velhagen (Basel: Öffentliche Kunstsammlung Basel, 1993), 10; and Pietro Paolo Vergerio, *Pierpaolo Vergerio the Elder and Saint Jerome: An Edition and Translation of Sermones pro sancto Hieronymo*, ed. John M. McManamon (Tempe: Arizona Center for Medieval and Renaissance Studies, 1999), especially the introduction.

82. Roland Stieglecker, *Die Renaissance eines Heiligen: Sebastian Brant und Onuphrius eremita*, ed. Dieter Wuttke, vol. 37, *Gratia: Bamberger Schriften zur Renaissanceforschung* (Wiesbaden: Harrassowitz, 2001).

83. "Et quanquam nullam literarum haberet noticiam, solebat tamen ex infusa desuper scientia, viros etiam peritissimos ex secretarum rerum ignorantia quandoque liberare." Wölflin, *Divi Nicolai vita*, BK 3, 142.

84. "Plus in deserto ecclesiae fonte, hoc est in heremo, quam in aurato synagogae templo, hoc est quam imprudentium huiusce seculi conventiculis reperit. Aliud est quod tibi respondere autumo: quam diverse videlicet sunt ad virtutem vie ad domini enim vineam conducti, iuxta ewangelium: alius sic ibat, alius sic, siquidem et margarite inter se differunt, hec fulgentior est et rotunda, illa vero haud parem habet

decorem, sed alium quendam et varium. Sic et varijs vivendi modis trahimur. Illi in solitudine ac heremo, in sua simplicitate, ut ex vitis sanctorum patrum habemus, coelum rapiunt, alij litterarum periti fulgidique, qui mundo vivunt, cum ipsorum peritia Augustini iuxta sententiam apud inferos sepeliuntur demergunturque." Gundelfingen, *Hystoria Nicolai*, BK 3, 116.

85. John W. O'Malley, "Grammar and Rhetoric in the *Pietas* of Erasmus," *Journal of Medieval and Renaissance Studies* 18 (1988): 81–98; John W. O'Malley, "Introduction," in *Spiritualia and Pastoralia*, ed. John W. O'Malley and Louis A. Perraud, *Collected Works of Erasmus* (Toronto: University of Toronto Press, 1999), ix–xxxi; and Hilmar M. Pabel, *Conversing with God: Prayer in Erasmus' Pastoral Writings*, vol. 13, *Erasmus Studies* (Toronto: University of Toronto Press, 1997), 6–18.

86. Gundelfingen, *Hystoria Nicolai*, BK 3, 115.

87. Desiderius Erasmus, "Eximii doctoris Hieronymi stridonensis vita," in *Omnia Opera: Supplementum*, ed. Wallace K. Ferguson (Hildesheim, Germany: Georg Olms, 1978), lines 308–38; and Desiderius Erasmus, "The Life of the Eminent Doctor Jerome of Stridon," in *Collected Works: Patristic Scholarship, the Edition of St. Jerome*, ed. James F. Brady and John C. Olin (Toronto: University of Toronto Press, 1992), 29.

88. Regarding animosity between the Habsburgs and the confederation, see Paul-Joachim Heinig, "Friedrich III., Maximilian I. und die Eidgenossen," in *Die Eidgenossen und ihre Nachbarn*, ed. Peter Rück (Marburg an der Lahn, Germany: Basilisken Presse, 1991), 267–94; Heinrich Koller, "Die politische Grundhaltung der Habsburger und der Südwesten des Reichs," in ibid., 37–60; and Guy P. Marchal, "Die schweizerische Geschichtsforschung und die österreichische Herrschaft: Ergebnisse und Fragen," in ibid., 16–29. The William Tell story, recounted in the *White Book of Sarnen*, orients the virtuous Tell against the count of Tyrol and his bailiff Gessler (i.e., Habsburg and Austrian), not the emperor. "Das Weisse Buch von Sarnen," in *Quellenwerk zur Entstehung der Schweizerischen Eidgenossenschaft*, ed. Hans Georg Wirz (Aarau, Switzerland: H. R. Sauerländer, 1947), 1–41; and Randolph C. Head, "William Tell and His Comrades: Association and Fraternity in the Propaganda of Fifteenth- and Sixteenth-century Switzerland," *Journal of Modern History* 67 (1995): 527–57.

89. Regarding the importance of the Middle Ages for the Swiss themselves in creating a sense of identity in the early modern period, see Guy P. Marchal, "Das Mittelalter und die nationale Geschichtsschreibung der Schweiz," in *Spannungen und Widersprüche*, ed. Susanna Burghartz, Hans-Jörg Gilomen et al. (Sigmaringen, Germany: Thorbecke, 1992), 91–108.

90. Adolf Gasser, "Ewige Richtung und Burgunderkrieg: Zur Klärung einer alten Streitfrage," *Schweizerische Zeitschrift für Geschichte* 23 (1973): 697–749; Gerrit Himmelsbach, *Die Renaissance des Krieges: Kriegsmonographien und das Bild des Krieges in der spätmittelalterlichen Chronistik am Beispiel der Burgunderkriege* (Zurich: Chronos, 1999), 57–58; Roger Sablonier, "The Swiss Confederation," in *The New Cambridge Medieval History, c. 1415–c. 1500*, ed. Christopher Allmand (New York: Cambridge University Press, 1998), 663–64; Walter Schaufelberger, "Krieg und Kriegertum im eidgenössischen Spätmittelalter," in *500 Jahre Stanser Verkommnis* (Stans, Switzer-

land: Der Historische Verein Nidwalden und der Historisch-Antiquarische Verein Obwalden, 1981), 40–46; Claudius Sieber-Lehmann, *Spätmittelalterlicher Nationalismus: Die Burgunderkriege am Oberrhein und in der Eidgenossenschaft*, vol. 116, *Veröffentlichungen des Max-Planck-Instituts für Geschichte* (Göttingen: Vandenhoeck und Ruprecht, 1995), 11–24, 337–40, 399–407; Claudius Sieber-Lehmann, " 'Teutsche Nation' und Eidgenossenschaft: Der Zusammenhang zu den Türken- und Burgunderkriegen," *Historische Zeitschrift* 253 (1991): 561–602; Norbert Stein, *Burgund und die Eidgenossenschaft zur Zeit Karls des Kühnen* (Frankfurt: Peter Lang, 1979), 108–21; and Alois Steiner, "Die Eidgenossenschaft im Kräftspiel von Österreich, Frankreich und Burgund," in *500 Jahre Stanser Verkommnis*, 13, 20–35.

91. Wilhelm. Baum, "Friedrich IV. von Österreich und die Schweizer Eidgenossen," in *Die Eidgenossen und ihre Nachbarn*, ed. Rück, 87; Alois Niederstätter, "Die ersten Regierungsjahre Kaiser Friedrichs III. und der Südwesten des Reiches," in ibid., 111–30; and Bernhard Stettler, "Reich und Eidgenossenschaft im 15. Jahrhundert," in *Vom "Freiheitskrieg,"* ed. Peter Niederhäuser und Werner Fischer (Zurich: Chronos, 2000), 13–15.

92. Stettler, "Reich," 15–19.

93. Regarding the consequences of this war on the developing Swiss identity and in particular its place in humanist historiography, see Florian Hitz, "Schwabenkrieg und Bündner Identität," in *Vom "Freiheitskrieg,"* ed. Niederhäuser and Fischer, 123–37; and Antje Niederberger, "Sebastian Brant, das Reich und die Eidgenossen," in *Humanisten am Oberrhein*, ed. Sven Lembke and Markus Müller (Leinfelden-Echterdingen, Germany: DRW Verlag, 2004), 189–207.

94. Stettler, "Reich," 19–27. The Peace of Westphalia in 1648 gave Swiss independence international recognition.

95. Regula Schmid, "Die schweizerische Eidgenossenschaft: Ein Sonderfall gelungener politischer Integration?," in *Fragen der politischen Integration im mittelalterlichen Europa*, ed. Werner Maleczek (Ostfildern, Germany: Thorbecke, 2005), 422–25, 433–39.

96. A series of documents from Swiss representatives at Stans attest to some intervention on Brother Claus's part, significant enough to warrant their written thanks. Where these documents were preserved as Gundelfingen and Lupulus were researching and writing cannot be determined; there is no evidence that either author knew of them. We know of them today through copies made and kept by the senders. As for political involvement more generally, some two dozen pieces of evidence exist, dated from 1467 to 1487, that document Brother Claus's political activity. See Ernst Walder, *Das Stanser Verkommnis: Ein Kapitel eidgenössischer Geschichte neu untersucht, die Entstehung des Verkommnisses von Stans in den Jahren 1477 bis 1481* (Stans, Switzerland: Historischer Verein Nidwalden, 1994), 208–16. See also BK 1, 115–20.

There is a growing literature on saints' serving as peacemakers. Most of it has focused on Renaissance Italian saints' negotiating reconciliation within cities, as in the case of Bernadino of Siena. In contrast, Nicholas here negotiated between warring states. Rosa Maria Dessì, "Pratiche della parola di pace nella storia dell'Italia urbana," in *Pace e guerra nel basso medioevo*, ed. Enrico Menestò (Spoleto: Fondazione Centro italiano di studi sull'alto medioevo, 2004), 271–312; Michael Goodich, "Foreigner, Foe, and Neighbor: The Religious Cult as a Forum for Political Reconciliation," in *Meeting the Foreign in the Middle Ages,* ed. Albrecht Classen (New York: Routledge, 2002), 11–26; Sean Kinsella, "'The Lord Give You Peace': The Preaching of Peace in the Writings and Early Lives of Saint Francis of Assisi," *Mediaevistik* 16 (2003): 51–99; Renée Nip, "Exile and Peace: Saint Arnulf of Oudenburg, Bishop of Soissons (d. 1087)," in *Exile in the Middle Ages,* ed. Laura Napran and Elisabeth van Houts, *International Medieval Research* (Turnhout, Belgium: Brepols, 2004), 199–212; and Cynthia Polecritti, *Preaching Peace in Renaissance Italy: Bernardino of Siena and His Audience* (Washington, D.C.: Catholic University of America Press, 2000).

97. Petermann Etterlin, "Kronica von der loblichen Eydtgnoschaft, jr harkommen und sust seltzam strittenn und geschichten," BK 2, 594–95; also ed. Eugen Gruber in *Quellenwerk zur Entstehung der Schweizerischen Eidgenossenschaft,* vol. 3, 3 (Aarau Switzerland, 1965). See August Bernoulli, "Etterlins Chronik der Eidgenossenschaft," *Jahrbuch für schweizerische Geschichte* 1 (1876): 47–49, 256; Feller and Bonjour, *Geschichtsschreibung,* 63–66; and Roland Gröbli, *Die Sehnsucht nach dem "einig Wesen": Leben und Lehre des Bruder Klaus von Flüe* (Zurich: NZN Buchverlag, 1990), 37. Etterlin's reference (1507) was followed by von Schilling (1509/1513). It was picked up by Trithemius and inserted into the *Hirsau Annals* (1511/1513). See *500 Jahre Stanser Verkommnis*; Sablonier, "Swiss Confederation," 647, 660; Schaufelberger, "Krieg und Kriegertum," 37–58; Steiner, "Die Eidgenossenschaft im Kräftspiel," 9–26; Ernst Walder, "Bruder Klaus als politische Ratgeber und die Tagsatzungsverhandlungen in Stans 1481," *Freiburger Geschichtsblätter* 65 (1987–1988): 113–14; and Walder, *Das Stanser Verkommnis.*

98. The German-language lives include those by Sebastian Rhaetus (1521, BK 3, 153–70) and Ulrich Witwyler (1571, BK 2, 769–91; VD16 S1327), both of which passed over Stans in silence, as did the documents of the unsuccessful canonization process in 1591. Hans Salat's legend of 1537 (BK 2, 664–71; VD16 S1326) and the canonization process of 1621, which resulted in Brother Claus's beatification, included no testimony of his witnesses at Stans.

99. Joachim Eichorn, *Historia Fratris Nicolai de Saxo, eremitae Vndervaldensis Helvetii, hominis angelica abstinentia, columbina innocentia, sanctitate admirabili* (Fribourg, Switzerland, 1608). See also Joseph Müller, "Johann Joachim Eichorns deutsche Lebensbeschreibung des seligen Nikolaus von Flüe," *Zeitschrift für schweizerische Kirchengeschichte* 22 (1928): 81–97.

100. Schmid, "Die schweizerische Eidgenossenschaft," 425–29.

101. Bonstetten, "Hystoria fratris Nicolai," BK 1, 82.

102. "Obedienciam summe laudat et pacem, ad quam quidem servare Confederatores apprime exhortatur et omnes ad eum applicantes." Ibid., 89.

103. "In bellis vexillifer, manipulariusque ac primipularius, in pace minister nonnunquam Underwaldensium extitisset spectatissimus." Gundelfingen, *Hystoria Nicolai,* BK 3, 107.

104. Ibid., 111.

105. Ibid.

106. Ibid.

107. Ibid.

108. Ibid., 112n133.

109. Wölflin, *Divi Nicolai vita,* BK 3, 122–23.

110. Ibid., 127.

111. For example, "Inferiores subsilvaticos, superiores vero incolas supra silvam suo more appellant. Legibus et plebiscitis ultro citroque ita datis et acceptis, ut subsivatica communitas unius partis, superior vero duarum partium totius Undervaldensis civitatis nomen et vices gerant ac sortiantur. Annuus utrinque magistratus totius populi deligitur suffragiis, quod et plures alii consueverunt confoederati. Eum vero qui praeest ammanum vocant. Hic cum omnis eius societatis sit supremus, nihil tamen, quod ad rempublicam spectet, absque senatorio ordine molitur aut definit." Ibid., 128.

112. Ibid., 130.

113. Ibid., 135.

114. C. Julius Caesar, *De bello gallico,* 1.1. Other classical references appear, for example, in Tacitus, *Germania,* 28; and Cicero, *Pro Balbo,* 14.32.

115. Conrad Türst, *De situ confoederatorum descriptio,* vol. 6, *Quellen zur Schweizer Geschichte* (Basel: Schneider, 1884).

116. Thomas Maissen, "Ein 'helvetisch Alpenvolck': Die Formulierung eines gesamteidgenössischen Selbstverständnisses in der Schweizer Historiographie des 16. Jahrhunderts," in *Historiographie in Polen und in der Schweiz,* ed. Krzysztof Baczkowski and Christian Simon, *Studia Polono-Helvetica* (Kraków: Uniwersytet Jagiellonski, 1994), 69–86; and Thomas Maissen, "Weshalb die Eidgenossen Helvetier wurden: Die humanistische Definition einer *natio,*" in *Diffusion des Humanismus,* ed. Johannes Helmrath, Ulrich Muhlack et al. (Göttingen: Wallstein, 2002), 210–49.

117. BK 3, 142.

118. Ibid.

119. Ibid., 135.

120. Concerning the derivation of Swiss self-identity from images of the Swiss as the enemy *(Feindbilder),* see Guy P. Marchal, "Über Feindbilder zu Identitätsbildern: Eidgenossen und Reich im Wahrnehmung und Propaganda um 1500," in *Vom "Freiheitskrieg,"* ed. Peter Niederhäuser and Werner Fischer (Zurich: Chronos, 2000), esp. 103–15; and Claudius Sieber-Lehmann, Christian Bertin, and Thomas Wilhelmi, *In Helvetios—wider die Kuhschweizer: Fremd- und Feindbilder von den Schweizern in antieidgenössischen Texten aus der Zeit von 1386 bis 1532,* vol. 14, *Schweizer Texte, n.s.* (Bern: Haupt, 1998).

121. Two works illuminate the patriotic idealization of the farmer in Swiss literature of the late Middle Ages and early modern era: Albert Tanner and Anne-Lise Head-König, eds., *Die Bauern in der Geschichte der Schweiz— Les Paysans dans l'histoire de la Suisse* (Zurich: Chronos, 1992); and Matthias Weishaupt, *Bauern, Hirten und "frume edle puren": Bauern- und Bauernstaatsideologie in der spätmittelalterlichen Eidgenossenschaft und der nationalen Geschichtsschreibung der Schweiz* (Basel: Helbing and Lichtenhahn, 1992), 207–11.

122. Confessional conflicts over Nicholas have emerged recurrently. In the nineteenth century the first efforts at source-critical biographical studies inspired contentious debates. Catholic historian Johann Ming, for example, used his research on Nicholas to argue against the Kulturkampf's insinuation that one could not be both faithfully Catholic and loyally Swiss; Johann Ming, *Der selige Bruder Nikolaus von Flüe: Sein Leben und Wirken*, 4 vols. (Lucerne: Räber, 1861–1878). Ernst Ludwig Rochholz retorted in his subsequent book that Brother Claus should be kept Swiss but that his "römisch-katholischer Musterpatriotismus" had to be debunked; Ernst Ludwig Rochholz, *Die Schweizerlegende vom Bruder Klaus von Flüe nach ihren geschichtlichen Quellen und politischen Folgen* (Aarau, Switzerland: H. R. Sauerländer, 1875), especially pp. 205–28. Ming's final volume appeared in 1878, some three years after Rochholz's one-volume work, allowing him to compare Rochholz's work in its veracity with the "'eternal lies'" (quoting Voltaire) about the Jesuits found in Pascal's *Lettres provinciales* (vol. 4, 286–318). For the an overview of the nineteenth-century Swiss interest in Nicholas, see Urs Altermatt, "Niklaus von Flüe als nationale Integrationsfigur: Metamorphosen der Bruder-Klausen-Mythologie," *Zeitschrift für schweizerische Kirchengeschichte* 81 (1987): 54–60. The concern over confessional affiliation surfaced again in the mid-1940s as Swiss Catholics appealed to Rome for Nicholas's canonization; eminent Reformed theologian Karl Barth denounced the canonization as a seditious attempt by Catholics to co-opt Nicholas from their non-Catholic fellow citizens; Karl Barth, "Ein Heiliger," *Leben und Glauben: Evangelisches Wochenblatt (Laupen)* 19, no. 45 (1944): 8–9. The canonization took place nonetheless. Even the conflicts, however, demonstrate that association with Nicholas made (and makes) one more Swiss, suggesting a cultural identity above the obvious confessional divisions.

CONCLUSION

1. Eugene F. Rice, *Saint Jerome in the Renaissance* (Baltimore: Johns Hopkins University Press, 1984), 197–99.

2. Ibid.

3. Kurth, 1 and 293.

4. Ibid., 301.

5. Ibid., 308.

6. Ibid., 293.

7. Ibid., 328, 329, 341.

8. Dürer's relationships to Renaissance humanism, on the one side, and to Evangelicalism, on the other, have been much discussed in recent scholarly literature. His recent biographer, Jane Hutchison, proposes that identifying Dürer–who died in 1528–as either Catholic or Evangelical is fundamentally anachronistic. Mary Kirn and Jeffrey Chipps Smith refrain from assigning Dürer a confessional designation avant la letter in their recent encyclopedia articles. David Price's work has been lauded for identifying how Dürer not only was influenced by Renaissance humanism but also shaped its appropriation and development in Germany through art. Price further argues not merely that Dürer was (even after the Leipzig disputation of 1519) highly

sympathetic to Luther but also that "he was Lutheran." Price relies on the presumptive connection between early German humanism and Luther's theology. Berndt Hamm's "normative centering"—a model of explaining how fifteenth- and sixteenth-century Christian sensibilities were changing in ways that led sixteenth-century Catholics and Evangelicals to be different from fifteenth-century Christians in similar respects—allows the thematic and iconographic developments in Dürer's works in the 1510s and 1520s to as accurately be called Catholic as Evangelical. Alternatively, Dürer may have simply been in matters theological (and in contrast to his stance vis-à-vis humanist learning) passive, a point one can take from chapter eight of Price's *Albrecht Dürer's Renaissance.* Jane Campbell Hutchison, *Albrecht Dürer: A Biography* (Princeton, N.J.: Princeton University Press, 1990), 178; Mary Em Kirn, "Dürer, Albrecht," in *Oxford Encyclopedia of the Reformation,* ed. Hans J. Hillerbrand (New York: Oxford University Press, 1996), vol. 2, 13; David Price, *Albrecht Dürer's Renaissance: Humanism, Reformation, and the Art of Faith; Studies in Medieval and Early Modern Civilization* (Ann Arbor: University of Michigan Press, 2003), 1–6, 225–48; and Jeffrey Chipps Smith, "Dürer, Albrecht," in *Encyclopedia of the Renaissance,* ed. Paul F. Grendler (New York: Charles Scribner's Sons, 1999), vol. 2, 229. See also Hamm, Berndt. "Normative Centering in the Fifteenth and Sixteenth Centuries: Observations on Religiosity, Theology, and Iconology." *Journal of Early Modern History* 3 (1999): 307–354.

9. Heinrich Denzinger and Peter Hünermann, eds., *Enchiridion symbolorum definitionum et declarationum de rebus fidei et morum,* 38th ed. (Freiburg, Germany: Herder, 1999), 1821–25.

10. Peter Burke, "How to Be a Counter-Reformation Saint," in *Religion and Society in Early Modern Europe, 1500–1800,* ed. Kaspar von Greyerz (London: George Allen and Unwin, 1984); Donald Weinstein and Rudolph M. Bell, *Saints and Society: The Two Worlds of Western Christendom, 1000–1700* (Chicago: University of Chicago Press, 1982). But see also Simon Ditchfield, "How Not to Be a Counter-Reformation Saint," *Papers of the British School in Rome* 60 (1992): 379–422; and Simon Ditchfield, "Sanctity in Early Modern Italy," *Journal of Ecclesiastical History* 47 (1996): 98–112.

11. The first saint from the empire to be canonized was the Bohemian John Nepomucen (1330–1383) by Benedict the XIII in 1729. Benedict XIV issued the bull of solemn canonization for the Swabian Fidelis of Sigmaringen (1577–1622) in 1746.

12. VD16 W3930. Georg Witzel, *Hagiologium, seu de sanctis Ecclesiae* (Mainz: Franciscus Behem, 1541), 2r–5v.

13. Regarding his hagiographical writings see Barbara Henze, *Aus Liebe zur Kirche, Reform: Die Bemühungen Georg Witzels (1501–1573),* ed. Klaus Ganzer, vol. 133, *Reformationsgeschichtliche Studien und Texte* (Münster: Aschendorff, 1995), 103–106, 355–56. Regarding his "irenic theology" and his attempts at reconciling Evangelicals and Catholics before the Council of Trent, see Gerrit Walther, "Humanismus und Konfession," in *Späthumanismus: Studien über das Ende einer kulturhistorischen Epoche,* ed. Notker Hammerstein and Gerrit Walther (Göttingen: Wallstein, 2000), 114.

14. Witzel, *Hagiologium,* ccxlviii–ccxlix. Indeed, Witzel made the opening line of Pope Hadrian VI's bull ("Excelsus dominus militantem ecclesiam preciosorum lapidum vivorum") his own and then took lines from its first part, a synopsis of Benno's

life in the form of an earlier letter to Pope Leo X, beginning "Solebant maiores nostri, beatissime Pater." These words were, in fact, Emser's: His colleague in the canonization campaign and the dean of the Meissen chapter, John Hennig, had greatly abbreviated and slightly revised Emser's vita into what has since been called the *Epitome vetus actorum*. In his avoidance of the use of miracles, Witzel removed several traditional touches that Hennig had apparently returned to Emser's version of Benno's life. I inspected the canonization documents in the manuscript at Dresden (Sächsische Landesbibliothek, Staats und Universitätsbibliothek Dresd. ms. a 12). See partial editions in AASS, June 3: 146E, 148–49. See also Christoph Volkmar, *Die Heiligenerhebung Bennos von Meissen (1523/24): Spätmittelalterliche Frömmigkeit, landesherrliche Kirchenpolitik und reformatorische Kritik im albertinischen Sachsen in der frühen Reformationszeit*, ed. Heribert Smolinsky, vol. 146, *Reformationsgeschichtliche Studien und Texte*, 99n382.

15. Petrus Canisius, *Catechismi latini et germanici*, ed. Friedrich Streicher, 2 vols., *Societatis Jesu selecti scriptores* (Rome: Pontificia Universitas Gregoriana, 1933), vol. 1, 89, 95–97. VD16 C710, Petrus Canisius, *De Maria Virgine incomparabili, et Dei genitrice sacrosancta, libri quinque* (Ingolstadt, Germany: David Sartorius, 1577).

16. For example, Petrus Canisius, *I fioretti di santa Ida di Fischingen*, ed. Roberto Busa, trans. Ilsemarie Brandmair Dallera (Brescia, Italy: Morcelliana, 1996); Petrus Canisius, "Zwey und neunzig Betrachtung und Gebett deß gottseligen fast andächtigen Einsidels Bruder Clausen von Unterwalden," in *Bruder Klaus*, ed. Robert Durrer (Sarnen, Switzerland: Louis Ehrli, 1917), 817–34; Petrus Canisius, *Zwo warhaffte, lustige, recht christliche Historien, auss vilen alten Scribenten zusammen gezogen, ietzunder aber auffs new verbessert, unnd in Druck verfertiget. Die erste vom dem uralten apostolischen Mann S. Beato ersten Prediger im Schweitzerland, die ander von dem berümten Abbt S. Fridolino ersten Prediger zu Glaris und Seckingen* (Fribourg, Switzerland: Abraham Gemperlin, 1590). See, for example, VD16 C759, M1284, N1534, N1535.

17. Trevor Johnson, "Holy Fabrications: The Catacomb Saints and the Counter-Reformation in Bavaria," *Journal of Ecclesiastical History* 47 (1996): 274–97; Edmund Kern, "Counter-Reformation Sanctity: The Bollandists' *Vita* of Blessed Hemma of Gurk," *Journal of Ecclesiastical History* 45 (1994): 412–34; Floridus Röhrig, "Der Kult des heiligen Leopold im Dienste der Gegenreformation," in *Die Kirche in bewegter Zeit*, ed. Rudolf Zinnhobler (Graz, Austria: Syria Medien Service, 1994), 341–54; Philip M. Soergel, *Wondrous in His Saints: Counter-Reformation Propaganda in Bavaria*, vol. 17, *Studies on the History of Society and Culture* (Berkeley: University of California Press, 1993).

18. Paul Holt, "Die Sammlung von Heiligenleben des Laurentius Surius," *Neues Archiv* 44 (1922): 341–64.

19. VD16 S10252–S10257. Laurentius Surius, *De probatis sanctorum historiis*, 1st ed., 6 vols. (Cologne: Calenius and Quentel, 1570–1575).

20. Eight volumes published in Venice between 1551 and 1560; two, in Louvain, Belgium, in 1564.

21. René Aigrain, *L'hagiographie: Ses sources, ses méthodes, son histoire*, ed. Robert Godding, vol. 80, *Subsidia hagiographica* (Brussels: Société des Bollandistes, 2000), 325–27.

22. VD16 S10258–S10263; ZV11179; and VD16 S10264–S10275. Laurentius Surius, *Bewerte Historien der lieben Heiligen Gottes von irem christlichem, gottseligem Leben, warhaffter Bekantnüß, herrlichen Thaten, bestendigem Leiden*, trans. Johannes a Via (Munich: Adam Berg, 1574–1580); Laurentius Surius, *De probatis sanctorum historiis*, 2d ed., 6 (plus index) vols. (Cologne: Calenius and Quentel, 1576–1581).

23. In this regard, Surius's work requires the same reassessment that the *Sanctuarium* of Bonino Mombrizio has recently undergone. Mombrizio's legendary vita was long considered one of the most philologically original works of its kind from the late Middle Ages on account of its redactor's faithful reproduction of the manuscript texts, including scribal errors. Recent scholarship, however, has identified irregularities that are better explained with reference to Mombrizio's political concerns in Milan than to his philological integrity. Alison Knowles Frazier, *Possible Lives: Authors and Saints in Renaissance Italy* (New York: Columbia University Press, 2005), 101–68.

24. Surius, *De probatis sanctorum historiis*, 1st ed., vol. 3, 509–36.

25. VD16 S10243, S10244, ZV14820. Laurentius Surius, *Commentarius brevis rerum in orbe gestarum ab anno salutis 1500 usque in annum 1568* (Cologne: Quentel, 1568). See Soergel, *Wondrous in His Saints*, 96–97.

26. See Joassart's recent historical analysis of "Bollandism," the guiding principles of Bollandist editing; Bernard Joassart, "Jacques Sirmond et les débuts du bollandisme," *Analecta bollandiana* 119 (2001): 345–56. The French Benedictine Congregation of Saint Maurus undertook a similar historical project vis-à-vis writings about the saints in the seventeenth century with less wide-reaching influence: Luc d'Achéry and Jean Mabillon, *Acta sanctorum Ordinis s. Benedicti*, 6 vols. (Paris, 1668–1701). Knowles's narrative history of the Maurists remains the most accessible; David Knowles, *Great Historical Enterprises* (London: Nelson, 1964), 33–62. Chaussy's work is the most current general history; Yves Chaussy, *Les Bénédictins de Saint-Maur*, 2 vols. (Paris: Études augustiniennes, 1989).

27. AASS, Jan. 1: xixxxv.

28. Ibid., Mar. 3: 629–30.

29. Ibid., June 3: 146–231.

Selected Bibliography

MANUSCRIPTS

Augsburg, Bischöfliche Ordinariatsbibliothek, cod. 50.
Bamberg, Staatsbibliothek Bamberg, RB, ms. 122, 123, 124; HV ms. 132
  (Mro. 2137).
Berlin, Staatsbibliothek zu Berlin, Preussischer Kulturbesitz, ms. theol. lat.
  fol. 706; ms. theol. lat. oct. 171
Brussels, Bibliothèque royale de Belgique, ms. 8930–31 (3494)
Cologne, Dombibliothek Köln, cod. 271
Cologne, Historisches Archiv der Stadt Köln, codices 164, 164a, 164b
Dresden, Sächsische Landesbibliothek, Staats- und Universitätsbibliothek
  Dresden, ms. Dresd. a 12, nr. 2
Frauenfeld, Kantonsbibliothek Thurgau, Y 68, Y 68a
Frauenfeld, Staatsarchiv des Kantons Thurgau, Schachtelsignatur 7' 41' 102
Fulda, Hessische Landesbibliothek, cod. Aa 96
Jena, Thüringer Universitäts- und Landesbibliothek, ms. Sag. q. 5
Koblenz, Landeshauptarchiv, D 01, Bestand 701, nr. 12 and nr. 13.
Lippetal-Herzfeld, St.-Ida-Pfarrarchiv, unnumbered cod.
Munich, Bayerische Staatsbibliothek München, cgm. 409, clm. 692, clm.
  901, clm. 4353, clm. 27044, clm. 27045, clm. 27372
Münster, Nordrhein-Westfälisches Staatsarchiv, Altertumsverein Münster
  (Dep.), mss. 136 and 356, and Manuskriptensammlung, ms. VII 1032
Nuremberg, Staatsarchiv Nürnberg, Rep. 52a, nr. 2; Rep. 14, St. Sebald, nr.
  465; and Reichstadt Nürnberg, Ratskanzlei, A-Laden, 142, nr. 16 (Rep.
  15a) (Film S3484)
Nuremberg, Stadtbibliothek Nürnberg, cod. cent. III, 69; cod. cent. VII, 43;
  cod. Solger 37

Paderborn, Erzbischöfliche Akademische Bibliothek, cod. Theod. Ba 2
Paris, Bibliothèque Nationale de France, ms. 5656; ms. lat. 10161
Rome, Vat. Pal. lat. cod. 850
St. Gallen, Stiftsbibliothek 603
Trier, Stadtbibliothek, ms. 2002/92
Vienna, Nationalbibliothek, cod. ser. nr. 35753–56
Weimar, Thüringisches Hauptstaatsarchiv HS Reg. O 157, HS Reg. O 29a, HS Reg. O 29b, and QE 42/10.
Würzburg, Universitätsbibliothek, M ch. q. 95/2

INDICES OF SOURCES

Bibliotheca Hagiographica Latina (BHL)

109	4148	4927	5394	6406
227	4149	4937	5878	6407
1028	4165	4939	6227z	7535
1064	4812	4955	6228	7536d
1066	4922	4956	6394	7640
1166d	4923	4957	6395	7775
1204	4924	4958	6397	7941
1467	4925	4959	6404	8362
4143	4926	5096	6405	8990

Gesamtkatalog der Wiegendrucke (GW)

4919	M27567	M31630	M38692
4920	M27572	M3175210	M38774
5067	M29712	M31754	M38775
5068	M29714	M31765	M40784
5579	M30412	M31766	M51767
6466	M30431	M32672	V, 573
7075	M30434	M32676	
M27563	M31627	M33835	
M27564	M31628	M38537	

Verzeichnis der im deutschen Sprachbereich erschienenen Drucke des 16. Jahrhunderts (VD16)

B1184	C757	E2968	K2477
B2050	E1085	F2716	L868
B3153	E1117	G2924	M936
B5746	E1118	H3482	M5078
B5756	E1216	H5278	S2392
B8095	E1217	K2476	S2393

S2394	S10257–75	W3408	ZV11179
S10243	V1739	W3409	ZV14820
S10244	V1741	W3930	
S10252	W3344	ZV9238	

VITAE OF HOLY MEN AND WOMEN IN GERMANY, COMPOSED AND/OR
PRINTED BETWEEN 1470 AND 1530 IN THE GERMAN LANDS OF THE
HOLY ROMAN EMPIRE

Adelaide: *Vita s. Adelhaydis*. Durlach, Germany, 1516.

Adelph: Wimpheling, Jakob. *Vita s. Adelphi*. 1506.

Afra: Bild, Veit, ed. *Gloriosorum Christi confessorum Uldarici et Symperti, necnon beatissime martyris Aphre, Augustane sedis patronorum fidelissimorum historie*. Augsburg: S. Otmar, 1516.

Albert: Petrus de Prussia. *Legenda venerabilis domini Alberti magni*. Cologne: Johannes Guldenschaiff, 1486/1487.

Albert: Rudolphus de Novimagio. *Legenda litteralis Alberti magni*. Cologne: Johannes Koelhoff de Lübeck, 1490.

Basin: Scheckmann, Johannes. *Vita s. Basini ep. Treverensis*, ca. 1510.

Beat: Agricola, Daniel. *Almi confessoris et anachorete Beati, Helveciorum primi evangeliste et apostoli a sancto Petro missi vita iam pridem exarata*. Basel: Adam Peter von Langendorff, 1511.

Benno: Emser, Hieronymus. *Epitome ad sanctissimum dominum nostrum papam Julium secundum super vita, miraculis et testimonia divi patris Bennonis episcopi quondam insignis et ingenue ecclesie Missnensis*. Leipzig: Melchior Lotter der Ältere, 1505.

Benno: Emser, Hieronymus. *Divi Bennonis vita*. Leipzig: Melchior Lotter der Ältere, 1512.

Boniface: *Legenda s Bonifacii patroni Germaniae*. ca. 1500.

Bruno: Blomevenna, Petrus. *Vita s. Brunonis*. Cologne: Charterhouse St. Barbara, 1516.

Christina: *Legenda ss. virginum Christianae, Kunegundis, Mechtundis, et Wibrandis*. Basel: Michael Furter, after 1504.

Corbinian: Freiberger, Johann. *Vita s. Corbiniani*. Before 1520.

Elizabeth: Montanus, Jacobus. *Vita illustris ac dive Helisabeth Hungarorum regis filie*. Münster, Germany, 1511.

Elizabeth: Montanus, Jacobus. *Divae Helisabet Hungarorum regis filiae vita*. Cologne: Eucharius Cervicornus, 1521.

Fridolin: Seckinganus, Baltherus. *Vita s. Fridolini*. Basel: Peter Kollecker; Nuremberg: Anton Koberger, 1483–1485.

Gerold: Bonstetten, Albrecht von. *Legenda b. Geroldi, heremite olim quoque Saxonie ducis*. ca. 1484.

Hildegard: *Vita s. Hildegardis reginae*. 1472.

Ida of Herzfeld: Cincinnius von Lippstadt, Johannes. *Vita et sancta conversatio b. Idae*. 1517.

Ida of Toggenburg: Bonstetten, Albrecht von. *Vita b. Idae*. 1481.

Ida of Toggenburg: Bonstetten, Albrecht von. *Legenda b. Idae.* 1485.

Irmina: Trithemius, Johannes. *Vita s. Hiriminae.* [lost].

Kunegund: *Legenda ss. virginum Christianae, Kunegundis, Mechtundis, et Wibrandis.* Basel: Michael Furter, after 1504.

Lambert:Engelbrecht, Philipp "Engentinus." *Divi Lamberti episcopi traiectensis vita.* Basel, 1519.

Ludger: Cincinnius von Lippstadt, Johannes. *Vita d. Ludgeri Memigardevordensis ecclesie.* Cologne: Quentel, 1515.

Macharius: Trithemius, Johannes. *Vita domini Macharii primi abbatis.* ca. 1514.

Maximus: Trithemius, Johannes. *Vita s. Maximi.* 1515.

Maximilian: *Vita ac legenda s. Maximiliani.* Cologne: Bartholomaeus von Unckel. After 1484.

Mechtund: *Legenda ss. virginum Christianae, Kunegundis, Mechtundis, et Wibrandis.* Basel: Michael Furter, after 1504.

Meinrad: Bonstetten, Albrecht von. *Passio s. Meginradi.* 1481.

Nicholas: Bonstetten, Albrecht von. *Historia fratris Nicolai de Rupe.* 1479–1481.

Nicholas: Gundelfingen, Heinrich. *Historia Nicolai Underwaldensis heremite.* 1488.

Nicholas: Wölflin, Heinrich "Lupulus." *De vita Nicolai Undervaldensis.* 1501.

Otto: Lang, Andreas. *Vita s. Ottonis ep. Babenbergensis.* [1]1474

Otto: Lang, Andreas. *Vita s. Ottonis ep. Babenbergensis.* [2]1498–1499.

Rhabanus: Trithemius, Johannes. *Vita b. Rhabani Mauri.* 1515.

Sebald: Meisterlin, Sigismund. *Vita s. Sebaldi.* [1]1484.

Sebald: Meisterlin, Sigismund. *Vita s. Sebaldi.* [2]1488.

Servatio: Rolevinck, Werner. *Legenda minor s. Servationis ep. Tungrensis.* 1472.

Simpert: Bild, Veit, ed. *Gloriosorum Christi confessorum Uldarici et Symperti, necnon beatissime martyris Aphre, Augustane sedis patronorum fidelissimorum historie.* Augsburg: S. Otmar, 1516.

Swithbert: Pseudo-Marcellinus. *Vita divi Swiberti Verdensis ecclesie episcopi, Saxonum Frisorumque apostoli,* ed. Gerardus de Harderwyck and Ortwinus Gratius. Cologne: Heinrich von Neusse, 1508.

Ulrich: Bild, Veit, ed. *Gloriosorum Christi confessorum Uldarici et Symperti, necnon beatissime martyris Aphre, Augustane sedis patronorum fidelissimorum historie.* Augsburg: S. Otmar, 1516.

Wibrand: *Legenda ss virginum Christianae, Kunegundis, Mechtundis, et Wibrandis.* Basel: Michael Furter, after 1504.

Wolfgang: *Legenda s. Wolfgangi ep. Ratisponensis.* Burgdorf, Switzerland: Drucker des Jacobus de Paradiso, 1475.

Wolfgang: *Vita d. Wolfgangi praesulis eximii.* Landhut, Germany: Johann Weyssenburger, 1516.

Legendaries in Manuscript

Cologne Legendary of the Windesheim Congregation, 1463–1465. Cologne, Historisches Archiv der Stadt, cod. 164, 164a, 164b.

Kreuzenstein Legendary, 1452–1483. Vienna, Österreichische Nationalbibliothek, cod. ser. nr. 35753–56.

Magnum legendarium Bodecense, 1460. Fragments: Paderborn, Erzbischöfliche Akademische Bibliothek, cod. Theod. Ba. 2.

Martyrologium Greveni. Berlin, Staatsbibliothek zu Berlin, Preussischer Kulturbesitz, ms. theol. lat. fol. 706.

Passionale decimum of Blaubeuren, ca. 1496. Fulda, Hessische Landsbibliothek, cod. Aa96.

SELECT PRIMARY LITERATURE ANTEDATING 1806 (INCLUDING LATER EDITIONS)

Aeneas Silvius "Germania" und Jakob Wimpfeling "Responsa et replicae ad Eneam Silvium," ed. Adolf Schmidt. Cologne: Böhlau, 1962.

Agricola, Daniel. *Almi confessoris et anachorete Beati, Helveciorum primi Evangeliste et Apostoli a sancto Petro missi vita iam pridem exarata.* Basel: Adam Peter von Langendorff, 1511.

Agricola, Rudolph. *Anna mater* (1484). In *Opuscula, orationes, epistolae,* ed. Alardus Amstelredamus, 297–306. Frankfurt: Minerva, 1975.

———. *Anna mater* (1484), edited by Angelika Dörfler-Diercken and Wolfgang Schibel. In Wilhelm Kühlmann, ed. *Rudolf Agricola, 1444-1485: Protagonist des nordeuropäischen Humanismus zum 550. Geburtstag,* 294-311. Memoria. Bern: P. Lang, 1994.

"Aktenstücke zur Geschichte der *Vita Bennonis Misnensis,"* ed. Richard Doebner. *Neues Archiv für Sächsische Geschichte und Alterthumskunde* 7 (1886): 131–44.

Altfridus. "Vita sancti Ludgeri." In *Die Vitae sancti Liudgeri,* ed. Wilhelm Diekamp. Münster, Germany: Theissing'schen Buchhandlung, 1881.

Argumentum oder Inhalt der Comedi von S. Benno, zehenden Bischoff der Kirchen zu Meissen in Sachsenlandt, welches heiliger Leib jetzundt allhie in unser lieben Frawen Hauptkirchen herrlich auffbehalten. Munich: N. Henricus, 1598.

Bebel, Heinrich. *Liber hymnorum.* Tübingen, Germany, 1501.

Bild, Veit. *Gloriosorum Christi confessorum Uldarici et Symperti, necnon beatissime martyris Aphre, Augustane sedis patronorum fidelissimorum historie.* Augsburg: S. Otmar, 1516.

———. *Leben, verdienen vnd wunderwerck der hailigen Augspurger Bistumbs bischoffen, sant Ulrichs und Symprechts, auch der säligen martrerin sant Aphre, irer muter Hilarie geschlecht und gesellschafft, in unserm daselbst loblichen gotshauß rastend, Das.* Augsburg: S. Otmar, 1516.

Blomevenna, Petrus. *Sermo de sancto Brunone.* Cologne, 1516.

———. "Sermo de sancto Brunone" (facsimile). *Analecta Cartusiana* 130 (1995): 104–43.

———. *Vita sancti Brunonis.* Cologne: St. Barbara Charterhouse, 1516.

———. "Vita sancti Brunonis" (facsimile). *Analecta Cartusiana* 130 (1995): 32–103.

Brant, Sebastian. *Carmina in laudem b. Mariae Virginis multorumque sanctorum.* Basel: Johann Bergmann, no earlier than 1494.

————. "In divi Onophrii laudem." In *Die Renaissance eines Heiligen: Sebastian Brant und Onuphrius eremita*, ed. Roland Stieglecker, 541. Wiesbaden: Harrassowitz, 2001.

————. *Varia Carmina.* Basel: Johann Bergmann von Olpe, 1498.

Braun, Placidus. *Notitia historico-literaria de codicibus manuscriptis in bibliotheca liberi ac imperialis monasterii ordinis s. Benedicti ad ss. Udalricum et Afram Augustae extantibus.* 6 vols. Vol. 3. Augsburg, 1793.

Brouwer, Christoph. *Sidera illustrium et sanctorum virorum qui Germaniam praesertim magnam olim gestis rebus ornarunt.* Mainz: J. Albini, 1616.

Bruder Klaus, ed. Robert Durrer and Rupert Amschwand. Sarnen, Switzerland: Regierungsrat des Kantons Obwalden, 1917–1918, 1987.

Brugman, Johannes. *Vita alme virginis Lijdwine.* Teksten en Documenten, vol. 2. Groningen, the Netherlands: Rijksuniversiteit te Utrecht, 1963.

Bulla Canonizationis Sancti Leopoldi Marchionis. Vienna, 1485.

Caesarius of Heisterbach. *Dialogus miraculorum*, ed. Joseph Strange. 2 vols. Cologne: H. Lempertz, 1851.

Canisius, Heinrich. *Thesaurus monumentorum ecclesiasticorum et historicorum*, 2d ed., ed. Jacques Basnage. Antwerp: Rudolphum and Gerhardum Wetstenios, 1725.

Canisius, Peter. *Catechismi latini et germanici*, ed. Friedrich Streicher. 2 vols., *Societatis Jesu selecti scriptores.* Rome: Pontificia Universitas Gregoriana, 1933.

————. *De Maria Virgine incomparabili, et Dei genitrice sacrosancta, libri quinque.* Ingolstadt, Germany: David Sartorius, 1577.

————. *I fioretti di santa Ida di Fischingen*, ed. Roberto Busa; trans. Ilsemarie Brandmair Dallera. Brescia, Italy: Morcelliana, 1996.

————. *Kurze Beschreibung der gottseligen Frau Sankt Yta Gräfin von Kirchberg.* s. 1, 1600.

————. "Zwey und neunzig Betrachtung und Gebett deß gottseligen fast andächtigen Einsidels Bruder Clausen von Unterwalden." In *Bruder Klaus*, ed. Robert Durrer, 817–34. Sarnen, Switzerland: Louis Ehrli, 1917.

————. *Zwo warhaffte, lustige, recht christliche Historien, auss vilen alten Scribenten zusammen gezogen, ietzunder aber auffs new verbessert, unnd in Druck verfertiget. Die erste vom dem uralten apostolischen Mann S. Beato ersten Prediger im Schweitzerland, die ander von dem berümten Abbt S. Fridolino ersten Prediger zu Glaris und Seckingen.* Fribourg, Switzerland, 1590.

Celtis, Conrad. *Oratio in Gymnasio in Ingolstadio publice recitata, cum carminibus ad orationem pertinentibus.* Bibliotheca scriptorum medii recentisque aevorum saec, ed. Hans Rupprich, 15–16. Leipzig: Teubner, 1932.

————, ed. *Opera Hrosvite, illustris virginis et monialis Germane, gente Saxonico orte.* Nuremberg: Sodalitas Celtica, 1501.

Cincinnius von Lippstadt, Johannes. *Vita beate Ide.* In "Renaissance Revisions: A Brief Analysis and Critical Edition of Cincinnius's *Vita s. Ida*, a Revision of BHL 4143." *Analecta bollandiana* 124 (2006): 343-58.

————. *Vita divi Ludgeri Mimigardevordensis ecclesie.* Cologne: Quentel, 1515.

————. "Vita sancti Ludgeri." In *Die Vitae sancti Liudgeri*, ed. Wilhelm Diekamp. Münster, Germany: Theissing'schen Buchhandlung, 1881.

Cochlaeus, Johannes. *Psalterium beati Brunonis episcopi quondam Herbipolensis.* Leipzig: Schmidt, Nickel, 1533.

d'Achéry, Luc, and Jean Mabillon. *Acta sanctorum ordinis s. Benedicti.* 6 vols. Paris, 1668–1701.

Eichorn, Joachim. *Historia fratris Nicolai de Saxo, eremitae vndervaldensis helvetii, hominis angelica abstinentia, columbina innocentia, sanctitate admirabili.* Fribourg, Switzerland, 1608.

Emser, Hieronymus. *Antwurt auff das lesterliche Buch wider Bischoff Benno zu Meyßen unnd Erhebung der Heiligen jungst außgegangen.* Dresden: Emserpresse, 1524.

———. *Divi Bennonis Misnensis quondam episcopi vita miracula et alia quedam non tam Misnensibus quam Germanis omnibus decora.* Leipzig: Melchior Lotter the Elder, 1512.

———. *Epitome ad sanctissimum dominum nostrum papam Julium secundum super vita miraculis et sanctimonia divi patris Bennonis Episcopi quondam insignis et ingenue ecclesie Missnensis.* Leipzig: Melchior Lotter the Elder, 1505.

———. *Das heilig leben und legend des seligen Vatters Bennonis weylund Bischoffen tzu Meyssen.* Leipzig: Melchior Lotter the Elder, 1517.

Engelbrecht, Philipp "Engentinus." *Divi Lamberti episcopi traiectensis vita.* Basel: Johann Froben, 1519.

Erasmus, Desiderius. "Hieronymi Stridonensis vita." In *Erasmi Opuscula,* ed. Wallace K. Ferguson, 134–90. The Hague: Nijhoff, 1933.

Flugschriften gegen die Reformation (1525-1530), eds. Adolf Laube and Ulman Weiss. 2 vols. Berlin: Akademie Verlag, 2000.

Freiberger, Johannes. *Origo christiane religionis ecclesie Frisingensis.* Landshut: Johann Weißenburger, 1520.

Gewiß: vnd Approbirte Historia von S. Bennonis, etwo Bischoffen zu Meissen, Leben vnd Wunderzaichen, so er vor vnd nach seinem seligen Absterben, an mancherlay orthen, durch die Gnad Gottes gewircket, auch sein Canonization vnd Fest betreffent. Munich: N. Henricus, 1606.

Glaubwirdig: und approbirte Historia von S. Bennonis, etwo Bischoffen zu Meissen, Leben vnd Wunderzeichen, so er vor vnd nach seinem seligen Absterben, durch die Gnad Gottes geweürcket, auch sein Canonization vnd Fest betreffent. Munich: N. Henricus, 1601.

Gundelfingen, Heinrich. "Historia Nicolai Underwaldensis eremitae." In *Bruder Klaus,* ed. Rupert Amschwand, 105–16. Sarnen, Switzerland: Regierungsrat des Kantons Obwalden, 1987.

———. *L'office chante de Nicolas de Flue: 1488–1650–1950, das Offizium von Gundelfingen 1488, édition critique mit Reproduktionen des Offiziums und der Historia Nicolai des Bologneser Originals,* ed. Jean-Marie Curti. Geneva: Opéra-Studio de Genève, 1991.

Hartmann, Christopher. *Annales heremi Dei Parae Matris monasterii in Helvetia.* Freiburg, Germany, 1612.

Heidenreich, Martin. *Benno, episcopus olim Misenensis, redivivus, seu vita Bennonis: ex probatæ fidei monumentis et codicibus manuscriptis eruta.* Dresden and Leipzig: Hekelius, 1694.

Hennig, Johannes (?). "Vita beati Bennonis episcopi Misnensis ad Leonem X." Rome, 1521.

Hinderbach, Johannes. "Ein Brief von Johannes Hinderbach an den Gurker Bischof Ulrich III. Sonnenberger," ed. Jakob Obersteiner. *Carinthia I: Mittheilungen des Geschichtsvereins für Kärten* 175 (1985): 212–13.

Hugo, Pierre. *Beati Nicolai de Rupe.* Rome, 1691.

Jacobus de Gouda. "Legenda copiosa et metrica." In *Beati Alberti Magni episcopi quondem Ratisbonensis tractatus de forma orandi eiusdem Legenda metrica praemissa,* ed. Albert Wimmer, vii–x. Regensburg, 1902.

———. "Legenda metrica Alberti." In *Legenda litteralis Alberti Magni,* A'-ii-r–B'-i-r. Cologne: Johannes Koelhoff de Lübeck, 1490.

Justinianus, Vincentius. *Biblia Mariae: Opus a b. Alberto magno . . . conscriptum. Accessere compendiosa vitae descripto et panegyricis propter publicos applausus et apotheosis eiusdem b. Alberti extensionem nunc primum in lucem edita.* Cologne: Boetzer, 1625.

Lampertus Hersfeldensis. "Annales." In *Opera,* ed. Oswald Holder-Egger. MGH SRG 38. Hannover: Hahn, 1894 (reprint, 1984).

Lang, Andreas. "De vita et operibus beatissimi Ottonis Babenbergensis episcopi, et confessoris Christi ac Pomeranicae gentis apostoli." In *Scriptores rerum episcopatus Bambergensis,* ed. Johann Peter Ludewig. Frankfurt and Leipzig, 1718.

———. "De vita s. Ottonis" (2d rev. ed.). In *Divi Bambergenses s Henricus imperator s Kundegundis imperatrix s Otho episcopus,* ed. Jakob Gretser. Ingolstadt, Germany: Adam Sartorius, 1611.

———. *De vita s. Ottonis Babenbergensis ecclesiae episcopi ac Pomeranorum gentis apostolic libri quatuor* (1st ed.), ed. Valerius Jasche. Kolberg (Kołobrzeg, Poland): Röderus, 1681.

"Legenda patroni Germaniae sancti Bonifacii, libris II." In *Scriptores rerum Germanicarum praecipue Saxonicarum,* ed. Johann Burchard Menke, vol. 1, 833–51. Leipzig: Joannes Christianus Martinus, 1728.

"Legenda sancti Bonifacii." *Zeitschrift des Vereins für thüringische Geschichte und Alterthumskunde* 6 (1865): 238–48.

"Legenda sanctissime matrone Anne." Louvain, Belgium, 1496. Also, Leipzig, 1497, 1498.

Libelli tres perutiles. Heidelberg, 1500. (Hain 10070.)

Loër, Dirk. *D. Dionysii Carthusiani, doctoris extatici vita, simul et operum eius fidissimus catalogus.* Cologne: Jasper von Gennep, 1532.

———. *Elucidissima in divi Pauli epistolas commentaria Dionysij, olim Carthusiani apud cedlebrem Ruremundam. . . . Vita authoris, simul et operum illius cathologus, cum indice, et illustrissimi principis Caroli, ducis Geldriae etc. epistola hortatoria, necnon et sacrae facultatis theologicae Coloniensis, approbatione, commentarijs ipsis praemittunt.* Cologne: Quentel, 1532.

Major, Georg. *Vitae patrum, in usum ministrorum verbi, quo ad eius fieri potuit repurgatae.* Wittenberg, Germany: Seitz, 1544.

Mamphrasius, Wolfgang. *De miraculis Bennonis episcopi olim Misnensis.* Leipzig: Johann Börner the Younger, 1606.

Meisterlin, Sigismund. "Vita s. Sebaldi" (1484 and 1488 editions). In Arno Borst, "Die Sebaldslegenden in der mittelalterlichen Geschichte Nürnbergs." *Jahrbuch für fränkische Landesforschung* 26 (1966): 122–28.

Menke, Johann Burkhard, ed. *Scriptores rerum Germanicarum praecipue Saxonicarum.* Leipzig: Johann Christian Martin, 1728.

Montanus, Jacobus. *De passione ac morte Christi fasciculus mirrhe coccineo lugubris metri funiculo colligatus.* Cologne: Quentel, 1511.

———. *Divae Helisabet Hungarorum regis filiae vita.* Cologne: Eucharius Cervicornus Agrippinatis, 1521.

———. *Divi Pauli apostoli vita, carmine Heroico foelicissime descripta.* Cologne: Eucharius Cervicornus, 1518.

———. *Vita illustris ac divae Elisabeth hungarorum regis filiae,* ed. Herrman Müller. Heilbronn: Gebr. Henninger, 1878.

Myconius, Oswald. *Vom Leben und Sterben Huldrych Zwinglis: Das älteste Lebensbild Zwinglis,* ed. Ernst Gerhard Rüsch. Vol. 50, *Mitteilungen zur vaterländischen Geschichte.* St. Gallen, Switzerland: Fehr'sche Buchhandlung, 1979.

Oettinger, Rebecca Wagner. *Music as Propaganda in the German Reformation.* Burlington, Vt.: Ashgate, 2001.

Pavinis, Johannes Franciscus de. *Defensorium canonisationis S. Leopoldi.* Passau, Germany: Johann Petri, 1491.

———. *Oratio in laudem Leopoldi Marchionis Austrie.* Rome: Eucharius Silber, 1484.

———. *Rede auf den Heiligen Leopold,* ed. Ludwig Bieler. Innsbruck: Tyrolia, 1936.

Petrus de Prussia. *Beati Alberti doctoris Magni ex ordine Praedicatorum episcopi Ratisponensis de adhaerendo Deo libellus. Accedit eiusdem Alberti vita, deo adhaerentes exemplar.* Antwerp, 1621.

———. *Legenda venerabilis domini Alberti Magni.* Cologne: Johannes Guldenschaff, 1486–1487.

Pius II [Aeneas Silvius Piccolomini]. "De gravamine Germanicae nationis." In *Opera quae extant omnia,* 836–71. Basel: Heinrich Petri, 1551.

———. "Europa in qua sui temporis varias historias complectitur." In *Opera quae extant omnia,* 387–471. Basel, Heinrich Petri, 1551.

———. *Germania,* ed. Adolf Schmidt. Cologne: Böhlau, 1962.

———. "Historia de Europa." In *Opera geographica et historica,* 218–374. Helmstadt, Germany: Süstermann, 1699.

Poggio Bracciolini, Gian Francesco. *Epistolae,* ed. Tommaso De Tonelli. 3 vols. Florence: L. Marchini, 1832–1861.

Polzmann, Balthasar. *Compendivm vitae, miracvlorvm S. Leopoldi, sexti marchionis Avstriae, cognomento Pii.* Klosterneuburg, Austria, 1591.

Pseudo-Marcellinus. *Vita divi Swiberti Verdensis ecclesie episcopi, Saxonum Frisorumque apostoli,* ed. Gerardus de Harderwyck and Ortwinus Gratius. Cologne: Heinrich von Neusse, 1508.

Ptolemy. "Geography." In *Ptolemy's Geography: An Annotated Translation of the Theoretical Chapters,* ed. J. Lennart Berggren and Alexander Jones. Princeton, N.J.: Princeton University Press, 2000.

Puteus, Franciscus [François Dupuy]. *Vita beati Brunonis primi institutoris ordinis Carthusiensium.* Basel, 1515.

Quetif, Jacobus, and Jacobus Echard. *Scriptores ordinis praedicatorum recensiti.* Paris: Ballard and Simart, 1719–1723.

Rader, Matthaus, and Raphael Sadeler. *Bavaria pia.* Munich: Raphael Sadeler, 1628.

———. *Bavaria sancta.* Munich: Raphael Sadeler, 1615.

Reuchlin, Johann. "Sergius." In *Johann Reuchlins Komödien: Ein Beitrag zur Geschichte des lateinischen Schuldramas,* ed. Hugo Holstein. Halle a. Saale, Germany: Verlag der Buchhandlung des Waisenhauses, 1973.

Rhenanus, Beatus. *Libri tres rerum germanicarum nov-antiquarum, historico-geographicarum.* Frankfurt am Main: Samuel Tobias Hocker, 1712.

Rolevinck, Werner. *Ein Buch zum Lobe Westfalens des alten Sachsenlands: Der Text der lateinischen Erstausgabe vom Jahre 1474 mit deutschen Übersetzung,* ed. Hermann Bücker. Münster: Regensbergsche Verlagsbuchhandlung, 1982.

Rosweyde, Heribert. *Fasti sanctorum quorum vitae in Belgicis bibliothecis manuscriptae.* Antwerp: Officina Plantiniana, 1607.

———. *Vitae patrum.* Leiden, the Netherlands: Durand, 1617.

Rudolphus de Novimagio. *Legenda beati Alberti magni,* ed. Heribert Christian Scheeben. Cologne, 1928.

———. *Legenda litteralis Alberti Magni.* Cologne: Johannes Koelhoff de Lübeck, 1490.

Schevius, Henricus. *In divi Brunonis primi Carthusianae religionis fundatoris ac patroni montisque Carthusiae praecomium.* Cologne, 1519.

Schiner, Matthäus. *Korrespondenzen und Akten zur Geschichte des Kardinals Matthäus Schiner,* ed. Albert Büchi. 2 vols. Basel: Rudolf Geering, 1920, 1925.

Seckinganus, Baltherus. *Vita s. Fridolini.* Basel: Peter Kollecker; Nuremberg: Anton Koberger, 1483–1485.

Seyffarth, Carolus Fridericus. *Ossilegium s. Bennonis episcopi quondam Misnensis seu vita et acta ipsius.* Munich: Jacobus Otto, 1765.

Spalatin, Georg. *Magnifice consolatoria exempla, et sententiae, ex vitis et passionibus sanctorum et aliorum summorum virorum, brevissime collecta opera.* Wittenberg, Germany: Schirlent, 1544.

Stretzinger, Thomas. *Oratio de divo Leopoldo III Austriae marchione in Universitate Vindobonensi habita. Bibliotheca scriptorum Medii Recentisque Aevorum . . . Saec. XVI,* ed. Hermann Maschek. Leipzig: Teubner, 1934.

Surius, Laurentius. *Bewerte Historien der lieben Heiligen Gottes von irem christlichem, gottseligem Leben, warhaffter Bekantnüß, herrlichen Thaten, bestendigem Leiden,* trans. Johannes a Via. Munich: Adam Berg, 1574–1580.

———. *Commentarius brevis rerum in orbe gestarum ab anno salutis 1500 usque in annum 1568.* Cologne: Quentel, 1568.

———. *De probatis sanctorum historiis.* 6 vols. Cologne: Calenius and Quentel, 1570–1575.

———. *De probatis sanctorum historiis,* 2d ed., 6 vols. (plus index). Cologne: Calenius and Quentel, 1576–1581.

"Translatio beati Alberti Magni." *Analecta sacri ordinis Fratrum Praedicatorum* 3 (1897): 349–51.

Trithemius, Johannes. *Annales Hirsaugienses*. 2 vols. St. Gallen, Switzerland: Schlegel, 1690.

———. *De laudibus sanctissime matris Anne tractatus perquam utilis*. Mainz, 1494.

———. "De viris illustribus ordinis sancti Benedicti (1492)." In *Joannis Trithemii opera pia et spiritualia*, ed. Johannes Busaeus, 16–149. Mainz: Johannes Albinus, 1604–1605.

———. *Opera Historica*, ed. Marquard Freher. 1601. Reprint, Frankfurt: Minerva 1966.

———. "Vita beati Maximi, episcopi Moguntini." In *De probatis sanctorum historiis*, ed. Laurentius Surius, 407–14. Cologne, 1581.

Tuberinus, Johannes Matthias. *Historia completa de passione et obitu pueris Simonis*. Trent, Italy: Albrecht Kunne für Hermann Schindeleyp, 1476.

Türst, Conrad. *De situ confoederatorum descriptio*. Vol. 6, *Quellen zur Schweizer Geschichte*. Basel: Schneider, 1884.

Uffing. "Ex Vita s. Idae." MGH SSf 2 (1829): 569–76.

———. "Leben und die Wunder der heiligen Ida von Herzfeld (um 980), Das." In *Heilige Ida von Herzfeld, 980–1980*, ed. Géza Jászai, 9–25. Münster, 1980.

———. "Vita sanctae Idae." In *Die Kaiserurkunden der Provinz Westfalen, 777–1313*, ed. Roger Wilmans, 2 vols., vol. 1, 470–88. Münster: Friedrich Regensberg, 1867.

Urkunden und Aktenstücke zum Kanonisationsprozeß des Margrafen Leopold III. des Heiligen, ed. Vinzenz Oskar Ludwig. Jahrbuch des Stiftes Klosterneuburg, vol. 9. Klosterneuburg, Austria, 1919.

Vergerio, Pietro Paolo. *Pierpaolo Vergerio the Elder and Saint Jerome: An edition and translation of Sermones pro sancto Hieronymo*, ed. John M. McManamon. Tempe: Arizona Center for Medieval and Renaissance Studies, 1999.

Vita beati Hartmanni episcopi Brixinensis (1140–1164), ed. Anselm Sparber. *Schlern-Schriften*, vol. 46. Innsbruck: Universitäts-Verlag Wagner, 1940.

"Vita brevis et compendiosa Alberti Magni" from the *Legenda Coloniensis*, ed. Paulus von Loë. *Analecta bollandiana* 19 (1900): 272–84.

"Vita Lebuini presbiteri et confessoris." MGH SS 30.2 (1934): 791–95.

"Vita prima Bennonis," ed. David J. Collins. *Revue Bénédictine* 111 (2001): 551–56.

" 'Vita sancte Adelhaydis': Ein Druck des 16. Jahrhunderts aus Durlach, Die," ed. Herbert Paulhart. *Mitteilungen des Instituts für österreichische Geschichte* 69 (1961): 100–104.

Vitae sancti Liudgeri. Die Geschichtsquellen des Bisthums Münster, Die, ed. Wilhelm Diekamp. Münster: Theissing'schen Buchhandlung, 1881.

von Bonstetten, Albrecht. *Briefe und ausgewählte Schriften*, ed. Albert Büchi. Basel: Adolf Geering, 1893.

———. *Deux visites à Nicolas de Flue*, ed. Johann von Waldheim; trans. Eduard Fick. Geneva: Fick, 1864.

———. "Legenda beati Geroldi, heremite olim quoque Saxonie ducis." In *Der gute Gerhart*, ed. Rudolf Bentzinger, Christina Meckelnborg, Franzjosef Pensel, and Anne-Beate Riecke, 124–38. Berlin: Akademie, 2002.

———. "Legenda beate Ite (1485)." *Thurgauische Beiträge zur vaterländischen Geschichte* 64/65 (1928): 60–83.

———. "Legenda beate Ite comitisse in Toggenburg (1485)." *Thurgauische Beiträge zur vaterländischen Geschichte* 112 (1976): 62–72.

———. *Septem horae canonicae virgineae matris Mariae.* Freiburg: Friedrich Riederer, 1493.

———. "Vita divae Iddae ex antiquis codicibus descripta (1481)." *Thurgauische Beiträge zur vaterländischen Geschichte* 64/65 (1928): 60–83.

von dem Busche, Hermann. *Epigrammata.* Cologne, 1498.

"Von der wirdigen frowen sanct Yta leben (1470)." *Thurgauische Beiträge zur vaterländischen Geschichte* 64/65 (1928): 62–83.

"Weisse Buch von Sarnen, Das." In *Quellenwerk zur Entstehung der Schweizerischen Eidgenossenschaft,* ed. Hans Georg Wirz, 1–41. Aarau, Germany: Sauerländer, 1947.

Werinharius. "La vie de saint Adelphe de Metz par Werinharius d'après un manuscrit de Neuwiller (Cod. Vindobonensis 563, xii-e s.)," ed. Guy Philippart. *Analecta bollandiana* 100 (1982): 431–42.

"Werner von Themar, ein Heidelberger Humanist," ed. Karl Hartfelder. In *Karl Hartfelder: Studien zum pfälzischen Humanismus,* ed. Wilhelm Kühlmann and Hermann Wiegand, 73–173. Heidelberg: Manutius, 1993.

Wimpfeling, Jacob. "Catalogus archiepiscoporum Moguntinorum (1514)." In *Commentatio de catalogo archiepiscoporum Moguntinensium Wimpfelingiano,* ed. Georg Englert. Aschaffenburg, Germany, 1882.

———. *De vita et moribus episcoporum aliorumque praelatorum et principum libellus, etiam privatis personis utilis, lectuque iucundus.* Strassburg: Ren. Beck, 1512.

———. *De vita et viraculis Joannis Gerson. Defensio Wymphelingii pro divo Joanne Gerson. et clero seculari: qui in libro (cui titulus supplementum celifodine) graviter taxati sunt et reprehensi.* Strassburg: Johann Prüss the Elder, 1506.

———. *Epithoma rerum Germanicarum usque ad nostra tempora.* Strassburg: Jean Pruss, 1505.

———. "Germania." In *Declamatio de tribus fratribus,* ed. Philippus Beroaldus. Strassburg: Johann Prüss the Elder, 1501.

———. *Opera selecta: Epistolae (187–358),* ed. Otto Herding and Dieter Mertens, vol. 3/2. Munich: Wilhelm Fink, 1990.

———. *Vita sancti Adelphi patroni Collegii Novillarensis.* Strassburg, 1506.

Witzel, Georg. *Chorus sanctorum omnium.* Cologne: Quentel and Calenium, 1563.

———. *Hagiologium, seu de Sanctis Ecclesiae: Historiae diuorum toto terrarum orbe celeberrimorum.* Mainz, 1541.

Wölflin, Heinrich "Lupulus." "Divi Nicolai de Saxo vita." In *Bruder Klaus,* ed. Rupert Amschwand, 126–50. Sarnen, Switzerland: Regierungsrat des Kantons Obwalden, 1987.

Index

Page numbers in **bold** indicate figures. Proper names with various spellings are generally listed alphabetically as they appear in the text. If there are striking variations in spellings, the names have been multiply listed and cross-referenced (see page 139, note 15). Written works are generally indexed under the author's name. Anonymous works and minor primary texts are listed by title. Select authors of secondary works are listed. Endnotes are indexed when they include content in addition to citations. Entries to saints and corresponding vitae are mixed. Written sources about saints are also indexed under "lives of the saints" by name of saint. Persons are designated as saints in the index only if they are addressed in the text as saints; and in such cases no distinction is made between the canonized and the uncanonized.

eremitism
  Bruno of Cologne, 83
  and coenobitism, 55, 63
  and episcopal vita, 74, 126–127
  eremitical vita, 124, 126–127
  Gerold of Saxony, 78
  Gundelfingen vita, 112–113
  and holiness, 53
  Ida of Toggenburg, 166–167n73
  Nicholas of Flue, 100, 108–109
  revisions in medieval writing, 156n1
  vita contemplativa, 105
  vitae sanctorum, 73–74
  Vitaspatrum, 110
Eschweiler, Adam (abbot), 85
Etterlin, Petermann, 117
Evangelicals. *See* Protestantism. *See also*
    Christianity, medieval *and* Roman
    Catholicism.

Farmer, Sharon A., 169n14
Fasti sanctorum. See Rosweyde, Heribert.
fasting saints. *See* asceticism.
Ferrari, Michele C., 145n7
Festival Calendar of the Saints. See Rosweyde,
    Heribert.
Fidelis of Sigmaringen (saint), 191n11
Filelfo, Francesco, 104
Fischingen, 66, 68
Florent, Hadrian (van Trusen). *See*
    Hadrian VI (pope).
France, **60**, 95, 116. *See also* Francia.
Francia, 90, 94
Francis of Assisi (saint), 53
Franciscans, 53, 106
Franconia, 57
Frazier, Alison Knowles, 12–13, 28,
    141n25, 193n23
Frederick III (emperor), 24, 65, 116, **130**,
    137n4, 156n112
Frederick the Victorious (count palatinate),
    47–48, 156n112
Frederick the Wise, elector of (ernestine)
    Saxony, 44
Freiburg (Breisgau), 104, **125**
Freiburger, John, 22
Freitäger, Andreas, 172n46, 173n58
Fribourg (Üchtland), 116
Friesland, 39, 91, 94
Frisians, 79

Gaue (districts), 95
Gaul, 90–91
Geary, Patrick J., 156n1
Geiler von Kaysersberg, John, 100, 104
genealogy. *See* chorography.
Genevieve of Brabant (saint), 68–69,
    166n63
Geographia (Ptolemy), 77–78, 86, 91, **92–93**,
    175n76
geography. *See* chorography.
George the Bearded, duke of (albertine)
    Saxony
  Benno canonization, 3–4, 19, 29
  church reform, 46–48
German vernaculars. *See* languages.
*The German Wars of Charles, Duke of
    Burgundy, and His Death. See*
    Bonstetten, Albert von.
Germania (Aeneas Silvius Piccolomini).
    See Pius II.
Germania (Tacitus), 76, 189n114
Germania illustrata project. *See also*
    chorography; cities and towns; *and*
    regions and principalities.
  Celtis's address, 77
  and chorography, 79–80, 96–97, 127
  founding of Cologne, 83
  history writing, 58, 64, 96, 113, 124
  Germany, 17, 50
Germany (and the Holy Roman Empire).
    See also chorography; cities and
    towns; *and* regions and principalities.
  ancient history of, 76, 81, 86–87, 94
  bishops, 20–21, 41, 38, 44–50,
    141–142n26, 143n38
  canonization, 3–4, 41, 131, 137n4, 158n9,
    191n11
  christianization of, 21, 39, 46, 50, 59, 61
  frontiers, 39, 44, 90–91, 143n38
  Germania illustrata project, 17, 75–77,
    85, 90, 96, 124, 127
  Habsburgs, 68, 115–116, **130**, 137n4,
    186n88
  hagiography, 15, 17, 95–96, 110, 124,
    131, 133, 135, 174n71
  history writing, 58, 64, 75–76, 96, 113, 124
  humanism, 13–17, 25, 55, 65, 73–77, 96,
    124, **125**, 127, 135–136
  map, **92–93**
  religious life in, 55, 56, 63, 162n42